Money Makers

They Did It!

Vit Westworth

ISBN: 978-1-77961-913-6
Imprint: Babycakes Pancakes
Copyright © 2024 Vit Westworth.
All Rights Reserved.

Contents

Methodology and Approach 7
Structure of the Book 15

Chapter 2: The Role of Entrepreneurs in Economic Success 19
Chapter 2: The Role of Entrepreneurs in Economic Success 19
The Entrepreneurial Mindset 23
Case Studies of Successful Entrepreneurs 31
The Impact of Entrepreneurship on Economic Growth 40

Chapter 3: Innovations that Transformed Industries 51
Chapter 3: Innovations that Transformed Industries 51
The Power of Innovation 54
Revolutionary Technological Innovations 67
Case Studies of Industry Transformations 77

Chapter 4: Financial Market Innovations and Economic Success 87
Chapter 4: Financial Market Innovations and Economic Success 87
The Evolution of Financial Markets 90
Financial Market Innovations 96
Case Studies of Financial Market Success 103

Chapter 5: Globalization and Economic Success 113
Chapter 5: Globalization and Economic Success 113
The Rise of Globalization 116
Economic Success in the Globalized World 121
Case Studies of Global Economic Success 131

Chapter 6: Sustainable Development and Economic Success 141
Chapter 6: Sustainable Development and Economic Success 141

The Concept of Sustainable Development 144
Sustainable Business Practices 149
Case Studies of Sustainable Economic Success 160

Chapter 7: Government Policies and Economic Success 171
Chapter 7: Government Policies and Economic Success 171
The Role of Government in Economic Development 174
Fiscal and Monetary Policy 182
Case Studies of Government-led Economic Success 193

Chapter 8: Education and Human Capital Development 207
Chapter 8: Education and Human Capital Development 207
The Importance of Education in Economic Success 211
Innovations in Education 219
Case Studies of Education for Economic Success 229

Chapter 9: Inclusive Growth and Economic Success 237
Chapter 9: Inclusive Growth and Economic Success 237
Understanding Inequality and Poverty 239
Policies for Inclusive Growth 244
Case Studies of Inclusive Economic Success 252

Chapter 10: Future Perspectives on Economic Success 263
Chapter 10: Future Perspectives on Economic Success 263
Emerging Trends and Challenges 268
Innovations for Future Economic Success 278
Lessons from the Past for Future Success 289

Index 299

CONTENTS

The Importance of Makin' Moolah

In today's rapidly changing global economy, economic success stories play a crucial role in inspiring and motivating individuals, businesses, and societies at large. These stories offer real-life examples of how individuals and nations have overcome challenges, taken risks, and implemented innovative strategies to achieve remarkable economic outcomes. They provide valuable insights into the factors that contribute to economic success and offer a wealth of knowledge that can guide future endeavors.

At its core, economic success can be defined as the achievement of sustainable economic growth, improved living standards, and increased well-being for individuals and societies. However, the path to economic success is often complex and multifaceted, influenced by a variety of factors such as technological advancements, entrepreneurial activities, policy frameworks, and global trends. Economic success stories help us understand and analyze these factors by providing concrete examples of how they have contributed to positive economic outcomes.

One of the key reasons why economic success stories are important is their ability to inspire and motivate individuals. By highlighting the achievements of successful entrepreneurs, innovators, and policymakers, these stories demonstrate that anyone with passion, determination, and the right strategies can overcome obstacles and create significant economic impact. They showcase the power of human agency and the potential for positive change, fostering an entrepreneurial mindset and encouraging individuals to embrace new opportunities and take calculated risks.

Moreover, economic success stories offer practical lessons that can be applied in various contexts. They provide insights into the strategies, best practices, and innovative approaches that have proven successful in different industries and countries. By studying these stories, individuals and policymakers can gain valuable knowledge on how to foster economic growth, promote innovation, and create favorable conditions for businesses to thrive. This knowledge can inform policy decisions, guide business strategies, and shape education and training programs to cultivate the skills and competencies needed for economic success.

Economic success stories also play a vital role in shaping public perceptions and discourse around economic issues. They help demystify the world of economics by making complex concepts and theories more relatable and accessible to a wider audience. By illustrating the practical applications and real-life impact of economic principles, these stories engage and captivate readers, fostering a deeper understanding of economic phenomena and their implications. This understanding can facilitate informed decision-making at both the individual and societal levels, leading to more effective economic policies and practices.

It is worth noting that economic success stories are not without their limitations. While they offer valuable insights into the factors that contribute to economic success, they cannot guarantee similar outcomes in different contexts. Economic success is influenced by a myriad of factors, including the political, social, and cultural landscapes in which it occurs. Therefore, it is important to critically analyze and contextualize these stories, considering the unique circumstances and challenges faced by each individual or nation.

To study economic success stories, a mix of research methodologies and approaches can be utilized. Case studies and interviews with key individuals can provide in-depth insights into their strategies, decision-making processes, and experiences. Statistical analysis and data visualization can offer a quantitative understanding of the economic impact and trends associated with various success stories. Comparative studies and cross-country analysis can help identify common patterns and factors that contribute to economic success across different contexts.

In this book, we will explore a range of economic success stories from around the world, spanning different industries, regions, and time periods. We will examine the role of entrepreneurs in driving economic growth, the transformative power of innovations in industries, the impact of financial market innovations, the influence of globalization on economic success, the importance of sustainable development, the role of government policies, the significance of education and human capital development, the pursuit of inclusive growth, and the future perspectives on economic success.

Through a comprehensive exploration of these topics, we aim to provide readers with a deeper understanding of the multidimensional nature of economic success and inspire them to pursue their own journeys, pioneer new research, and contribute to the revolutionary ideas that continue to transform the modern economy. So let's dive into the stories that have shaped our economic world and use them as a stepping stone to our own success.

Historical Context of Economic Success Stories

In order to understand the significance and impact of economic success stories, it is essential to delve into the historical context in which they emerged. The study of economic history helps us recognize patterns, analyze trends, and draw valuable lessons from the past. This section provides an overview of the historical context of economic success stories, exploring the major factors that contributed to their emergence and proliferation.

The Evolution of Economic Systems

Throughout history, different economic systems have emerged and evolved, each with its own characteristics, strengths, and limitations. From agrarian societies to modern industrial economies, the transformation of economic systems has played a crucial role in shaping the landscape of economic success stories.

One of the earliest economic systems was subsistence farming, where individuals produced only enough to meet their basic needs. As societies grew more complex and trade expanded, mercantilism emerged, emphasizing exports, colonization, and accumulation of wealth. The Industrial Revolution marked a significant turning point, as economies shifted from agrarian to industrial, with the development of factories and machinery.

The rise of capitalism, with its principles of private ownership, profit motive, and market competition, paved the way for economic success stories. Capitalism provided individuals and entrepreneurs the freedom to innovate, invest, and accumulate wealth, leading to the emergence of powerful economic actors who shaped the course of history.

Key Historical Events

Various historical events have been instrumental in shaping economic success stories around the world. These events created the conditions necessary for innovation, growth, and prosperity.

The Renaissance and the Age of Enlightenment in Europe, for example, fostered a climate of intellectual curiosity and innovation. It paved the way for groundbreaking discoveries in science, philosophy, and technology, which in turn sparked economic progress.

The Industrial Revolution, particularly in the 18th and 19th centuries, brought about a radical transformation in manufacturing and production processes. This era witnessed the introduction of new technologies, such as steam power and machinery, which revolutionized industries and led to significant economic growth.

The post-World War II era, also known as the "Golden Age of Capitalism," witnessed rapid economic expansion, especially in the United States and Western Europe. Massive investments in infrastructure, technological advancements, and government policies promoting economic stability laid the foundation for economic success stories during this period.

Globalization and Economic Interconnectedness

In recent times, the increasing interconnectedness of nations through trade, finance, and technology has played a crucial role in shaping economic success stories. Globalization has opened up new avenues of economic growth, allowing businesses to tap into larger markets, access resources and talent globally, and generate greater profits.

Advancements in transportation and communication technology, such as the internet and air travel, have made it easier for businesses to connect with customers, suppliers, and partners around the world. This has facilitated the spread of ideas, expertise, and innovations, leading to the creation of economic success stories in diverse sectors.

However, it is important to note that the benefits of globalization have not been evenly distributed. The phenomenon has also contributed to economic inequality, as certain regions and individuals have gained disproportionately from global economic integration. Understanding the complexities and challenges of globalization is crucial in order to foster inclusive economic success.

Lessons from History

Studying the historical context of economic success stories provides valuable insights and lessons for both policymakers and individuals seeking to achieve economic success. It highlights the role of innovation, entrepreneurship, and adaptability in driving economic growth and development.

History also emphasizes the importance of institutions and governance structures that foster an enabling environment for economic success. A transparent legal system, protection of property rights, and market-oriented policies are often key factors in promoting economic prosperity.

Additionally, historical analysis helps us recognize the interconnectedness of different disciplines within economics. The study of economic history reveals the symbiotic relationships between technological advancements, financial innovations, government policies, and social development.

By analyzing the successes and failures of the past, we can identify best practices and avoid pitfalls. However, it is important to consider the unique characteristics and contextual factors of each situation, as no one-size-fits-all approach guarantees economic success.

Example: The Industrial Revolution and Economic Transformation

An exemplary historical event that showcases the transformative power of economic progress is the Industrial Revolution. This period, spanning from the 18th to the 19th century, witnessed the transition from handmade, labor-intensive production methods to machine-based mass production.

The Industrial Revolution began in Great Britain and eventually spread to other parts of Europe, North America, and beyond. The invention and widespread adoption of new technologies, such as the steam engine and mechanized textile production, revolutionized industries and increased productivity.

This period of industrialization brought about significant economic changes. It led to the growth of urban centers, the rise of the working class, and the expansion of global trade networks. The manufacturing sector boomed, and new industries emerged, creating employment opportunities and stimulating economic growth.

The Industrial Revolution also fueled scientific and technological advancements, such as the development of the telegraph and the steam-powered locomotive. These innovations not only transformed manufacturing but also revolutionized transportation, communication, and commerce.

While the Industrial Revolution brought about significant progress, it also had its downsides. The rapid pace of industrialization led to adverse environmental impacts, exploitation of workers, and increased social inequality. These challenges underscore the need for sustainable development and a holistic approach to economic success.

In conclusion, understanding the historical context of economic success stories helps us appreciate the factors that contributed to their emergence and learn from the lessons of the past. By examining the evolution of economic systems, key historical events, the impact of globalization, and the lessons from history, we gain valuable insights into the dynamics of economic success. Applying these insights to contemporary challenges can guide policymakers, entrepreneurs, and individuals on the path toward sustainable economic development and prosperity.

The Role of Individual Stories in Understanding Economic Success

The study of economic success is an intricate and complex field, requiring a multidimensional approach that incorporates various perspectives and methodologies. One crucial aspect of understanding economic success is through the exploration of individual stories. These stories not only serve as inspiration but also provide valuable insights into the factors and strategies that contribute to success in the modern economy.

Individual stories offer a unique perspective on the challenges, triumphs, and strategies employed by successful individuals in their journey towards economic success. By analyzing these stories, we can better understand the underlying principles and approaches that have led to their achievements. Additionally, these stories serve as a source of motivation and inspiration for aspiring entrepreneurs and individuals seeking to make a mark in the business world.

One notable example of the role of individual stories in understanding economic success is the rise of Steve Jobs and the Apple revolution. Jobs' story is a remarkable tale of perseverance, innovation, and entrepreneurial spirit. Through his journey, we can identify key traits and characteristics that are often associated with successful entrepreneurs, such as visionary thinking, calculated risk-taking, and relentless pursuit of excellence.

Furthermore, analyzing Jobs' story allows us to gain insights into the challenges and obstacles faced by entrepreneurs. We learn how Jobs overcame setbacks and failures, constantly pushing himself and his team to create revolutionary products that transformed the technology industry. His story highlights the importance of resilience, adaptability, and the ability to learn from failures in achieving economic success.

Individual stories also shed light on the broader social and economic context in which success occurs. They provide a rich understanding of the historical, cultural, and economic factors that have shaped the journeys of successful individuals. By contextualizing these stories, we can identify patterns and trends that may have contributed to economic success.

For example, examining the story of Jeff Bezos and the rise of Amazon reveals the significant role of technological innovation in reshaping the retail industry. Bezos' foresight in recognizing the potential of e-commerce and his relentless focus on customer experience positioned Amazon as a global powerhouse. This story highlights the impact of technological advancements and the need for continuous adaptation in a rapidly changing business landscape.

Individual stories also contribute to our understanding of the interplay between individual actions and broader economic systems. They provide real-world examples of how entrepreneurs and innovators can leverage their skills and resources to create value, generate employment, and drive economic growth.

Moreover, studying individual stories helps to demystify economic success and challenges the notion that success is solely determined by external factors such as luck or privileged backgrounds. By showcasing diverse individuals from different backgrounds and industries, we understand that economic success is attainable through a combination of factors, including individual aspirations, skills, knowledge, and opportunities.

To facilitate a comprehensive analysis of individual stories, a multidisciplinary approach is necessary. This involves combining qualitative methods such as case studies and interviews with quantitative analysis, statistical tools, and data visualization. By integrating these approaches, we can extract valuable insights from individual stories and validate them with empirical evidence.

In conclusion, individual stories play a vital role in understanding economic success. They offer valuable insights into the strategies, challenges, and dynamics involved in achieving economic prosperity. By examining these stories, we gain a deeper understanding of the traits and characteristics associated with success, the impact of technological innovations, and the interplay between individual actions and broader economic systems. Incorporating individual stories into our analysis enhances our comprehension of economic success and serves as a source of inspiration for future entrepreneurs and individuals aiming to make a difference in the modern economy.

Methodology and Approach

Case Studies and Interviews

In order to understand the real-life journeys of economic success and the revolutionary ideas that have shaped the modern economy, it is essential to delve into the experiences of individuals who have achieved remarkable feats. In this section, we will explore the role of case studies and interviews in uncovering valuable insights and lessons from these economic success stories.

Case studies provide in-depth analysis and examination of specific individuals, companies, or industries, allowing us to gain a deep understanding of their strategies, challenges, and achievements. By investigating these real-world examples, we can extract valuable knowledge that can be applied to different contexts and settings.

One example of a case study is the examination of Steve Jobs and the Apple Revolution. By studying Jobs' entrepreneurial journey, we can gain insights into his innovative mindset, his ability to anticipate customer needs, and his relentless pursuit of excellence. This case study allows us to understand the impact of Jobs' visionary leadership on the success of Apple, as well as the lessons that can be learned from his approach to product development and marketing.

Interviews with successful individuals also play a crucial role in identifying the key factors that contribute to economic success. By engaging with these individuals directly, we can gain firsthand knowledge of their experiences, decision-making processes, and strategies. Through interviews, we can uncover valuable insights that are not easily observable or documented in traditional research.

For example, consider an interview with Elon Musk, the visionary entrepreneur behind companies like SpaceX and Tesla. By speaking with Musk about his journey and the challenges he faced, we can gain insights into his determination, risk-taking mentality, and ability to disrupt traditional industries. These interviews give us a unique perspective on the mindset and strategies of successful entrepreneurs, providing inspiration and guidance for aspiring entrepreneurs.

In addition to individual case studies and interviews, comparative studies and cross-country analysis are valuable tools for examining economic success stories. By comparing the experiences of different countries, regions, or industries, we can identify common trends, best practices, and potential pitfalls.

For instance, a comparative study of successful start-up ecosystems in Silicon Valley and Israel's "Startup Nation" reveals key ingredients for nurturing innovation and entrepreneurship. Through this analysis, we can identify the role of government policies, access to capital, supportive infrastructure, and collaborative networks in creating an environment conducive to economic success.

To enhance the rigor and credibility of case studies and interviews, it is important to incorporate quantitative analysis and data visualization methods. Statistical analysis can provide empirical evidence and support the qualitative findings obtained through case studies and interviews. Data visualization techniques, such as graphs and charts, can help to communicate complex information in a visually appealing and easily understandable manner.

For example, in a case study exploring the impact of entrepreneurship on economic growth, statistical analysis can be used to measure the correlation between entrepreneurial activity and indicators of economic performance. By presenting the findings in a visual format, such as a line graph showing the relationship between the number of new start-ups and GDP growth over time, we can effectively convey the key insights derived from the analysis.

In summary, case studies and interviews are essential tools for understanding economic success stories and extracting valuable insights. Through the detailed examination of specific individuals, companies, and industries, we can uncover the strategies, challenges, and achievements that have shaped the modern economy. Comparative studies and cross-country analysis provide further context and enable us to identify common trends and best practices. By incorporating quantitative analysis and data visualization techniques, we can enhance the rigor and credibility of these studies. Ultimately, these methods allow us to learn from the past and pave the way for future economic success.

Statistical Analysis and Data Visualization

Statistical analysis and data visualization are two essential tools in understanding and interpreting economic success stories. In this section, we will explore the concepts behind statistical analysis and data visualization, their importance in economic research, and how they can be used effectively.

The Role of Statistical Analysis

Statistical analysis is a powerful tool that allows economists to analyze and interpret data to uncover patterns, relationships, and trends. It provides a systematic framework for understanding complex economic phenomena, making informed decisions, and testing hypotheses.

One of the fundamental concepts in statistical analysis is probability theory. Probability theory enables economists to quantify uncertainty and randomness, allowing them to make predictions and draw conclusions based on data. Concepts such as probability distributions, hypothesis testing, and confidence intervals are crucial for analyzing economic data and drawing reliable conclusions.

Moreover, statistical analysis also involves the use of various statistical techniques, such as regression analysis, time series analysis, and panel data analysis. These techniques enable economists to model relationships between variables, estimate parameters, and make predictions. They provide a rigorous framework for analyzing economic relationships and understanding the impact of different factors on economic success.

Data Visualization: Communicating Insights

Data visualization plays a vital role in economic research by transforming complex data into visual representations that are easy to understand and interpret. It helps economists communicate their findings effectively, uncover patterns and trends, and make data-driven decisions.

Visualizations such as charts, graphs, and maps provide a clear and intuitive way to present large amounts of data. They enable economists to identify patterns and trends that may not be apparent in raw data. By using visual elements such as colors, shapes, and sizes, data visualizations can convey information quickly and facilitate the understanding of complex relationships.

One popular data visualization technique is the scatter plot, which represents the relationship between two variables. Scatter plots can reveal correlations, outliers, and other patterns that may be crucial in understanding economic success.

Additionally, line graphs are often used to display time series data, allowing economists to observe trends and changes over time.

In recent years, interactive and dynamic visualizations have gained popularity. These visualizations allow users to explore the data interactively, change parameters, and view different perspectives. Interactive visualizations provide a more engaging and immersive experience, enabling users to gain deeper insights into the data.

Challenges and Considerations

While statistical analysis and data visualization are powerful tools, they also come with challenges and considerations that economists need to be aware of.

Firstly, it is crucial to ensure the quality and reliability of data used for statistical analysis. Data errors, missing values, and sampling biases can significantly impact the accuracy of results. Economists should carefully clean and preprocess the data, apply appropriate weighting techniques if necessary, and address any missing or erroneous data points.

Another challenge is the interpretation of statistical results. It is essential to avoid drawing incorrect or misleading conclusions from statistical analysis. Economists should consider the limitations of their analysis, acknowledge potential confounding factors, and use statistical significance and effect sizes to determine the strength of relationships.

Additionally, the choice of data visualization techniques should be carefully considered. Different types of visualizations are suitable for different types of data and research questions. Economists should select visualizations that effectively communicate the key insights and support the research objectives. Labels, legends, and captions should be used appropriately to provide context and clarity.

Example: Analyzing the Impact of Education on Economic Success

To illustrate the importance of statistical analysis and data visualization, let's consider an example of analyzing the impact of education on economic success. Suppose we have a dataset that includes information on educational attainment and income levels for a sample of individuals.

Using statistical analysis, we can run a regression analysis to model the relationship between education and income. By estimating regression coefficients, we can quantify the effect of education on income, controlling for other relevant factors such as age, gender, and work experience. This analysis allows us to determine whether higher levels of education lead to higher income levels.

Next, we can use data visualization techniques to present our findings. We can create a scatter plot with education level on the x-axis and income on the y-axis. Each point on the plot represents an individual in our sample. By visualizing the relationship between education and income, we can observe any patterns or trends, such as a positive correlation between education level and income.

Furthermore, we can enhance our visualization by including additional information, such as color-coding the points based on gender or overlaying a trend line to illustrate the overall relationship. These visual enhancements can provide additional insights and facilitate a more comprehensive understanding of the impact of education on economic success.

In conclusion, statistical analysis and data visualization are crucial tools in understanding and interpreting economic success stories. They enable economists to analyze data, uncover relationships, and communicate findings effectively. By using these tools appropriately and addressing challenges, economists can gain valuable insights and make informed decisions to drive economic success.

Exercises

1. Consider a dataset that includes information on GDP per capita and education expenditure for a sample of countries. Use statistical analysis techniques to test the hypothesis that countries with higher education expenditure have higher GDP per capita.

    2. Create a line graph to visualize the trend in unemployment rates over the past decade for a given country. Identify any patterns or changes that can be observed from the graph.

    3. Discuss the limitations and potential biases that may arise when analyzing data from survey-based sources, such as self-reported income levels or education attainment. How can economists address these limitations in their analysis?

    4. Investigate a real-world economic success story and analyze the key factors that contributed to its success. Use statistical analysis and data visualization techniques to support your analysis and present your findings effectively.

    5. Explore different types of data visualizations, such as bar charts, pie charts, or heat maps. Choose a specific economic research question and select the most appropriate visualization technique to represent the data effectively.

Additional Resources

1. "The Visual Display of Quantitative Information" by Edward Tufte provides a comprehensive guide to effective data visualization techniques.

2. "Principles of Econometrics" by R. Carter Hill, William E. Griffiths, and Guay C. Lim offers a detailed introduction to statistical analysis techniques in economics.

3. The World Bank's Open Data initiative provides a wide range of economic and development data that can be used for statistical analysis and data visualization.

4. "Data Visualization: A Practical Introduction" by Kieran Healy offers practical guidance on creating effective visualizations using R and ggplot2.

5. "Statistics for Business and Economics" by Paul Newbold, William L. Carlson, and Betty Thorne covers statistical concepts and techniques specifically tailored for business and economics students.

Comparative Studies and Cross-Country Analysis

In order to gain a deeper understanding of economic success and its underlying factors, economists and researchers often employ comparative studies and cross-country analysis. These approaches allow us to examine different countries and their economic systems, policies, and outcomes in order to identify patterns, trends, and potential causal relationships. By comparing the experiences of various nations, we can uncover valuable insights and lessons that can inform policy-making, guide decision-making, and contribute to economic success.

The Importance of Comparative Studies

Comparative studies play a crucial role in economics as they provide a systematic framework for analyzing and interpreting economic data across countries. This method allows researchers to identify similarities and differences in economic performance, policies, institutions, and other relevant factors that can shape outcomes. By examining a range of countries, from diverse regions of the world, we can gain a broader perspective on the factors that contribute to economic success and understand how different contexts and circumstances can affect outcomes.

One of the key advantages of comparative studies is their ability to control for confounding factors. By comparing countries with similar characteristics, such as levels of development, natural resources, or cultural backgrounds, researchers can isolate the effects of specific variables and identify their impact on economic success. This approach helps us move beyond anecdotal evidence and provide robust and empirically grounded explanations of economic phenomena.

Cross-Country Analysis: Methods and Approaches

Cross-country analysis involves the systematic comparison of economic data and indicators from multiple countries. It allows us to evaluate the relationships between various economic variables, such as GDP growth, inflation rates, trade openness, education levels, infrastructure development, and many others. There are several key methods and approaches used in cross-country analysis.

Firstly, researchers employ statistical techniques to analyze and compare data across different countries. Descriptive statistics, such as mean, median, and standard deviation, provide a summary of the data and allow for an initial understanding of the patterns and variations. Econometric methods, such as regressions and panel data analysis, enable researchers to estimate the relationships between variables and test hypotheses.

Secondly, researchers often utilize data visualization techniques to present their findings in a clear and intuitive manner. Graphs, charts, and maps can effectively illustrate patterns, trends, and variations in economic data across countries. These visual representations can enhance the understanding of complex economic relationships and facilitate the communication of research findings to a wider audience.

Thirdly, comparative studies often involve qualitative analysis, including case studies and interviews. This approach allows researchers to delve deeper into the unique experiences of individual countries and explore the specific factors that have contributed to their economic success or failure. Qualitative analysis provides valuable insights into the context-specific factors that statistical analysis may not capture fully.

Examples of Comparative Studies and Cross-Country Analysis

Let's consider two examples of comparative studies and cross-country analysis to better illustrate the practical applications of these approaches.

In the first example, researchers might examine the relationship between educational attainment and economic growth across different countries. By collecting data on educational indicators, such as literacy rates, enrollment rates, and educational expenditure, and combining it with macroeconomic data, researchers can test the hypothesis that higher levels of education contribute to higher levels of economic growth. By comparing countries with varying levels of educational attainment, such as Finland, South Korea, and Germany, researchers can identify the specific policies and practices that have led to educational success and economic prosperity.

In the second example, researchers might investigate the impact of trade policy on economic development. By analyzing trade data, such as export and import volumes, trade balances, and tariff rates, in conjunction with other economic indicators, researchers can assess the relationship between trade openness and economic performance. By comparing countries with different trade policies, such as China, India, and Brazil, researchers can identify the potential benefits and drawbacks of different approaches to trade liberalization.

Limitations and Caveats

While comparative studies and cross-country analysis provide valuable insights, it is important to recognize their limitations and caveats. Firstly, the presence of confounding factors can complicate the interpretation of findings. Even when controlling for certain variables, there may be unobserved or omitted variables that influence outcomes. Researchers need to exercise caution when making causal claims based solely on cross-country analysis.

Secondly, the availability and quality of data can vary across countries, which can introduce biases and limitations. Researchers must carefully select and verify data sources to ensure the reliability and comparability of the data used in cross-country analysis.

Lastly, the dynamic nature of economic systems and policies means that comparative studies can only provide a snapshot of a particular moment in time. Economic conditions, policies, and outcomes can change over time, requiring ongoing analysis and updated research.

Conclusion

Comparative studies and cross-country analysis are powerful tools for understanding economic success and the factors that contribute to it. By comparing diverse countries and analyzing their economic systems, policies, and outcomes, researchers can uncover valuable insights and inform policy-making. However, caution must be exercised in interpreting findings, accounting for confounding factors, and recognizing the limitations of available data. Despite these challenges, comparative studies remain an essential component of economic research and contribute to our understanding of economic success stories.

Structure of the Book

Overview of Chapters and Sections

In this section, we will provide an overview of the chapters and sections covered in this book, "Economic Success Stories: Real-Life Journeys, Pioneering Research, and the Revolutionary Ideas That Transformed the Modern Economy". We will explore the importance of economic success stories, defining economic success, the historical context of economic success stories, and the role of individual stories in understanding economic success. Additionally, we will discuss the methodology and approach used in this book, as well as the structure of the chapters and sections.

Chapter 2 focuses on "The Role of Entrepreneurs in Economic Success". We will delve into the entrepreneurial mindset, discussing the traits and characteristics of successful entrepreneurs. It is important to understand the challenges and risks faced by entrepreneurs and how they overcome obstacles to achieve success. Through case studies of prominent entrepreneurs such as Steve Jobs, Jeff Bezos, and Elon Musk, we will highlight their journeys and the impact of entrepreneurship on economic growth.

Chapter 3 explores "Innovations that Transformed Industries". We will first examine the power of innovation, defining it and discussing its different types. Research and development play a critical role in innovation, and we will explore the importance of intellectual property protection. Through case studies of industry transformations, such as Netflix, Uber, and Airbnb, we will showcase how these companies disrupted traditional industries and revolutionized their respective sectors.

Moving on to Chapter 4, we will delve into "Financial Market Innovations and Economic Success". This chapter provides a historical overview of financial market development and the role of financial intermediaries. We will discuss significant financial market innovations like securitization, high-frequency trading, and online banking. Through case studies of successful investors like Warren Buffett, George Soros, and Ray Dalio, we will examine their strategies and the impact of their investment approaches on economic success.

Chapter 5 focuses on "Globalization and Economic Success". We will provide a definition of globalization and explore its historical context. Understanding the drivers of globalization is crucial, and we will examine advanced manufacturing, global trade, and foreign direct investment as key components. Case studies of countries like South Korea, Singapore, and China will highlight their experiences and demonstrate the relationship between globalization and economic success.

In Chapter 6, we will discuss "Sustainable Development and Economic

Success". This chapter explores the concept of sustainable development and its environmental, social, and economic dimensions. We will highlight the importance of sustainable business practices such as corporate social responsibility, circular economy, and green technologies. Case studies of companies like Patagonia, Novozymes, and Costa Rica will illustrate their successful approaches to sustainable economic development.

Chapter 7 examines "Government Policies and Economic Success". We will explore the role of government in economic development, particularly in addressing market failures. The chapter will delve into fiscal and monetary policy, discussing taxation, central banking, and government debt management. Through case studies of countries like the Nordic countries, Singapore, and Brazil, we will analyze the impact of government-led policies on economic success.

"Education and Human Capital Development" is the focus of Chapter 8. We will showcase the importance of education in economic success, by introducing education and human capital theory. Investment in education is a key factor, and we will explore innovations in education such as online learning, vocational education, and lifelong learning. Case studies of countries like Finland, South Korea, and Germany will exemplify their approaches to education for economic success.

In Chapter 9, we will discuss "Inclusive Growth and Economic Success". Understanding inequality and poverty is crucial, and we will explore the measurement, causes, and consequences of inequality. Examining policies for inclusive growth, such as redistribution, access to quality education and healthcare, and financial inclusion, we will highlight their impact on economic success. Case studies of countries like Costa Rica, Rwanda, and Sweden will demonstrate their efforts towards inclusive economic development.

Finally, in Chapter 10, we will provide "Future Perspectives on Economic Success". Emerging trends and challenges, such as technological disruptions, climate change, and global economic cooperation and governance, will be explored. We will discuss innovations for future economic success, including artificial intelligence, genetic engineering, and blockchain technology. Lessons from the past will be examined, emphasizing historical patterns, sustainable development, and collaboration for global economic success.

Throughout this book, we aim to provide a comprehensive understanding of economic success through real-life stories, pioneering research, and revolutionary ideas. By examining the role of entrepreneurs, innovations, financial market developments, globalization, sustainable development, government policies, education, and inclusive growth, readers will gain insights into the factors that contribute to economic success.

Connecting Themes and Concepts Across Chapters

In this section, we will explore the key themes and concepts that connect the chapters in this book. By examining the interplay between various disciplines and ideas, we aim to provide a comprehensive understanding of the factors driving economic success.

The Interdisciplinary Nature of Economic Success

Economic success is a complex phenomenon that cannot be understood through a single lens. It requires an interdisciplinary approach that combines insights from economics, entrepreneurship, innovation, finance, globalization, sustainability, government policies, education, and inclusive growth. These different disciplines contribute unique perspectives and tools that collectively enhance our understanding of how economies thrive.

Entrepreneurship as a Catalyst for Economic Success

Chapter 2 highlights the crucial role of entrepreneurs in driving economic success. Entrepreneurs bring innovative ideas, take calculated risks, and create new opportunities that lead to job creation, wealth generation, and industry transformation. Their mindset, characterized by traits like resilience, creativity, and adaptability, is a connecting theme across various chapters. Understanding the entrepreneurial process and its impact on economic growth is essential to grasp the dynamics behind economic success stories.

Innovation as a Driver of Economic Transformation

Innovation is another vital theme that runs across different chapters. Chapter 3 emphasizes the power of technological breakthroughs in reshaping industries and driving economic growth. The types of innovation, such as incremental, radical, and disruptive innovations, play a pivotal role in determining the success of businesses and economies. The importance of research and development, intellectual property protection, and the impact of innovation on job creation and sustainable development are topics that connect various chapters in the book.

Financial Markets and Globalization as Catalysts for Economic Growth

Chapter 4 delves into the role of financial market innovations in promoting economic success. These innovations, such as securitization, high-frequency trading, and online banking, have reshaped the financial landscape and facilitated capital allocation and investment. The interconnectedness of financial markets and globalization is explored further in Chapter 5. Globalization, driven by advanced manufacturing, global trade, and foreign direct investment, has opened up new avenues for economic growth and expanded global market opportunities. The dynamics of financial markets and globalization are interwoven throughout the book, highlighting their critical influence on economic success.

Sustainable Development and Inclusive Growth as Imperatives for the Future

Chapters 6 and 9 tackle the themes of sustainable development and inclusive growth, emphasizing the importance of balancing economic prosperity with environmental and social considerations. The concept of sustainable development, encompassing environmental, social, and economic dimensions, provides a framework for creating long-term success. Inclusive growth, characterized by reducing inequalities and ensuring access to education, healthcare, and financial services, is crucial for sustainable and equitable economic development. These themes, along with discussions on government policies and education, offer insights into the necessary conditions for future economic success.

Lessons from the Past and Future Perspectives

Throughout the book, lessons from historical success stories and present-day case studies provide valuable insights for future economic success. Chapter 10 examines emerging trends and challenges, such as technological disruptions, climate change, and global economic cooperation. It also explores the potential of artificial intelligence, genetic engineering, and blockchain technology as drivers of future economic success. Staying mindful of historical patterns, embracing sustainable development principles, and fostering collaboration will be critical to securing long-term prosperity.

By connecting the themes and concepts discussed in different chapters, this book aims to provide a holistic understanding of economic success. It encourages readers to think beyond disciplinary boundaries and develop a broader perspective on the intricate factors that shape economies and drive sustainable growth. Through case studies, analysis, and real-world examples, we invite readers to explore the diverse pathways to economic success and identify key principles that can guide them in their own journeys.

Chapter 2: The Role of Entrepreneurs in Economic Success

Chapter 2: The Role of Entrepreneurs in Economic Success

Chapter 2: The Role of Entrepreneurs in Economic Success

Entrepreneurs play a critical role in driving economic success. Their innovative ideas, risk-taking mindset, and ability to create new businesses contribute to job creation, economic growth, and societal development. In this chapter, we will explore the significance of entrepreneurs in the modern economy, their unique traits and characteristics, the challenges they face, and how they overcome obstacles to achieve success.

The Importance of Entrepreneurs

Entrepreneurs are the engines of economic growth and development. They identify untapped market opportunities, introduce new products and services, and promote competition, which stimulates innovation and increases productivity. By starting new businesses, entrepreneurs create job opportunities, enhance income levels, and improve overall living standards within a society.

Moreover, entrepreneurs contribute to economic stability and resilience. They bring diversity to the economy by introducing new industries, which reduces dependence on a single sector. This diversification helps buffer against economic downturns and enhances the economy's ability to adapt to changing circumstances.

Defining Entrepreneurship

Entrepreneurship is a multifaceted concept that encompasses various dimensions. At its core, entrepreneurship involves the process of identifying, evaluating, and exploiting business opportunities. It requires individuals with a vision, creativity, and the ability to take calculated risks.

Entrepreneurs are driven by the desire to create value and make a difference. They are willing to challenge the status quo, disrupt traditional industries, and push boundaries in pursuit of their goals. Successful entrepreneurs possess a combination of traits and characteristics that set them apart from others.

Traits and Characteristics of Successful Entrepreneurs

While every entrepreneur is unique, research has identified several common traits and characteristics that contribute to their success. These include:

- **Passion and Persistence:** Entrepreneurs are deeply passionate about their ideas and are willing to persevere in the face of challenges and setbacks. This determination helps them overcome obstacles and stay focused on their goals.

- **Creativity and Innovation:** Entrepreneurs possess a high degree of creativity, enabling them to generate novel ideas and innovative solutions to problems. They are not afraid to think outside the box and challenge conventional wisdom.

- **Risk-Taking and Tolerance for Uncertainty:** Entrepreneurship inherently involves risk, and successful entrepreneurs have a willingness to take calculated risks. They can tolerate uncertainty and make decisions in the face of incomplete information.

- **Flexibility and Adaptability:** Entrepreneurs need to be adaptable and able to pivot their strategies in response to changing circumstances. They can quickly adjust their business models and take advantage of emerging opportunities.

- **Leadership and Vision:** Entrepreneurs are natural leaders who can inspire and motivate others to join their vision. They have a clear sense of purpose and can articulate a compelling vision for their businesses.

Challenges and Risks Faced by Entrepreneurs

While entrepreneurship offers great rewards, it also comes with significant challenges and risks. Some of the common challenges faced by entrepreneurs include:

- **Access to Capital:** Securing funding to start and grow a business is often a major hurdle for entrepreneurs. Traditional sources of capital, such as banks, may be hesitant to invest in unproven ventures, making it difficult for entrepreneurs to access the necessary resources.

- **Market Uncertainty:** Entrepreneurs face the challenge of understanding market dynamics, identifying target customers, and predicting their needs. It can be challenging to gauge customer demand, stay ahead of competitors, and navigate changes in consumer preferences.

- **Regulatory and Legal Constraints:** Compliance with regulations and legal requirements is a significant challenge for entrepreneurs. Understanding the complex web of rules and regulations can be time-consuming and costly, particularly for startups with limited resources.

- **Team Building and Talent Acquisition:** As businesses grow, entrepreneurs need to build effective teams and attract top talent. Hiring skilled employees, fostering a positive work culture, and retaining key personnel can be challenging, especially in highly competitive industries.

- **Failure and Resilience:** Entrepreneurship involves a high degree of uncertainty, and failure is a common risk. Entrepreneurs need to develop resilience and the ability to learn from failures, adapt their strategies, and persevere in the face of adversity.

Overcoming Obstacles and Achieving Success

Despite the challenges they face, entrepreneurs can overcome obstacles and achieve success. Here are some strategies and approaches commonly employed by successful entrepreneurs:

- **Building a Strong Network:** Entrepreneurs recognize the importance of surrounding themselves with mentors, advisors, and peers who can provide guidance and support. Building a strong network enables entrepreneurs to access knowledge, resources, and potential business opportunities.

- **Continuous Learning and Skill Development:** Successful entrepreneurs are lifelong learners who seek to expand their knowledge and skills. They invest in their personal development through reading, attending workshops, and participating in networking events.

- **Embracing Failure and Learning from Mistakes:** Rather than seeing failure as a setback, entrepreneurs view it as an opportunity to learn and grow. They analyze their mistakes, identify lessons learned, and apply this knowledge to future endeavors.

- **Adapting to Market Changes:** Entrepreneurs must stay attuned to market trends and adapt their strategies accordingly. This may involve pivoting their business models, exploring new markets, or leveraging emerging technologies to gain a competitive edge.

- **Seeking Feedback and Being Open-Minded:** Successful entrepreneurs actively seek feedback from customers, industry experts, and their team members. They maintain an open mind, embracing constructive criticism and using it to refine their products, services, and business strategies.

Entrepreneurs are vital drivers of economic success, and understanding their role and contributions is crucial for both aspiring entrepreneurs and policymakers. By recognizing the importance of entrepreneurship and supporting entrepreneurial endeavors, societies can foster an environment conducive to innovation, economic growth, and societal progress.

Resources and Further Reading

For further exploration of the role of entrepreneurs in economic success, the following resources provide valuable insights and knowledge:

- *The Lean Startup* by Eric Ries: This renowned book offers practical guidance for entrepreneurs looking to build successful businesses by embracing the principles of lean startup methodology.

- *Zero to One: Notes on Startups, or How to Build the Future* by Peter Thiel: In this book, Thiel provides unique insights on entrepreneurship and shares his perspectives on what it takes to build transformative companies.

- *Entrepreneurship: Theory, Process, and Practice* by Donald F. Kuratko: This comprehensive textbook offers a deep dive into the theoretical foundations of entrepreneurship and provides practical guidance for aspiring entrepreneurs.

- *StartUp Podcast*: This popular podcast series features real-life stories of entrepreneurs, their challenges, and their journeys to success. It provides a wealth of inspiration and insights into the world of entrepreneurship.

Exercises

1. Think of a successful entrepreneur you admire. Identify and analyze three key traits or characteristics that you believe have contributed to their success.

2. Research and explore the entrepreneurial ecosystem in your local area. Identify support organizations, such as incubators or accelerators, that assist entrepreneurs in launching and growing their businesses. What resources do they offer, and how do they contribute to entrepreneurial success?

3. Imagine you have a business idea that you want to pursue. Develop a plan outlining the key steps you would take to overcome the challenges and risks associated with launching and growing your venture. Consider factors such as funding, market research, team building, and marketing strategies.

4. Reflect on a failure or setback you have experienced in your life. How did you respond to it? What lessons did you learn from the experience, and how would you apply those lessons to future entrepreneurial endeavors?

Remember, entrepreneurship is not solely about starting a business; it is a mindset and a way of thinking that can be applied in various contexts. Embracing and cultivating an entrepreneurial mindset can lead to personal and professional growth, allowing you to seize opportunities and make a positive impact in your chosen field.

The Entrepreneurial Mindset

Traits and Characteristics of Successful Entrepreneurs

Entrepreneurs are the driving force behind economic growth and innovation. They possess a unique set of traits and characteristics that enable them to identify opportunities, take risks, and create successful ventures. In this section, we will explore the key traits that contribute to the success of entrepreneurs.

Passion and Vision

One of the most important traits of successful entrepreneurs is passion. They are deeply committed to their ideas and have a genuine enthusiasm for their work.

This passion fuels their determination and perseverance, allowing them to overcome obstacles and setbacks.

Additionally, successful entrepreneurs possess a clear vision for the future. They have a strong sense of purpose and can articulate their goals and objectives. This vision inspires and motivates others to join their journey, whether it be employees, investors, or customers.

Creativity and Innovation

Entrepreneurs thrive in environments where they can think outside the box and come up with innovative solutions to problems. They possess a high level of creativity, which allows them to see opportunities and possibilities that others may overlook.

Furthermore, successful entrepreneurs are not afraid to challenge conventional wisdom and disrupt existing industries. They constantly seek new ways of doing things and are willing to take risks in pursuit of their ideas. They are open to experimentation and embrace failure as a learning opportunity.

Resilience and Persistence

Starting and growing a business is not easy, and entrepreneurs face numerous challenges along the way. Successful entrepreneurs possess a high level of resilience and are able to bounce back from failures and setbacks. They view obstacles as temporary roadblocks, and their persistence enables them to keep moving forward despite the difficulties.

Entrepreneurs also have a high tolerance for ambiguity and uncertainty. They are comfortable with taking calculated risks and making decisions in the face of incomplete information. This ability to navigate through uncertainty is crucial for success in the ever-changing business landscape.

Adaptability and Flexibility

In today's fast-paced and dynamic business environment, successful entrepreneurs must be adaptable and flexible. They are quick to recognize changes in the market and are willing to adjust their strategies and tactics accordingly. They embrace innovation and are not afraid to pivot their business models if necessary.

Moreover, successful entrepreneurs are lifelong learners. They continually seek new knowledge and stay updated with the latest industry trends. They are open to feedback and are willing to seek help and advice from mentors and experts in their field.

Strong Leadership and Communication Skills

Entrepreneurs are often at the helm of their ventures, and strong leadership skills are crucial for success. They have the ability to inspire and influence others, rallying their teams towards a common goal. They are effective communicators and can articulate their ideas clearly and persuasively.

Furthermore, successful entrepreneurs are adept at building and nurturing relationships. They understand the importance of networking and forming partnerships, whether it be with suppliers, customers, or investors. They have the ability to create a strong support network that can provide valuable resources and opportunities.

Examples and Case Studies

To illustrate the traits and characteristics of successful entrepreneurs, let's look at a few examples:

Elon Musk is known for his passion and vision. His passion for space exploration and sustainable energy led to the founding of SpaceX and Tesla, two highly successful companies that are transforming their respective industries.

Sara Blakely, the founder of Spanx, demonstrated creativity and innovation. She identified a gap in the market for comfortable and flattering undergarments, and came up with a unique solution that revolutionized the industry.

Richard Branson exemplifies resilience and persistence. Despite facing numerous setbacks and failures, he continued to pursue his entrepreneurial ventures, including Virgin Records, Virgin Atlantic, and Virgin Galactic.

Oprah Winfrey demonstrates strong leadership and communication skills. She built a media empire through her ability to connect with and inspire her audience, using her platform to promote positive change and empowerment.

Resources and Further Reading

If you're interested in learning more about the traits and characteristics of successful entrepreneurs, here are some recommended resources:

- "The Lean Startup" by Eric Ries: This book explores the entrepreneurial mindset and provides strategies for building successful businesses.

- "Grit: The Power of Passion and Perseverance" by Angela Duckworth: This book investigates the role of grit, a combination of passion and persistence, in achieving long-term success.

- TED Talks: TED features a wide range of talks on entrepreneurship and leadership by successful entrepreneurs, including Elon Musk, Richard Branson, and Sara Blakely.

- Entrepreneurship courses on platforms like Coursera and edX: These online courses provide comprehensive insights into the world of entrepreneurship, covering topics such as opportunity recognition, business models, and scaling ventures.

Exercises

1. Think of a successful entrepreneur who has inspired you. Identify and discuss the key traits and characteristics that have contributed to their success.

2. Reflect on a recent challenge or setback you have faced. How could applying the traits of resilience and persistence have helped you overcome this obstacle?

3. Take a look at a successful startup in your industry. Analyze the traits and characteristics exhibited by the founder(s) and how they have contributed to the company's success.

4. Research a case study of an entrepreneur who failed in their first venture but went on to achieve great success. Explore the traits and characteristics that enabled them to bounce back and achieve their goals.

Remember, entrepreneurship is a journey that requires a combination of skills, traits, and characteristics. As you embark on your own entrepreneurial path, continue to develop and nurture these qualities, and always be open to learning and growing.

Challenges and Risks Faced by Entrepreneurs

Being an entrepreneur is not an easy path to choose. While the rewards can be great, the journey is filled with numerous challenges and risks. In this section, we will explore some of the common challenges entrepreneurs face and the risks they must navigate in order to achieve success.

Financial Challenges

One of the primary challenges faced by entrepreneurs is securing funding for their ventures. Starting a business requires capital, whether it is for product development, marketing, or hiring a team. Many entrepreneurs struggle to find the necessary funding, especially in the early stages when they may not have a proven track record or collateral to secure a loan.

Moreover, entrepreneurs often face difficulty in accurately estimating the costs associated with their business. Budgeting and financial planning are crucial skills for entrepreneurs to master in order to avoid running out of funds before achieving profitability. They must carefully manage their cash flow, monitor their expenses, and make strategic decisions to ensure the long-term financial stability of their venture.

Market Challenges

Navigating the market can be a daunting task for entrepreneurs. They often face stiff competition from established players or disruptive startups. Identifying a target market, understanding customer needs, and developing a unique value proposition are essential for success. Entrepreneurs must conduct market research to gain insights into consumer preferences, industry trends, and competitive dynamics.

Market challenges also include effectively positioning their product or service, pricing it competitively, and building a brand that resonates with their target market. This requires effective marketing strategies, strong branding efforts, and continuous innovation to stay ahead of the competition.

Operational Challenges

Entrepreneurs face various operational challenges as they strive to build and grow their businesses. These include managing day-to-day operations, developing efficient systems and processes, and establishing a solid organizational structure. Scaling a business brings additional complexities, such as hiring and retaining talent, managing supply chains, and optimizing production or service delivery.

Furthermore, entrepreneurs must be adaptable and able to navigate unforeseen challenges and changes in the business environment. These can range from technological advancements that disrupt their industry to shifts in consumer behavior or regulatory changes. Entrepreneurs must be agile and have the ability to pivot their business strategies to stay relevant and capitalize on new opportunities.

Personal and Professional Risks

Entrepreneurs often take on significant personal and professional risks. Starting a business requires a deep personal commitment, as it involves investing time, energy, and resources into an uncertain future. Many entrepreneurs face the risk of financial insecurity, as they may need to use personal savings or take on debt to finance their ventures.

Moreover, entrepreneurs often sacrifice stability and work-life balance in pursuit of their entrepreneurial dreams. They may face long working hours, high levels of stress, and a constant need to juggle multiple responsibilities. The pressure to succeed and the fear of failure can take a toll on their mental and emotional well-being.

Mitigating Risks and Overcoming Challenges

Entrepreneurs can mitigate risks and overcome challenges by adopting certain strategies and mindset. Here are some recommendations:

1. Building a Strong Support Network: Entrepreneurs should surround themselves with mentors, advisors, and like-minded individuals who can provide guidance and support throughout their journey. Collaborating with others can help them navigate challenges and learn from the experiences of others.

2. Continuous Learning: Entrepreneurs must have a thirst for knowledge and a commitment to lifelong learning. They should stay updated on industry trends, acquire new skills, and seek out opportunities for personal and professional growth. This will enable them to adapt to changing market conditions and stay ahead of the curve.

3. Embracing Failure: Failure is an inevitable part of the entrepreneurial journey. Entrepreneurs should view failure as a learning opportunity and not let it discourage them. They should be willing to take risks, learn from their mistakes, and iterate their business strategies based on feedback and market dynamics.

4. Building Resilience: Resilience is key to overcoming the challenges and setbacks that entrepreneurs face. They should develop emotional intelligence and cultivate a positive mindset. Engaging in self-care activities and seeking support when needed can help them maintain their mental and emotional well-being.

5. Seeking Professional Advice: Entrepreneurs should not hesitate to seek professional advice when needed. Consulting with experts in areas such as finance, legal, or marketing can provide valuable insights and help them make informed decisions.

In conclusion, entrepreneurs face a multitude of challenges and risks on their path to success. However, by understanding these challenges, developing the necessary skills, and adopting a resilient mindset, entrepreneurs can navigate these obstacles and increase their chances of achieving their entrepreneurial goals. The journey may be tough, but the rewards can be immense.

Overcoming Obstacles and Achieving Success

In the journey towards economic success, entrepreneurs face numerous challenges and obstacles. However, it is their ability to overcome these hurdles and find innovative solutions that ultimately leads to their success. In this section, we will explore some common obstacles faced by entrepreneurs and strategies they use to overcome them.

Identifying and Assessing Risks

One of the first obstacles entrepreneurs encounter is the identification and assessment of risks associated with their business ventures. Starting a new business involves inherent risks, such as market uncertainty, financial instability, and competition. It is essential for entrepreneurs to have a clear understanding of these risks and their potential impact on their businesses.

To address this challenge, entrepreneurs employ various strategies. They conduct thorough market research to identify potential opportunities and risks. They also analyze their financial resources and develop contingency plans to mitigate potential risks. Additionally, entrepreneurs often seek advice from mentors or consultants who can provide valuable insights and help them navigate through challenging situations.

Managing Financial Constraints

Financial constraints are a common hurdle for entrepreneurs, especially during the early stages of their ventures. Limited access to capital, high operational costs, and difficulties in securing funding can hinder the growth and success of a business.

To overcome financial constraints, entrepreneurs adopt different approaches. They explore alternative sources of funding such as venture capital, angel investors, or crowdfunding platforms. They also bootstrap their operations by minimizing costs and seeking cost-effective solutions. Moreover, entrepreneurs may leverage networking and strategic partnerships to access resources and financial support.

Building a Strong Team

Entrepreneurs often face the challenge of assembling a competent and motivated team. Hiring and retaining talented individuals with the necessary skills and experience is crucial for the success of any business.

To overcome this challenge, entrepreneurs focus on building a strong company culture that attracts and retains top talent. They offer competitive compensation packages, provide opportunities for professional growth, and create a supportive work environment. Additionally, entrepreneurs invest time and effort in recruiting and selecting the right candidates who align with their vision and values.

Adapting to Market Changes

In today's dynamic business environment, entrepreneurs must continuously adapt to market changes and evolving customer preferences. Failure to adapt can lead to the decline or failure of a business.

To overcome this obstacle, entrepreneurs stay vigilant and proactive. They closely monitor market trends, conduct regular competitor analysis, and gather customer feedback to identify new opportunities and potential challenges. They embrace innovation and continuously refine their products or services to meet changing market demands. Additionally, entrepreneurs cultivate a culture of learning and agility within their organizations to ensure they can quickly respond to emerging trends.

Persistence and Resilience

Entrepreneurship is a journey filled with ups and downs, and setbacks are inevitable. Overcoming failure and maintaining resilience in the face of adversity is crucial for long-term success.

To overcome these challenges, entrepreneurs cultivate a mindset of persistence and resilience. They view failures as learning opportunities and leverage their experiences to make improvements. Entrepreneurs build a strong support network of mentors, peers, and advisors who can provide guidance and moral support during challenging times. Moreover, they maintain a positive attitude and stay focused on their long-term goals, allowing setbacks to serve as motivation for growth and improvement.

Example: Elon Musk and SpaceX

An inspiring example of overcoming obstacles and achieving success is the story of Elon Musk and SpaceX. Musk faced significant challenges in revolutionizing the space industry, dominated by well-established players. He encountered technical difficulties and financial constraints that jeopardized the success of SpaceX.

To address these obstacles, Musk displayed exceptional problem-solving skills and resilience. He invested his own resources, co-founding SpaceX with the aim of reducing the cost of space exploration. Musk leveraged his expertise in engineering and technology to develop innovative solutions, such as reusable rockets, to overcome the high costs associated with space travel. Despite multiple setbacks and failed launches, Musk remained determined, fostering a culture of learning and improvement within SpaceX.

Eventually, SpaceX achieved groundbreaking milestones, becoming the first privately-funded company to send a spacecraft to the International Space Station and successfully landing reusable rockets. Musk's ability to overcome obstacles and his unwavering determination played a pivotal role in the success of SpaceX, revolutionizing the space industry and paving the way for future exploration.

Conclusion

Entrepreneurs face numerous obstacles on their journey to economic success. However, by overcoming these challenges, they demonstrate resilience, innovation, and determination. Strategies such as identifying and assessing risks, managing financial constraints, building strong teams, adapting to market changes, and maintaining persistence are essential for navigating through obstacles and achieving success. The example of Elon Musk and SpaceX serves as an inspiration, showcasing the transformative power of perseverance and innovation in the face of adversity.

Case Studies of Successful Entrepreneurs

Steve Jobs and the Apple Revolution

In the realm of entrepreneurship and technological innovation, few names carry as much weight as Steve Jobs and Apple Inc. Steve Jobs, the co-founder and former CEO of Apple, was a visionary leader who revolutionized the way we live, work, and communicate. His entrepreneurial journey and the subsequent success of Apple have become iconic in the business world.

The Visionary Mindset of Steve Jobs

One of the key factors that contributed to Steve Jobs' success was his unique mindset as an entrepreneur. Jobs possessed a rare combination of creativity, passion, and perfectionism that drove him to push the boundaries of what was possible. He believed in designing products that were not just functional, but also aesthetically pleasing and user-friendly.

Jobs famously stated, "Design is not just what it looks like and feels like. Design is how it works." This emphasis on design and user experience set Apple apart from its competitors. Jobs had an unwavering commitment to excellence and believed in delivering products that exceeded customer expectations.

The Apple Revolution

Under Jobs' leadership, Apple witnessed several groundbreaking innovations that transformed the technology industry. One of the most significant milestones in Apple's history was the launch of the Macintosh in 1984, which introduced the concept of personal computing to the masses with its user-friendly graphical interface.

However, it was the launch of the iPod in 2001 that truly set the stage for the Apple revolution. The iPod, a portable music player, revolutionized the way people consumed music. With its sleek design, intuitive user interface, and the introduction of the iTunes Store, Apple disrupted the traditional music industry and propelled digital music into the mainstream.

Building on the success of the iPod, Jobs introduced the iPhone in 2007, a revolutionary device that combined a mobile phone, an iPod, and an internet communication device into a single package. The iPhone not only transformed the telecommunications industry but also paved the way for the app revolution, creating a new ecosystem of mobile applications that reshaped various industries.

Apple's Impact on Industries

The impact of Apple's products goes far beyond the technology sector. Apple's relentless focus on innovation and user experience has disrupted and transformed several industries.

The introduction of the App Store created a platform for developers to create and distribute applications, giving rise to a booming app economy. Today, mobile applications are integral to various sectors such as education, entertainment, healthcare, and transportation, among others.

Apple's foray into the music industry with iTunes and later Apple Music led to a paradigm shift in the way music is consumed and distributed. The traditional model of physical CDs and music stores was replaced by digital downloads and streaming services. Artists and musicians now have a direct relationship with their audience and can distribute their work globally with ease.

The introduction of the iPad in 2010 revolutionized the tablet market, making it a mainstream device for personal and professional use. The iPad's impact can be seen in industries such as education, healthcare, and retail, where it has transformed workflows and enabled new possibilities for productivity and creativity.

Lessons from Steve Jobs and Apple

The success of Steve Jobs and Apple offers valuable lessons for aspiring entrepreneurs and business leaders.

First and foremost, Jobs' obsession with quality and design highlights the importance of delivering products that not only meet customer needs but also evoke an emotional connection. Jobs' attention to detail and relentless pursuit of excellence serve as a reminder that success stems from a passion for creating exceptional experiences.

Secondly, Jobs believed in focusing on a few core products and making them truly exceptional rather than pursuing a wide range of mediocre offerings. This strategy of simplicity and focus allowed Apple to maintain a strong brand identity and create a loyal customer base.

Furthermore, Jobs understood the significance of user experience and the integration of hardware, software, and services. By controlling every aspect of the Apple ecosystem, from the design of the hardware to the development of the operating system and the creation of the App Store, Apple ensured a seamless and cohesive user experience.

Lastly, Jobs was not afraid to take risks and disrupt established industries. From challenging the music industry with the iPod to revolutionizing the smartphone market with the iPhone, Jobs demonstrated the value of thinking differently and daring to envision a future that others may not yet see.

Conclusion

Steve Jobs and the Apple revolution have left an indelible mark on the business world. The visionary mindset of Jobs, coupled with Apple's commitment to innovation, design, and user experience, transformed multiple industries and set new standards for excellence.

The story of Steve Jobs and Apple serves as an inspiration for entrepreneurs and innovators, reminding us that with passion, perseverance, and a relentless pursuit of excellence, we can create products and experiences that shape the world and leave a lasting legacy. As we explore other success stories in this book, we will continue to draw upon the principles and lessons learned from Jobs and Apple's remarkable journey.

Jeff Bezos and the Rise of Amazon

In the realm of entrepreneurs who have revolutionized the modern economy, one name that stands out prominently is Jeff Bezos. Bezos is the founder and driving force behind Amazon, the e-commerce giant that has transformed the way people shop and do business. This section will delve into the rise of Amazon under Bezos' leadership, exploring the key strategies and innovations that propelled the company to its current position as a global powerhouse.

The Visionary Mindset of Jeff Bezos

One cannot discuss the success of Amazon without first understanding the entrepreneurial mindset of its founder, Jeff Bezos. Bezos is known for his long-term vision, unwavering commitment to customer satisfaction, and relentless pursuit of innovation. His ability to think big and take calculated risks has been instrumental in Amazon's exponential growth.

One of Bezos' core principles from the early days of Amazon was to prioritize long-term growth and market domination over short-term profits. This philosophy meant reinvesting revenues back into the company to fund ambitious projects, expand infrastructure, and customer-centric initiatives.

Trailblazing Strategies and Innovations

Amazon started as an online bookstore but quickly diversified its product offerings to become the "everything store" we know today. Bezos recognized early on the potential for e-commerce to disrupt traditional retail and transformed Amazon into a one-stop-shop for consumers' needs.

One of the key innovations that set Amazon apart was its customer-centric approach. Bezos understood the importance of personalization and convenience in the digital age. Amazon's recommendation system, powered by sophisticated algorithms, analyzes customer behavior and preferences to provide tailored product suggestions. This level of customization has significantly contributed to Amazon's success in capturing and retaining customers.

Additionally, Bezos recognized the importance of logistics and supply chain management. Amazon invested heavily in building a robust infrastructure, including fulfillment centers and distribution networks. This allowed the company to offer fast and reliable delivery, a critical factor in customer satisfaction. Furthermore, Amazon's foray into developing its own logistics capabilities, such as Amazon Prime and Amazon Flex, has enabled the company to exert greater control over the entire delivery process.

Disruption and Expansion

Under Bezos' leadership, Amazon has continuously disrupted various industries beyond retail. One notable example is Amazon Web Services (AWS), the company's cloud computing division. AWS provides scalable and cost-effective solutions for businesses, revolutionizing the way organizations manage their IT infrastructure. The success of AWS has not only propelled Amazon's growth but also transformed the landscape of cloud computing worldwide.

Furthermore, Bezos pushed the boundaries of innovation through ambitious projects like Kindle e-readers, Kindle Fire tablets, and the introduction of Alexa, Amazon's voice-controlled virtual assistant. These ventures allowed Amazon to diversify its revenue streams and establish a strong presence in the rapidly evolving tech industry.

Sustainable Growth and Corporate Social Responsibility

As Amazon expanded its global reach, concerns about its environmental impact and labor practices surfaced. Bezos recognized the importance of sustainability and corporate social responsibility, committing to ambitious goals such as carbon neutrality by 2040 and significant investments in renewable energy.

In terms of labor practices, Amazon has faced criticism regarding employee working conditions and unionization. Bezos acknowledged these concerns and committed to improving the well-being of Amazon's workforce by increasing wages and implementing safer working environments.

Lessons from Jeff Bezos and Amazon

Jeff Bezos and Amazon provide invaluable lessons for aspiring entrepreneurs and business leaders. Bezos' unwavering commitment to long-term growth, customer-centricity, innovation, and disruption serves as a blueprint for success in the digital economy.

Furthermore, the rise of Amazon highlights the importance of adaptability and continuous evolution in the face of changing market dynamics. By diversifying its product offerings, leveraging cutting-edge technologies, and prioritizing customer satisfaction, Amazon has maintained its position as an industry leader.

It is worth noting that Amazon's journey has not been without challenges and controversies. The company's dominance has raised concerns about competition, privacy, and the future of brick-and-mortar retailers. These dilemmas underscore the need for responsible business practices and effective regulation to ensure a fair and balanced marketplace.

In conclusion, Jeff Bezos and Amazon's rise to prominence exemplify the transformative power of entrepreneurship and innovation. Through visionary leadership, disruptive strategies, and a relentless focus on customer satisfaction, Bezos has shaped Amazon into a global juggernaut that continues to push boundaries and redefine the modern economy.

Elon Musk and the Vision for the Future

Elon Musk, the renowned entrepreneur and innovator, has emerged as one of the most influential figures in the modern business world. Through his various ventures, including SpaceX, Tesla, and Neuralink, Musk has demonstrated a visionary approach to technology and a bold determination to reshape the future of multiple industries. In this section, we will explore Elon Musk's vision for the future and the impact it may have on the economy and society as a whole.

The Visionary Mindset

To understand Musk's vision for the future, it is essential to delve into his mindset as an entrepreneur and innovator. Musk possesses a unique combination of traits and characteristics that have fueled his success and enabled his groundbreaking initiatives. Some of these key traits include:

1. **Determination and Resilience:** Musk is known for his relentless drive and unwavering commitment to his goals. Despite facing numerous setbacks and failures, he has consistently pursued his vision with determination and resilience.

2. **Big Picture Thinking:** Musk has the ability to think on a grand scale and envision possibilities beyond the conventional boundaries. He strives for transformative solutions that have the potential to disrupt entire industries and change the course of history.

3. **Risk-Taking:** Musk is not afraid to take risks and embrace uncertainty. He recognizes that revolutionary ideas often come with inherent risks, but he believes that the potential rewards outweigh the dangers.

4. **Multi-Disciplinary Approach:** Musk draws upon knowledge and expertise from various fields, seamlessly blending insights from engineering, physics, computer science, and business. This multidisciplinary approach enables him to tackle complex problems from different angles.

Space Exploration and Colonization

One of Elon Musk's most ambitious ventures is SpaceX, a private aerospace company with the goal of making space exploration and colonization a reality. Musk envisions a future where humans become a multi-planetary species, enabling the colonization of Mars and potentially other celestial bodies. This vision holds several significant implications:

1. **Human Survival and Planetary Resilience**: Musk believes that establishing a self-sustaining colony on Mars is crucial for the long-term survival of humanity. By creating an interplanetary civilization, the risk of extinction due to natural disasters or other catastrophic events on Earth can be mitigated.

2. **Technological Advancement**: The pursuit of space colonization requires the development of advanced technologies in areas such as rocket propulsion, life support systems, and sustainable resource utilization. These advancements have the potential to drive innovation and economic growth on Earth.

3. **Interplanetary Commerce**: In Musk's vision, Mars could become a hub for interplanetary commerce, facilitating trade and collaboration between Earth and Mars. This could open up new economic opportunities and markets beyond the confines of our planet.

While the colonization of Mars is undoubtedly a long-term goal, SpaceX has already made significant progress in space exploration and transportation. The company has successfully developed reusable rockets, drastically reducing the cost of launching payloads into space. This breakthrough has the potential to revolutionize the space industry and make space more accessible for scientific research, satellite deployment, and potentially space tourism.

The Electric Vehicle Revolution

Elon Musk's vision extends beyond space exploration and encompasses the transition to sustainable transportation on Earth. Tesla, the electric vehicle (EV) company founded by Musk, aims to accelerate the transition to a world powered by sustainable energy. Musk's vision for the future of transportation includes several key elements:

1. **Mass Adoption of Electric Vehicles**: Musk believes that electric vehicles are the future of transportation due to their lower carbon emissions and potential to be powered by renewable energy sources. Tesla's goal is to make electric vehicles mainstream and encourage the widespread adoption of sustainable transportation.

2. **Autonomous Driving Technology**: Musk envisions a future where vehicles are fully autonomous, capable of navigating without human intervention. Tesla's development of advanced driver-assistance systems and autonomous driving technology is a significant step towards realizing this vision.

3. **Energy Ecosystem Integration**: Tesla aims to create an integrated energy ecosystem that incorporates solar energy generation, energy storage through products like the Powerwall, and electric vehicle charging infrastructure. This

holistic approach aims to maximize energy efficiency and reduce reliance on fossil fuels.

The success of Tesla in the electric vehicle market has already had a significant impact on the automotive industry. Other major automakers have followed suit by investing in the development of electric vehicles, leading to increased competition and innovation in the sector. This shift towards sustainable transportation has the potential to reduce greenhouse gas emissions, improve air quality, and reduce dependence on fossil fuels.

Neuralink and the Future of Brain-Computer Interfaces

With Neuralink, Musk's neurotechnology company, he has set his sights on revolutionizing the way humans interact with computers and enhancing our cognitive abilities. Neuralink aims to develop implantable brain-machine interfaces that could bridge the gap between humans and artificial intelligence. Musk's vision for the future of brain-computer interfaces entails several key aspects:

1. **Enhancing Human Intelligence**: Musk believes that by connecting our brains directly to computers, we can enhance our cognitive abilities and augment human intelligence. This could enable us to access information more efficiently, learn at an accelerated pace, and potentially solve complex problems with greater ease.

2. **Medical Applications**: Neuralink also holds the promise of significant medical advancements. The technology could potentially provide solutions for neurological disorders, restore lost sensory capabilities, and enable communication for individuals with disabilities.

3. **Collective Intelligence**: In Musk's vision, brain-computer interfaces could facilitate the collective intelligence of humanity by enabling direct communication and information sharing between individuals. This could unlock new avenues for collaboration, problem-solving, and creativity on a global scale.

While the development of brain-computer interfaces is still in its early stages, Neuralink has made strides in implant technology and is engaged in ongoing research to advance the field. Musk's vision has the potential to reshape the boundaries of human cognition and bridge the gap between humans and artificial intelligence.

Caveats and Ethical Considerations

Although Elon Musk's vision for the future is undeniably captivating and exciting, it is essential to consider the caveats and ethical implications that arise from his ambitious pursuits. Some of the key concerns include:

1. **Technical Feasibility**: The realization of Musk's vision relies heavily on the development of cutting-edge technologies that are still in the early stages of development. The feasibility and scalability of some of these ideas are yet to be fully determined.

2. **Safety and Risk Assessment**: Musk's ventures, particularly in space exploration and brain-computer interfaces, involve inherent risks. Ensuring the safety of individuals and minimizing potential adverse effects should be a priority throughout the development process.

3. **Equitable Access and Distribution**: As transformative as Musk's vision may be, it is crucial to consider equitable access and distribution of the benefits it may bring. Ensuring that these advancements are accessible to all, regardless of socioeconomic status, is essential for a just and inclusive society.

Additionally, regulatory frameworks and ethical guidelines must be in place to address emerging challenges and dilemmas in areas such as privacy, security, and ownership of AI-generated content. Ethical considerations surrounding AI and automation, particularly in the context of job displacement, must also be carefully addressed.

Conclusion

Elon Musk's vision for the future encompasses an array of transformative ideas, from space exploration and sustainable transportation to neurotechnology and brain-computer interfaces. His entrepreneurial mindset, determination, and multidisciplinary approach have driven him to push the boundaries of what is possible. While the realization of his vision poses technical, ethical, and societal challenges, Musk's innovative thinking has the potential to reshape industries, drive economic growth, and shape the future of humanity. It is through individuals like Musk that society can aspire to achieve breakthroughs and create a better future for generations to come.

Resources: - Ashlee Vance, "Elon Musk: Tesla, SpaceX, and the Quest for a Fantastic Future" - Tesla website: https://www.tesla.com/ - SpaceX website: https://www.spacex.com/ - Neuralink website: https://www.neuralink.com/

Exercises: 1. Conduct further research on Musk's ventures and identify one technological challenge that he must overcome in each of his key areas of focus (space exploration, sustainable transportation, and brain-computer interfaces). 2. Discuss the potential economic and social impact of successfully colonizing Mars. Consider factors such as resource utilization, interplanetary commerce, and technological advancements. 3. Debate the ethical implications of brain-computer interfaces. Discuss the potential benefits and risks associated with integrating human brains with artificial intelligence. 4. Imagine you are an entrepreneur with a new sustainable transportation startup. Develop a pitch for potential investors, highlighting the environmental benefits and market potential of your venture.

Remember to approach these exercises with critical thinking and engage in constructive discussions to gain a deeper understanding of the topics.

The Impact of Entrepreneurship on Economic Growth

Job Creation and Innovation

Job creation and innovation are two interrelated concepts that play a crucial role in fostering economic success. In this section, we will explore the relationship between these two factors and discuss their implications for economic growth and development. We will also examine the various ways in which job creation and innovation can be promoted and supported.

The Importance of Job Creation

Job creation is a key driver of economic growth and prosperity. When new jobs are created, it not only provides individuals with employment opportunities but also contributes to the overall well-being of the society. Here are some key reasons why job creation is important:

- **Reducing unemployment:** Unemployment is a significant challenge faced by economies worldwide. Creating new jobs helps to alleviate unemployment, reducing social and economic inequalities.

- **Increased income and consumption:** When individuals are employed, they earn income, which allows them to consume goods and services. This increased consumption drives economic growth and stimulates demand in various sectors of the economy.

- **Enhancing productivity:** Job creation can lead to improvements in productivity. When businesses expand and hire more workers, the division of labor becomes more efficient, leading to higher levels of output per worker.

- **Boosting innovation and entrepreneurship:** New jobs often arise from innovative and entrepreneurial activities. These activities drive technological advancements, create new industries, and foster competition, all of which contribute to long-term economic growth.

The Role of Innovation

Innovation is a critical factor in driving economic success. It involves the development and implementation of new ideas, technologies, processes, or business models that bring about positive change. Here are some key aspects of innovation:

- **Technological innovation:** Technological advancements have a profound impact on job creation. New technologies often lead to the creation of entirely new industries and job opportunities. For example, the emergence of the internet and e-commerce has revolutionized the retail sector and created millions of jobs worldwide.

- **Product and process innovation:** Innovation can also involve the development of new products or the improvement of existing ones. This can lead to increased competitiveness, market expansion, and the creation of new jobs. Similarly, process innovation, such as the implementation of lean manufacturing techniques, can streamline operations and create more efficient job roles.

- **Innovation in business models:** Disruptive innovations, such as those seen in the sharing economy, have fundamentally changed traditional business models and created new job opportunities. Companies like Uber and Airbnb have leveraged innovative business models to transform the transportation and accommodation sectors, respectively.

- **Social innovation:** Innovation is not limited to technological advancements. Social innovation involves developing new solutions to address social challenges and improve the well-being of individuals and communities. This can include initiatives like microfinance, social enterprises, and sustainable business practices, which often create jobs and contribute to inclusive growth.

Strategies for Promoting Job Creation and Innovation

Promoting job creation and innovation requires a multi-faceted approach involving various stakeholders, including governments, businesses, educational institutions, and individuals. Here are some strategies that can facilitate job creation and foster innovation:

- **Investing in education and skills development**: A highly skilled workforce is crucial for fostering innovation and attracting investment. Governments and educational institutions should prioritize education and skills development programs that align with the changing needs of the labor market. This includes promoting science, technology, engineering, and mathematics (STEM) education and providing vocational training opportunities.

- **Supporting entrepreneurship**: Governments can create an enabling environment for entrepreneurship by implementing supportive policies and reducing regulatory barriers. This includes providing access to financing, establishing business incubators and innovation hubs, and offering mentorship and networking opportunities to aspiring entrepreneurs.

- **Encouraging research and development (R&D)**: Governments and businesses should invest in R&D activities to foster innovation. Funding for R&D can facilitate the development of new technologies, products, and processes, creating a fertile ground for job creation. Collaborations between universities, research institutions, and the private sector can expedite the transfer of research outcomes into commercial applications.

- **Promoting collaboration and knowledge sharing**: Collaboration between businesses, academia, and government entities is essential for fostering innovation. Knowledge sharing platforms, industry-academia partnerships, and the exchange of best practices can facilitate the diffusion of innovative ideas and improve the overall innovation ecosystem.

- **Creating a favorable business environment**: Governments should create a business-friendly environment that encourages investment and entrepreneurship. This includes simplifying regulations, reducing bureaucratic barriers, protecting intellectual property rights, and ensuring access to affordable infrastructure and resources.

Real-World Example: Silicon Valley

Silicon Valley is a prime example of the interplay between job creation, innovation, and economic success. Located in California, United States, Silicon Valley is home to numerous high-tech companies, including Apple, Google, and Facebook. The region has become synonymous with innovation and entrepreneurship, attracting talent and investment from around the world.

One of the main factors contributing to Silicon Valley's success is the presence of world-class educational institutions, such as Stanford University and the University of California, Berkeley. These institutions have played a crucial role in nurturing a skilled workforce and fostering research and development activities.

Furthermore, Silicon Valley has a vibrant startup ecosystem, with venture capital firms providing funding and support to early-stage companies. This has created a culture that celebrates risk-taking, innovation, and entrepreneurship, leading to the creation of thousands of jobs and the birth of groundbreaking technologies.

The success of Silicon Valley can be attributed to a combination of factors, including proximity to academic institutions, access to venture capital, a supportive regulatory environment, and a strong culture of collaboration and knowledge-sharing.

Exercise

Think of a recent technological innovation that has had a significant impact on job creation. Describe the innovation, its implications for job creation, and any potential challenges or drawbacks associated with it.

Hint: Consider innovations in sectors like e-commerce, renewable energy, artificial intelligence, or digital platforms.

Resources for further reading:

1. Acemoglu, D., & Autor, D. H. (2012). What does human capital do? A review of Goldin and Katz's The Race between Education and Technology. Journal of Economic Literature, 50(2), 426-463.

2. Mazzucato, M. (2015). The entrepreneurial state: Debunking public vs. private sector myths. PublicAffairs.

3. Porter, M. E., & Stern, S. (2001). Innovation policy for the 21st century. MIT Press.

Entrepreneurship Ecosystems and Policy Implications

Entrepreneurship is a vital driver of economic growth and innovation. In this section, we explore the concept of entrepreneurship ecosystems and discuss the policy implications for fostering a conducive environment for entrepreneurship to thrive. We will examine the components of a robust entrepreneurship ecosystem, the role of government policies, and the challenges involved in creating and sustaining an ecosystem that supports entrepreneurial activities.

Understanding Entrepreneurship Ecosystems

An entrepreneurship ecosystem can be seen as a dynamic network of interconnected actors, resources, and institutions that collectively support entrepreneurial activities. It comprises various elements, including entrepreneurs, investors, mentors, incubators, accelerators, educational institutions, research centers, and government agencies. These entities collaborate and interact to create an environment that stimulates and sustains entrepreneurial activities.

One key aspect of entrepreneurship ecosystems is the availability of financial capital. Startups often face challenges in accessing funding, especially in their early stages. Thus, the presence of angel investors, venture capitalists, and other sources of funding is crucial. These financial resources provide the necessary capital to support entrepreneurial ventures, fuel innovation, and enable growth.

Another vital component of entrepreneurship ecosystems is the presence of supportive institutions and infrastructure. This includes incubators and accelerators that provide startups with mentoring, networking opportunities, and shared office spaces. Educational institutions play a role in nurturing entrepreneurial talent by providing relevant training programs and courses. Research centers and technology transfer offices facilitate the commercialization of research and development outputs.

Furthermore, a strong ecosystem thrives on collaboration and knowledge sharing. Successful entrepreneurship ecosystems foster a culture of collaboration, where entrepreneurs, investors, and other ecosystem actors actively exchange ideas, experience, and resources. This collaboration leads to the creation of new ventures, joint ventures, and partnerships, thereby enhancing the overall ecosystem's innovation capacity.

Government Policies and Entrepreneurship Ecosystems

Government policies play a critical role in shaping entrepreneurship ecosystems. Policymakers can create an enabling environment for entrepreneurship to flourish by implementing supportive policies and regulations. Here, we discuss three key policy areas that have significant implications for fostering entrepreneurship ecosystems: regulatory environment, access to resources, and entrepreneurship education.

First, creating a favorable regulatory environment is essential. Excessive bureaucracy, complex regulations, and onerous licensing procedures can deter entrepreneurs from starting and scaling their ventures. Governments can streamline regulations, simplify procedures, and reduce administrative burdens to encourage entrepreneurial activities. Additionally, providing tax incentives, grants, and subsidies to startups and investors can facilitate the growth of entrepreneurial ventures.

Second, ensuring access to resources is vital for a vibrant entrepreneurship ecosystem. Access to finance, infrastructure, and talent are crucial factors for successful entrepreneurial ventures. Governments can establish funding programs specifically designed for startups and entrepreneurs, such as venture capital funds, angel investor networks, and microfinance schemes. Improving physical infrastructure, such as coworking spaces and high-speed internet connectivity, enhances the ecosystem's overall productivity. Moreover, policies focusing on attracting and retaining skilled talent, such as visa programs for international entrepreneurs, can further strengthen the ecosystem.

Third, entrepreneurship education is a key driver of a successful ecosystem. By incorporating entrepreneurship education into school curricula and higher education programs, governments can cultivate an entrepreneurial mindset and provide aspiring entrepreneurs with the necessary skills and knowledge. Entrepreneurship education can also include practical training, mentorship programs, and networking opportunities, further equipping individuals with the tools needed to succeed in the dynamic entrepreneurial landscape.

Challenges and Solutions

Creating and sustaining a flourishing entrepreneurship ecosystem is not without challenges. Some common obstacles include limited access to funding, lack of collaboration, talent gaps, and regulatory hurdles. Addressing these challenges requires a multi-faceted approach involving the collaboration of various ecosystem stakeholders.

To overcome funding constraints, governments can establish investment funds or venture capital firms dedicated to supporting startups. They can also work with financial institutions to develop innovative financing mechanisms tailored to the needs of entrepreneurs. Additionally, initiatives promoting networking events, pitch competitions, and hackathons can facilitate collaboration among entrepreneurs, investors, and other ecosystem actors.

Talent gaps can be mitigated through targeted education and training programs. Governments should collaborate with educational institutions and industry partners to develop specialized entrepreneurship courses and apprenticeship programs. Furthermore, policies promoting diversity and inclusion in entrepreneurship can help unlock untapped talent pools and foster innovation.

Regulatory hurdles can hinder entrepreneurial activities. Governments should regularly review and update regulations to create a more business-friendly environment. They should seek input from entrepreneurs and industry experts to identify and address regulatory bottlenecks. Moreover, establishing dedicated regulatory sandboxes, where startups can test their innovative solutions in a controlled environment, can help navigate regulatory requirements.

In conclusion, entrepreneurship ecosystems play a vital role in fostering economic growth and innovation. Governments have the power to shape these ecosystems through supportive policies and regulations. By ensuring a favorable regulatory environment, facilitating access to resources, and promoting entrepreneurship education, governments can create an environment where entrepreneurs can thrive. Overcoming challenges such as limited funding, lack of collaboration, talent gaps, and regulatory hurdles requires the collective effort of various ecosystem stakeholders. By addressing these challenges, governments can nurture vibrant entrepreneurship ecosystems that drive economic success and societal progress.

Exercises

1. Identify three components that are essential for a robust entrepreneurship ecosystem and explain their significance.

2. Discuss the role of government policies in creating an enabling environment for entrepreneurship. Provide examples of specific policies that can foster entrepreneurship ecosystems.

3. Explain the challenges that entrepreneurs often face in accessing funding. Suggest two policy measures that governments can implement to address this issue.

4. Describe three ways in which entrepreneurship education can contribute to the development of a successful entrepreneurship ecosystem.

5. Identify and explain two common challenges that hinder the growth of entrepreneurship ecosystems. Propose feasible solutions to overcome these challenges.

Additional Resources

1. The Startup Ecosystem Report 2021 by Startup Genome provides a comprehensive analysis of global entrepreneurship ecosystems and rankings of top startup hubs. Available at: https://startupgenome.com/report2021

2. The Global Entrepreneurship Monitor (GEM) is an annual survey that collects data on entrepreneurship activities worldwide. It offers valuable insights into the dynamics of entrepreneurship ecosystems. Access GEM reports at: https://www.gemconsortium.org/reports

3. The OECD Entrepreneurship Policy Review series provides in-depth assessments and recommendations for entrepreneurship policy development in specific countries. Explore reports at: https://www.oecd.org/cfe/leed/entrepreneurial-policies.htm

4. The Kauffman Foundation is a renowned organization focused on advancing entrepreneurship. Their website offers a wealth of resources, including research papers, educational materials, and ecosystem-specific insights. Visit: https://www.kauffman.org

Key Takeaways

- Entrepreneurship ecosystems consist of interconnected actors, resources, and institutions that support entrepreneurial activities. - Governments play a crucial role in shaping entrepreneurship ecosystems through supportive policies and regulations. - Key policy areas for fostering entrepreneurship ecosystems include the regulatory environment, access to resources, and entrepreneurship education. -

Challenges in entrepreneurship ecosystems, such as limited funding and regulatory hurdles, can be addressed through targeted policies and collaborative efforts. Successful entrepreneurship ecosystems enhance economic growth, innovation, and societal progress.

Lessons Learned from Successful Entrepreneurial Ventures

In this section, we will explore the valuable lessons that can be learned from successful entrepreneurial ventures. Entrepreneurs play a vital role in driving economic growth and innovation, and their stories can provide valuable insights for aspiring entrepreneurs and policymakers alike.

1. Embrace Failure as a Learning Opportunity

One of the key lessons that can be learned from successful entrepreneurs is the importance of embracing failure as a learning opportunity. Entrepreneurship is inherently risky, and setbacks and failures are often part of the journey. However, successful entrepreneurs understand that failure is not the end, but rather a stepping stone towards success. They view failure as a valuable learning experience that allows them to refine their approach, identify weaknesses, and develop resilience.

For example, take the case of Steve Jobs, co-founder of Apple. After being ousted from the company he helped create, Jobs faced numerous challenges and failures with his subsequent ventures. However, he used these experiences to learn and grow, eventually returning to Apple and leading it to unprecedented success. His ability to embrace failure and learn from it played a crucial role in his entrepreneurial journey.

2. Build a Strong Network of Mentors and Advisors

Successful entrepreneurs understand the importance of surrounding themselves with a strong network of mentors and advisors. These individuals provide guidance, support, and valuable insights based on their own experiences. They can offer advice on various aspects of entrepreneurship, including strategy, industry knowledge, and personal development.

Jeff Bezos, the founder of Amazon, is a prime example of an entrepreneur who recognized the value of mentorship. Throughout his career, Bezos sought advice and guidance from experienced business leaders, including Warren Buffett. Their mentorship played a significant role in shaping Bezos' approach to business and contributing to Amazon's success.

3. Foster a Culture of Innovation and Adaptability

One of the key lessons from successful entrepreneurial ventures is the importance of fostering a culture of innovation and adaptability. In today's rapidly changing business landscape, the ability to innovate and adapt is crucial for long-term success. Entrepreneurs who excel in this area are constantly seeking new ideas, exploring cutting-edge technologies, and adapting their strategies to meet evolving customer demands.

Elon Musk, the founder of Tesla and SpaceX, is a prime example of an entrepreneur who embraces innovation and adaptability. His ventures are driven by a mission to revolutionize industries and solve pressing global challenges. Musk's ability to constantly innovate and adapt has allowed his companies to thrive in highly competitive markets.

4. Focus on Customer Needs and User Experience

Successful entrepreneurs understand that meeting customer needs and delivering an exceptional user experience are critical factors for long-term success. They invest time and effort in understanding their target market, conducting market research, and gathering feedback from customers. This customer-centric approach allows them to develop products and services that truly address customer pain points and provide solutions that stand out from their competitors.

A notable example of this lesson is the story of Airbnb. The founders of Airbnb recognized the demand for alternative accommodation options and identified a gap in the market. By focusing on the needs and preferences of their users, they were able to create a platform that disrupted the hotel industry and revolutionized the way people travel and experience new places.

5. Persistence and Resilience Are Key

Entrepreneurship is a journey filled with challenges, setbacks, and obstacles. Successful entrepreneurs understand the importance of persistence and resilience in overcoming these hurdles. They possess the tenacity to keep going even in the face of adversity and are not easily discouraged by setbacks.

An inspiring example of persistence and resilience is the story of Oprah Winfrey. Despite facing numerous challenges throughout her career, including poverty, discrimination, and failures, she persevered and became one of the most influential media moguls of our time. Her ability to bounce back from setbacks and maintain her drive and determination played a crucial role in her entrepreneurial success.

Conclusion

In conclusion, the lessons learned from successful entrepreneurial ventures can provide valuable insights and guidance for aspiring entrepreneurs. Embracing failure as a learning opportunity, building a strong network of mentors and advisors, fostering a culture of innovation and adaptability, focusing on customer needs and user experience, and exhibiting persistence and resilience are some of the key lessons that aspiring entrepreneurs can take from successful ventures. By applying these lessons and learning from the experiences of successful entrepreneurs, aspiring entrepreneurs can increase their chances of achieving their own entrepreneurial success.

Chapter 3: Innovations that Transformed Industries

Chapter 3: Innovations that Transformed Industries

Chapter 3: Innovations that Transformed Industries

In this chapter, we explore the power of innovation in transforming industries and driving economic success. We will examine different types of innovation, the role of research and development, and the importance of intellectual property protection. Through case studies, we will analyze how specific innovations have reshaped various sectors, such as the film industry, transportation, and accommodation.

The Power of Innovation

Innovation is the process of creating and implementing new ideas, products, or processes that bring about significant changes in an industry or society. It is a driving force behind economic growth and progress, as it leads to the development of new markets, the creation of jobs, and the enhancement of productivity and efficiency.

Definition and Types of Innovation

Innovation encompasses a wide range of activities, and it can take different forms depending on the context. There are several types of innovation that are commonly observed in industries:

    1. **Product Innovation:** This type of innovation involves the introduction of new or improved products or services to the market. It may entail enhancing the functionalities, features, design, or performance of existing products, or developing entirely new ones.

2. **Process Innovation:** Process innovation focuses on improving the methods, techniques, or systems used to produce goods or deliver services. It aims to enhance efficiency, reduce costs, and optimize resource utilization.

3. **Business Model Innovation:** Business model innovation involves making fundamental changes to the way a business operates. It can include introducing new revenue streams, redefining value propositions, or adopting new distribution channels.

4. **Marketing Innovation:** Marketing innovation refers to the application of novel marketing techniques, strategies, or campaigns to promote products or services. It may involve the use of digital marketing, social media, or experiential marketing to reach and engage customers.

The Role of Research and Development

Research and development (R&D) plays a crucial role in driving innovation. It involves the systematic investigation, experimentation, and exploration of new ideas, technologies, or processes. R&D activities can be conducted by both private companies and public institutions.

R&D helps to expand the boundaries of knowledge and paves the way for breakthrough innovations. It involves a combination of scientific expertise, technological advancements, and creative thinking. By investing in R&D, organizations can gain a competitive edge, create intellectual property, and develop cutting-edge products or services.

Intellectual Property Protection and Innovation

Intellectual property (IP) refers to intangible assets that are the result of human creativity and innovation. It includes inventions, designs, trademarks, copyrights, and trade secrets. Protecting intellectual property is essential to incentivize innovation and enable individuals and organizations to reap the benefits of their creations.

Various legal mechanisms are in place to safeguard intellectual property rights. These include patents, which grant exclusive rights to inventors for a specified period, and trademarks, which protect distinctive symbols or designs associated with a brand. Copyrights protect original works of authorship, while trade secrets safeguard valuable confidential information.

Effective IP protection encourages investment in research and development by ensuring that innovators can profit from their creations. It also fosters competition and drives continuous improvement and innovation in industries.

Revolutionary Technological Innovations

Technological innovations have been a major driving force behind industry transformations. In this section, we will explore three groundbreaking technological innovations that have reshaped industries:

1. **The Internet and the Digital Age:** The advent of the internet has revolutionized communication, commerce, and information sharing. It has transformed industries such as media, retail, and entertainment. The internet has enabled the rise of e-commerce platforms, digital streaming services, and social media networks, fundamentally changing how businesses operate and individuals connect.

2. **Biotechnology and Medical Breakthroughs:** Biotechnology has revolutionized the healthcare industry by enabling the development of new drugs, treatments, and diagnostic tools. It has led to breakthroughs in personalized medicine, genetic engineering, and regenerative therapies, offering new hope for treating diseases and improving human health.

3. **Clean Energy Technologies and Sustainable Solutions:** The urgent need to address climate change and environmental concerns has spurred the development of clean energy technologies. Innovations in solar and wind power, energy storage, and sustainable materials have transformed the energy sector and paved the way for a greener and more sustainable future.

Case Studies of Industry Transformations

To better understand the impact of innovation on industries, let us examine a few case studies:

1. **Netflix and the Disruption of the Film Industry:** Netflix started as a DVD rental-by-mail service but transformed itself into a leading streaming platform. By leveraging the power of digital technology and data analytics, Netflix disrupted the traditional film and television industry. It pioneered the subscription-based streaming model and produced original content, challenging established players and transforming the way people consume entertainment.

2. **Uber and the Ride-Sharing Revolution:** Uber revolutionized the transportation industry with its ride-sharing platform. By leveraging smartphone technology and GPS, Uber disrupted the traditional taxi industry by offering a convenient, affordable, and on-demand service. It created a new business model that connects passengers with drivers, disrupting established transportation systems worldwide.

3. **Airbnb and the Sharing Economy**: Airbnb disrupted the hospitality industry by offering a platform for individuals to rent out their spare rooms or properties. It provided an alternative to traditional hotel accommodation, allowing travelers to access unique and affordable accommodations. Airbnb's disruptive innovation has transformed the way people travel and has influenced the entire tourism industry.

These case studies demonstrate how innovation can lead to the disruption and transformation of entire industries, creating new opportunities and challenging established players.

Conclusion

Innovations have the power to transform industries, drive economic growth, and shape the future. From technological advancements to novel business models, innovation provides organizations with a competitive advantage and opens new avenues for growth. Understanding the different types of innovation, the role of research and development, and the importance of intellectual property protection are crucial for fostering a culture of innovation. By embracing innovation, industries can stay ahead of the curve, adapt to changing market dynamics, and achieve lasting success.

The Power of Innovation

Definition and Types of Innovation

Innovation is a term that is frequently used in discussions about economic success and technological advancements. But what exactly is innovation? In simple terms, innovation refers to the process of creating something new or improving upon existing products, services, or processes. It involves the application of new ideas, methods, or technologies to bring about positive changes and drive economic growth.

Breaking Down the Definition

To understand the concept of innovation better, let's break down its definition into three key elements:

1. **Creating something new**: Innovation involves generating novel ideas, concepts, or solutions. It goes beyond mere replication and involves the

development of unique and original creations. This can range from the invention of new products or services to the introduction of new business models or processes.

2. **Improving upon existing products, services, or processes:** Innovation is not limited to creating something entirely new. It also encompasses the improvement and enhancement of existing products, services, or processes. This can involve making incremental changes or introducing significant breakthroughs to enhance performance, functionality, efficiency, or user experience.

3. **Application of new ideas, methods, or technologies:** Innovation requires the practical application of new ideas, methods, or technologies. These new elements can come from a variety of sources, including scientific research, technological advancements, creative thinking, or a combination of different disciplines. The application of these new elements is what brings about positive changes and drives economic success.

Types of Innovation

Innovation can take various forms depending on the scope, nature, and impact of the changes it brings. Let's explore some common types of innovation:

1. **Product Innovation:** This type of innovation involves the creation or improvement of products or services. It focuses on developing new features, functionalities, or designs that meet the changing needs and preferences of consumers. Product innovation can range from incremental improvements to radical breakthroughs.

2. **Process Innovation:** Process innovation refers to the improvement or introduction of new methods, techniques, or systems that streamline and enhance the efficiency of production or service delivery. It aims to optimize existing processes, reduce costs, increase productivity, and improve quality. Process innovation can involve reengineering workflows, adopting new technologies, or implementing lean principles.

3. **Business Model Innovation:** Business model innovation involves the creation or modification of the fundamental logic and structure of a business. It focuses on finding new ways to create value, deliver products or services, and capture revenue. Business model innovation can involve

changing the target market, adopting a new pricing strategy, embracing a collaborative ecosystem, or leveraging digital platforms.

4. **Marketing Innovation:** Marketing innovation involves the development of new marketing strategies, techniques, or channels to promote and sell products or services. It aims to reach and engage customers in novel ways, differentiate from competitors, and create unique brand experiences. Marketing innovation can include digital marketing campaigns, social media strategies, experiential marketing, or unconventional advertising methods.

5. **Organizational Innovation:** Organizational innovation focuses on improving the internal processes, structures, and culture of an organization. It aims to enhance employee productivity, foster creativity and collaboration, and drive continuous improvement. Organizational innovation can involve the implementation of flexible work arrangements, the adoption of agile methodologies, or the creation of innovation labs or cross-functional teams.

The Innovation Spectrum

Innovation can occur at different levels, ranging from incremental enhancements to radical breakthroughs. This concept is often visualized as the innovation spectrum, which represents the degree of novelty and impact of an innovation.

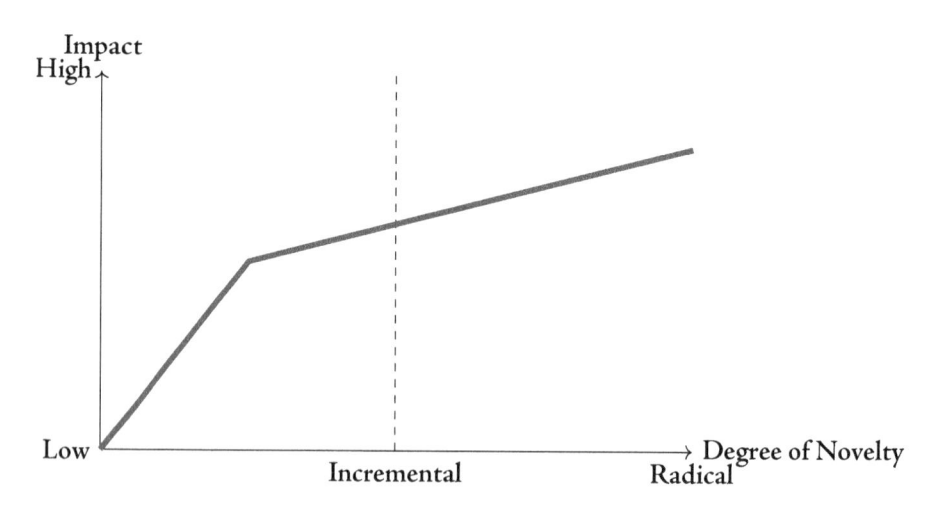

Figure 0.1: The Innovation Spectrum

Incremental innovations are small improvements or modifications made to existing products, services, or processes. They usually involve making minor adjustments to enhance functionality, performance, or user experience. Incremental innovations are important for continuous improvement and maintaining competitiveness in the market.

On the other end of the spectrum, radical innovations are groundbreaking and disruptive. They introduce entirely new ideas, products, or technologies that fundamentally change industries and create new markets. Radical innovations often involve high risks but can lead to significant economic success and transformation.

Between these two extremes, there are also disruptive innovations, which lie closer to the radical end of the spectrum. Disruptive innovations challenge existing norms and create new value propositions by offering simpler, more accessible, or more affordable alternatives. They often start in niche markets and gradually displace established players.

Innovation Ecosystem

Innovation does not occur in isolation but rather within a broader ecosystem that supports and fosters its development. An innovation ecosystem encompasses a range of actors, including individuals, organizations, institutions, and government bodies, all interacting and collaborating to enable, promote, and capitalize on innovation.

Key elements of an innovation ecosystem include:

- **Research and Development (R&D) Institutions:** These institutions play a crucial role in generating new knowledge, conducting scientific research, and developing new technologies. They provide the foundation for innovation by advancing the frontiers of knowledge and making breakthrough discoveries.

- **Entrepreneurs and Startups:** Entrepreneurs and startups are at the forefront of innovation, translating ideas into tangible products or services. They often operate in dynamic and risky environments, taking advantage of opportunities and disrupting traditional industries.

- **Investors and Venture Capitalists:** Investors and venture capitalists provide the necessary funding, resources, and expertise to support innovative ventures. They play a critical role in identifying high-potential opportunities, nurturing startups, and scaling up successful innovations.

- **Government Support and Policies:** Governments have a significant influence on innovation through policies, regulations, and funding initiatives. They often provide support for research and development, foster collaboration between academia and industry, and create an enabling environment for innovation to thrive.

- **Collaboration and Knowledge Networks:** Collaboration and knowledge sharing are vital for driving innovation. Establishing networks, partnerships, and platforms for sharing ideas, expertise, and resources can accelerate the innovation process and create a synergistic environment.

Case Study: Tesla and Electric Vehicle Innovation

One prominent example of innovation is the electric vehicle (EV) industry and the success of Tesla. Tesla revolutionized the automotive industry by introducing electric vehicles that offer a sustainable and high-performance alternative to traditional gasoline-powered cars.

Tesla's innovation can be analyzed using the framework discussed earlier:

- **Product Innovation:** Tesla's electric vehicles represent a significant product innovation. They incorporate advanced battery technology, cutting-edge design, and autonomous driving capabilities to provide a unique and compelling driving experience.

- **Process Innovation:** Tesla has pioneered new manufacturing processes that optimize efficiency and reduce costs. Their Gigafactories utilize advanced automation and vertically integrate the production of electric vehicle components, enabling economies of scale and faster time-to-market.

- **Business Model Innovation:** Tesla's business model stands out by combining the production of electric vehicles with a focus on sustainable energy solutions. The company leverages its expertise in battery technology to offer energy storage products for both residential and commercial use, establishing a diversified revenue stream.

- **Marketing Innovation:** Tesla's marketing strategy deviates from traditional approaches. Rather than relying on traditional advertising channels, Tesla emphasizes a direct-to-consumer sales model and utilizes online platforms and social media to engage with customers and build a passionate community.

- **Organizational Innovation:** Tesla has fostered a culture of innovation and disruption within the organization. The company encourages employee creativity, embraces a flat hierarchy, and promotes cross-functional collaboration to drive continuous improvement and adapt to changing market dynamics.

Tesla's success demonstrates how innovation, across different dimensions, can lead to transformative economic and industry-wide changes. By challenging the status quo and pushing the boundaries of technology, Tesla has not only achieved remarkable growth but has also catalyzed the widespread adoption of electric vehicles and clean energy solutions.

Conclusion

Innovation is a powerful engine that drives economic success and shapes our society. It encompasses the creation of new ideas, the improvement of existing products or processes, and the application of new methods or technologies. Various types of innovation, such as product, process, business model, marketing, and organizational innovation, contribute to economic growth and competitiveness.

Understanding the different dimensions and types of innovation is key to harnessing its potential. Whether incremental or radical, innovation can transform industries, create new markets, and improve the well-being of individuals and societies. By fostering an innovation ecosystem that supports collaboration, knowledge sharing, and risk-taking, we can unlock a world of possibilities and drive future economic success.

The Role of Research and Development

Innovation is a key driver of economic success, and research and development (R&D) plays a crucial role in fostering innovation. R&D is the systematic investigation and experimentation undertaken to gain new knowledge and create new products, processes, or services. It provides the foundation for technological advancements and helps businesses stay competitive in the global market. This section explores the importance of R&D in economic success and discusses various aspects related to its role.

Benefits of Research and Development

R&D has numerous benefits that contribute to economic success. Firstly, it promotes technological progress, which leads to the development of new products and services. It allows businesses to stay ahead of their competitors and meet the evolving needs and preferences of customers. For example, companies like Apple,

Google, and Tesla invest heavily in R&D to create innovative products that disrupt existing markets.

Secondly, R&D stimulates economic growth by creating new industries and job opportunities. Through the process of innovation, R&D drives productivity gains and fosters entrepreneurship. New industries emerge as a result of breakthrough scientific discoveries and technological advancements. This, in turn, leads to job creation, increased economic output, and higher living standards.

Moreover, R&D enhances the efficiency and effectiveness of production processes. It enables businesses to improve their operations, reduce costs, and increase productivity. By investing in R&D, businesses can identify innovative ways to streamline their processes, utilize resources more effectively, and achieve economies of scale. For example, companies in the manufacturing sector often use R&D to develop more efficient production techniques and machinery.

The Role of R&D in Innovation

Innovation is the process through which new ideas are transformed into commercially viable products, services, or business models. R&D plays a critical role in this process by providing the knowledge and expertise necessary for innovation to occur. It contributes to innovation in several ways:

1. Basic Research: Basic research, also known as pure or fundamental research, is conducted to gain a deeper understanding of the underlying principles of a phenomenon. It is the foundation of scientific knowledge and often leads to unexpected discoveries. Basic research is essential for innovation as it generates new ideas, theories, and concepts that can be applied to practical problems. For example, the discovery of the structure of DNA by James Watson and Francis Crick in the 1950s has revolutionized the fields of genetics and biotechnology.

2. Applied Research: Applied research focuses on solving specific problems or developing new products, processes, or services. It takes the knowledge generated through basic research and applies it to practical applications. Applied research is highly relevant to businesses as it helps them address market needs, improve existing products, and develop new technologies. For instance, pharmaceutical companies invest in applied research to discover and develop new drugs for various diseases.

3. Development: Development involves the translation of research findings into practical applications. It encompasses the design, prototyping, and testing of new products, processes, or services. Development bridges the gap between the theoretical knowledge generated through research and its commercialization. It is a crucial step in the innovation process as it transforms ideas into tangible outcomes. For example, the development phase in the tech industry involves converting innovative ideas into functional software or hardware products.

Financing R&D

R&D activities require substantial financial resources due to their long-term nature and high uncertainty. Financing R&D can be challenging for businesses, especially for small and medium-sized enterprises (SMEs) with limited budgets. However, there are various financing options available, such as:

1. Internal Funding: Many large corporations allocate a significant portion of their revenue towards R&D activities. They have dedicated departments and teams responsible for conducting research and developing new technologies. Internal funding provides businesses with control over the direction and scope of R&D projects. However, relying solely on internal funding may limit the capacity for innovation, as resources might not be sufficient to explore all potential opportunities.

2. Government Support: Governments play a vital role in promoting R&D by providing financial support to businesses through grants, tax incentives, and subsidies. These measures encourage businesses to invest in R&D and stimulate innovation. Governments also fund research institutions and universities, which conduct basic and applied research. This collaboration between the public and private sectors fosters knowledge-sharing and accelerates innovation.

3. External Funding: Businesses can also seek external funding sources for R&D, such as venture capital, angel investors, and crowdfunding. These sources are particularly beneficial for startups and SMEs that may not have access to large internal funds or government support. External funding often comes with expertise and industry connections, which can further enhance the success of R&D projects.

Challenges and Risks in R&D

While R&D offers significant benefits, it also presents challenges and risks that need to be managed effectively. Some of the key challenges and risks in R&D include:

1. Uncertainty: R&D projects are inherently uncertain, as they involve exploring unknown territories and dealing with unpredictable outcomes. Researchers and developers often face setbacks, failures, and unexpected results. Managing uncertainty requires resilience, flexibility, and the ability to learn from failures to make necessary adjustments.

2. Cost and Time Overruns: R&D projects can be resource-intensive and prone to cost and time overruns. The complexity and long duration of R&D activities make it difficult to accurately estimate budgets and timelines. Businesses need to carefully plan and allocate resources to ensure that R&D projects stay within budget and are completed on schedule.

3. Intellectual Property Protection: R&D often leads to the development of intellectual property (IP) in the form of patents, copyrights, trademarks, or trade secrets. Protecting IP is crucial for businesses to maintain a competitive advantage and monetize their innovations. However, it can be challenging to navigate the legal landscape of IP rights and enforce them effectively.

4. Talent Acquisition and Retention: Recruiting and retaining skilled researchers, scientists, engineers, and developers is vital for successful R&D. Talent shortages in specific fields or high competition for top talent can pose challenges for businesses. Developing attractive compensation packages, fostering a culture of innovation, and providing opportunities for professional growth can help overcome these challenges.

Case Study: SpaceX and R&D

Space Exploration Technologies Corp. (SpaceX) is a prime example of a company that relies heavily on R&D for its success. Founded by Elon Musk in 2002, SpaceX aims to revolutionize space technology and make space travel more accessible. R&D has been at the core of SpaceX's strategy from the beginning.

SpaceX invests a significant portion of its revenue in R&D to develop advanced rocket technologies, spacecraft, and associated infrastructure. The company conducts both basic and applied research to push the boundaries of space exploration. For example, SpaceX developed the Falcon 1 rocket through continuous iterations and improvements, leading to its successful launch in 2008.

Furthermore, SpaceX's development efforts have focused on reusable rocket technology. The company's Falcon 9 rockets are designed to land back on Earth after delivering their payloads to space, reducing the cost of access to space significantly. This achievement required extensive R&D, including iterative testing and design improvements.

SpaceX's commitment to R&D has resulted in numerous technological breakthroughs, such as the Dragon spacecraft and the Starship rocket. These innovations have transformed the space industry by increasing the reliability, reusability, and affordability of space launch systems. SpaceX's success serves as a testament to the critical role of R&D in driving innovation and shaping the future of space exploration.

Conclusion

Research and development are instrumental in driving economic success through innovation. R&D leads to technological advancements, creates new industries, and drives economic growth. It plays a vital role in the innovation process by generating new knowledge, solving practical problems, and translating research findings into practical applications. However, financing R&D, managing uncertainty, and protecting intellectual property are some of the challenges and risks associated with R&D. Through case studies like SpaceX, it is evident that R&D can have transformative effects on industries and shape the future of economic success. Hence, businesses, governments, and society as a whole should recognize the significance of R&D and foster an environment that promotes and supports it.

Intellectual Property Protection and Innovation

Intellectual property (IP) refers to creations of the mind, such as inventions, literary and artistic works, and symbols, names, and images used in commerce. Intellectual property protection plays a crucial role in fostering innovation and economic growth. It provides incentives for individuals and organizations to invest in research and development, as they can obtain exclusive rights to their creations, preventing others from using, copying, or profiting from their innovations without permission.

Types of Intellectual Property

There are several types of intellectual property rights, each designed to protect different forms of creativity and innovation:

- **Patents:** Patents grant exclusive rights to inventors for new inventions or improvements to existing inventions. To be granted a patent, an invention must be novel, non-obvious, and have practical utility. Patents typically last for 20 years from the filing date, during which the inventor has the right to prevent others from making, using, selling, or importing the patented invention.

- **Copyright:** Copyright protects original literary, artistic, and musical works, as well as software, databases, and other creations. It gives the creator exclusive rights to reproduce, distribute, display, and perform their work for a limited period of time. In most countries, copyright protection lasts for the life of the creator plus 50 to 70 years.

- **Trademarks:** Trademarks are used to protect distinctive signs, such as logos, names, and slogans, that distinguish goods or services of one enterprise from those of others. Trademark protection allows businesses to build and maintain brand recognition and prevent unauthorized use of their marks.

- **Trade Secrets:** Trade secrets refer to valuable and confidential information that provides a competitive advantage to a business. Unlike patents or copyrights, trade secrets are protected as long as they remain secret. Examples of trade secrets include formulas, recipes, manufacturing processes, and customer lists.

- **Industrial Design:** Industrial design rights protect the aesthetic aspects of a product, such as its shape, pattern, or color. This type of protection prevents others from copying or imitating the visual appearance of a product.

Importance of Intellectual Property Protection

Intellectual property protection encourages innovation by providing creators and inventors with the exclusive rights to their creations. These rights incentivize individuals and companies to invest time, money, and resources into research and development, knowing that they can enjoy the rewards of their innovations.

Effective IP protection also creates a conducive environment for collaboration and knowledge sharing. When creators can rely on their intellectual property rights, they are more willing to disclose their inventions and share their knowledge with others, leading to further advancements and discoveries.

Additionally, intellectual property protection promotes economic growth and competitiveness. It allows creators and businesses to monetize their innovations, attracting investment, creating jobs, and fostering technological advancements. IP protection also helps countries attract foreign direct investment (FDI) and facilitates international trade, as strong IP regimes provide assurance to foreign companies that their intellectual property will be protected in a given jurisdiction.

Challenges and Criticisms

While intellectual property protection is generally regarded as a vital component of innovation and economic success, it is not without challenges and criticisms. Some of the key concerns include:

1. **Balancing rights and access:** Striking the right balance between protecting IP rights and ensuring access to essential goods, services, and knowledge can be a challenge. Critics argue that overly restrictive IP laws can hinder access to medicines, education, and cultural resources, particularly in lower-income countries. Balancing the protection of IP rights with the public interest is a complex but crucial task.

2. **Patent quality and patent trolls:** The granting of low-quality patents can stifle innovation by creating barriers to entry and hindering competition. Patent trolls, also known as non-practicing entities, exploit weak or vague patents to claim infringement and extract licensing fees or settlements from alleged infringers. These practices divert resources from innovation and lead to costly legal battles.

3. **Digital piracy and counterfeiting:** The digital age has brought about new challenges in protecting intellectual property. Online piracy and counterfeiting of copyrighted works and trademarked goods have become widespread issues, causing significant economic losses for rights holders. Effective enforcement mechanisms and international cooperation are essential in tackling these problems.

4. **Disparities in global IP regimes:** There are significant differences in the level of IP protection and enforcement across different countries. These disparities can lead to issues of jurisdiction, enforcement challenges, and inadequate protection for creators and businesses operating in jurisdictions with weaker IP regimes. Addressing these disparities requires international cooperation and harmonization of IP laws.

Intellectual Property and Innovation Strategies

To promote innovation and navigate the challenges associated with IP protection, individuals and organizations can employ various strategies. Some of these include:

- **Developing a comprehensive IP strategy:** A well-defined IP strategy helps businesses identify and protect their valuable IP assets and manage their IP portfolio effectively. This strategy should align with the company's overall business objectives and consider both defensive and offensive IP measures.

- **Maintaining trade secret protection:** In certain cases, trade secret protection may be preferable to patent protection, especially when the innovation can be kept confidential and provides a competitive advantage. Companies should implement robust measures to safeguard their trade secrets, including confidentiality agreements, restricted access, and employee training.

- **Leveraging licensing and partnerships:** Licensing IP rights to other companies can generate revenue streams and allow for further innovation through collaboration. Partnerships and cross-licensing agreements can also facilitate technology transfer and the development of new products or services.

- **Monitoring and enforcing IP rights:** Effective monitoring and enforcement of IP rights are essential to combat infringement and unauthorized use of intellectual property. This involves actively searching for potential infringements, sending cease-and-desist letters, and, if necessary, pursuing legal action to protect IP assets.

- **Engaging in open innovation:** Open innovation involves actively seeking external collaborations, sharing knowledge, and licensing IP rights to foster innovation. By collaborating with other organizations, innovators can combine their expertise and resources, accelerate the development process, and create mutually beneficial outcomes.

Case Study: Apple Inc. and Intellectual Property Protection

A prominent example of the strategic use of intellectual property protection is Apple Inc. The company has built a reputation for its innovative products and has successfully utilized IP rights to protect its technology and maintain a competitive edge.

Apple has obtained numerous patents for its groundbreaking inventions, such as the iPhone, iPad, and Apple Watch. These patents have allowed Apple to prevent competitors from imitating or directly copying its products, ensuring its market dominance.

In addition to patents, Apple has also invested in design patents, which protect the unique visual appearance of its products. This has enabled Apple to differentiate its offerings through distinctive design elements, such as the rounded corners of the iPhone or the layout of its graphical user interfaces.

Furthermore, Apple has heavily relied on trademarks to build its brand recognition and create a sense of trust and quality among consumers. The iconic Apple logo, along with trademarks for product names like "iPhone" and "MacBook," has become synonymous with innovation and premium technology.

Apple's commitment to protecting its intellectual property has not been without challenges. The company has been involved in numerous legal battles worldwide, asserting its rights and defending against allegations of infringement. These legal disputes highlight the importance of maintaining a strong IP portfolio and enforcing IP rights to protect innovation and competitive advantage.

Conclusion

Intellectual property protection plays a crucial role in fostering innovation and economic success. It provides creators and innovators with exclusive rights to their inventions and creations, encouraging investment in research and development. However, balancing IP rights with accessibility, tackling challenges such as low-quality patents and digital piracy, and addressing disparities in global IP regimes are ongoing tasks.

By developing comprehensive IP strategies, leveraging licensing and partnerships, and actively monitoring and enforcing IP rights, individuals and organizations can navigate the complexities of intellectual property protection and harness its potential for driving innovation and achieving economic success.

Revolutionary Technological Innovations

The Internet and the Digital Age

The Internet and the digital age have revolutionized our society and transformed various aspects of the economy. In this section, we will explore the profound impact of the Internet on industries, business models, communication, and innovation. We will delve into the underlying principles of the Internet, its historical development, and its implications for economic success.

The Birth of the Internet

The Internet, as we know it today, emerged from a series of technological advancements and visionary ideas. Its inception can be traced back to the 1960s when the United States Department of Defense initiated the Advanced Research Projects Agency Network (ARPANET). ARPANET was designed to establish a robust and decentralized communication network that could withstand a nuclear attack. It connected various research institutions and allowed for the exchange of information across different locations.

The foundation of the Internet was laid with the development of the TCP/IP (Transmission Control Protocol/Internet Protocol) protocol suite in the 1970s. TCP/IP provided a set of rules for transmitting and receiving data packets over a network. This protocol made it possible to connect different computer networks, leading to the creation of a vast interconnected network of networks, which we now refer to as the Internet.

Principles of the Internet

The Internet operates on a set of fundamental principles that have facilitated its widespread adoption and transformative impact. These principles include:

1. **Openness:** The Internet is built on an open architecture that allows anyone to connect and participate. This openness promotes innovation, collaboration, and the exchange of ideas on a global scale. It enables individuals and organizations to create and share content freely, without gatekeepers or restrictions.

2. **Decentralization:** Unlike traditional communication networks, the Internet is decentralized, meaning that it has no central authority or control. Instead, it consists of a network of interconnected routers that direct data packets to their intended destinations. This decentralized structure ensures resilience, as the failure of a single node does not bring down the entire network.

3. **Interoperability:** The Internet enables different devices and systems to communicate and interact seamlessly. This interoperability is achieved through the use of standard protocols and formats, such as HTTP (Hypertext Transfer Protocol) for web browsing, SMTP (Simple Mail Transfer Protocol) for email, and TCP/IP for data transmission. It allows for the integration of diverse technologies and the exchange of information across platforms.

These principles have been instrumental in fueling innovation and driving the rapid development of the Internet.

Impact on Industries

The Internet has profoundly impacted various industries, transforming traditional business models and creating new opportunities. Let's explore some of the key sectors that have been revolutionized by the digital age:

1. **Retail and E-commerce:** The rise of the Internet has fundamentally changed the way we shop. E-commerce platforms like Amazon, Alibaba, and eBay have disrupted traditional brick-and-mortar retail by providing consumers with convenient online shopping experiences. The Internet has enabled small businesses to reach a global customer base and has facilitated the growth of online marketplaces.

2. **Media and Entertainment:** The Internet has revolutionized the media and entertainment industry, offering consumers new ways to access and consume content. Streaming services like Netflix and Spotify have gained popularity, offering on-demand access to a vast library of movies, TV shows, and music. User-generated content platforms like YouTube have empowered individuals to create and share their own videos, disrupting traditional media channels.

3. **Communication and Social Networking:** The Internet has transformed communication by enabling real-time, global connectivity. Social networking platforms like Facebook, Twitter, and Instagram have connected billions of people around the world, fostering new forms of online social interaction and communication. Instant messaging apps like WhatsApp and WeChat have revolutionized personal and business communication, making distance irrelevant.

4. **Finance and Fintech:** The Internet has revolutionized the financial industry, enabling the development of innovative financial technologies (fintech). Online banking services have made it easier for individuals and businesses to manage their finances, while mobile payment systems have simplified transactions. Cryptocurrencies like Bitcoin have emerged as a new form of digital currency, challenging traditional financial systems.

Challenges and Opportunities

While the Internet has brought about numerous benefits, it also presents a set of challenges that need to be addressed. These challenges include:

1. **Digital Divide:** The digital divide refers to the gap between those who have access to the Internet and digital technologies and those who do not. Bridging this divide is crucial for ensuring equal opportunities and inclusive growth.

2. **Privacy and Security:** With the proliferation of online activities, concerns about privacy and cybersecurity have become increasingly prominent. Protecting personal data and ensuring secure online transactions are critical for maintaining trust in the digital age.

3. **Disinformation and Fake News:** The Internet has made it easier for misinformation and fake news to spread rapidly. Addressing this issue requires promoting digital literacy, critical thinking, and reliable sources of information.

Despite these challenges, the Internet also presents exciting opportunities for future innovation and economic success. From the Internet of Things (IoT) to artificial intelligence (AI) and big data analytics, emerging technologies continue to shape the digital landscape and offer new avenues for growth and development.

Conclusion

The Internet and the digital age have had a transformative impact on the economy, society, and individual lives. Understanding the underlying principles of the Internet and its far-reaching implications is crucial for navigating the complexities of our interconnected world. By embracing the opportunities and addressing the challenges, we can harness the power of the Internet to drive economic success, foster innovation, and create a more inclusive and sustainable future.

Biotechnology and Medical Breakthroughs

Biotechnology has revolutionized the field of medicine, leading to remarkable advancements in health care and medical treatments. This section will explore the impact of biotechnology on the medical industry, highlighting key breakthroughs that have transformed the way we diagnose, treat, and prevent diseases.

Understanding Biotechnology

Biotechnology refers to the use of living organisms, or their products, to develop or improve processes, products, or services. It encompasses a wide range of applications, including genetic engineering, pharmaceuticals, diagnostics, and medical devices. Biotechnology has emerged as a powerful tool in medicine, providing innovative solutions to some of the most challenging health problems.

The Human Genome Project

One of the most significant breakthroughs in biotechnology is the completion of the Human Genome Project. This international research effort aimed to identify and map all the genes in the human genome. Completed in 2003, this monumental project has opened up new avenues for understanding human biology and developing personalized medicine.

The Human Genome Project has allowed scientists to identify genetic variations associated with diseases, paving the way for targeted therapies and precision medicine. It has revolutionized the field of genetics and provided insights into the genetic basis of various conditions, such as cancer, cardiovascular diseases, and neurological disorders.

Gene Therapy

Gene therapy is another groundbreaking application of biotechnology in the medical field. It involves introducing genetic material into a patient's cells to correct or replace a faulty gene. This innovative approach holds tremendous potential for treating genetic disorders and certain types of cancers.

For example, in recent years, gene therapy has shown promising results in the treatment of rare genetic disorders like spinal muscular atrophy (SMA) and inherited retinal diseases. By delivering a functional copy of the affected gene, gene therapy can restore normal cellular function and improve patients' quality of life.

Pharmaceutical Innovations

Biotechnology has also led to the development of numerous life-saving drugs. Through genetic engineering techniques, scientists can produce recombinant proteins, monoclonal antibodies, and other biotherapeutics with high specificity and efficacy.

One notable pharmaceutical innovation is the production of insulin using recombinant DNA technology. Previously, insulin was extracted from animal sources, leading to supply constraints and the risk of allergic reactions. However, with biotechnology, insulin can now be produced in large quantities using microbial fermentation, ensuring a stable and safe supply for patients with diabetes.

Diagnostic Advancements

Diagnostic technologies have greatly benefited from biotechnology, enabling early detection and accurate diagnosis of various diseases. Techniques such as polymerase chain reaction (PCR) and next-generation sequencing (NGS) have revolutionized molecular diagnostics, enhancing our ability to detect genetic mutations and infectious agents.

For instance, PCR-based tests have played a crucial role in diagnosing COVID-19 by detecting the presence of the SARS-CoV-2 virus in patient samples. NGS technologies have also allowed for rapid and comprehensive profiling of cancer genomes, facilitating personalized treatment strategies and targeted therapies.

Challenges and Ethical Considerations

While the advancements in biotechnology have brought immense benefits, they also introduce new challenges and ethical considerations. The use of genetic information raises concerns related to privacy, discrimination, and informed consent. Additionally, ensuring the safety and efficacy of gene therapies and other biotechnological interventions requires robust regulatory frameworks and rigorous clinical testing.

Resources and Further Reading

1. National Human Genome Research Institute: https://www.genome.gov/
2. Biotechnology Innovation Organization: https://www.bio.org/

3. World Health Organization - Biotechnology: `https://www.who.int/topics/biotechnology/en/`
4. The Pharmaceutical Research and Manufacturers of America: `https://www.phrma.org/`
5. National Institute of Biomedical Imaging and Bioengineering: `https://www.nibib.nih.gov/`

Conclusion

Biotechnology has transformed the medical field, offering innovative solutions to complex health challenges. From the completion of the Human Genome Project to gene therapy, pharmaceutical innovations, and diagnostic advancements, biotechnology continues to revolutionize the way we approach healthcare. However, ethical considerations and regulatory frameworks must keep pace with these developments to ensure the responsible and ethical application of biotechnology in medicine.

Clean Energy Technologies and Sustainable Solutions

Clean energy technologies and sustainable solutions play a crucial role in addressing the challenges of climate change and achieving long-term economic success. In this section, we will explore the importance of clean energy, the various technologies and solutions available, and their potential impact on the economy and environment.

The Global Energy Transition

The global energy landscape is undergoing a significant transformation, driven by the need to reduce greenhouse gas emissions and shift towards a sustainable and low-carbon future. This transition, often referred to as the "energy transition," involves a gradual shift away from fossil fuels towards cleaner and renewable sources of energy.

One of the main drivers of the global energy transition is the urgency to mitigate the effects of climate change. The burning of fossil fuels such as coal, oil, and natural gas for energy production releases significant amounts of carbon dioxide (CO_2) and other greenhouse gases into the atmosphere. These greenhouse gases trap heat, leading to global warming and climate change.

Clean energy technologies offer promising solutions to mitigate climate change and achieve sustainable economic growth. By harnessing renewable energy sources such as solar, wind, hydro, and geothermal power, countries can reduce their reliance on fossil fuels and significantly lower their carbon emissions.

Renewable Energy Technologies

Renewable energy technologies are at the forefront of the clean energy revolution. These technologies harness naturally replenishing sources of energy to generate power without depleting finite resources or emitting harmful greenhouse gases. Let's explore some of the key renewable energy technologies:

1. Solar Energy: Solar energy refers to the utilization of sunlight to generate electricity through photovoltaic (PV) panels or concentrated solar power (CSP) systems. PV panels convert sunlight directly into electricity, while CSP systems use mirrors or lenses to concentrate sunlight and generate steam for powering turbines. The falling costs of solar panels and advancements in efficiency have made solar energy increasingly competitive in the energy market.

2. Wind Energy: Wind energy involves harnessing the power of wind to generate electricity through wind turbines. As wind blows, it causes the turbine blades to rotate, thereby converting the kinetic energy of the wind into mechanical energy and eventually into electrical energy. Wind energy is a rapidly growing sector, with large-scale wind farms becoming a common sight in many countries.

3. Hydroelectric Power: Hydroelectric power uses the force of flowing water, typically from rivers or dams, to turn turbines and generate electricity. This technology has been in use for many decades and is a reliable and proven source of clean energy. Large-scale hydroelectric dams can generate significant amounts of electricity, but smaller-scale systems like run-of-river and micro-hydro plants are also viable options.

4. Geothermal Energy: Geothermal energy harnesses the heat from the Earth's core to generate electricity or provide heating and cooling for buildings. This technology relies on drilling deep into the Earth to access hot water or steam, which is then used to drive turbines and produce electricity. Geothermal energy is a reliable and constant source of power, but its widespread utilization is limited to regions with geothermal activity.

5. Biomass Energy: Biomass energy utilizes organic materials such as crop residues, wood, and agricultural waste to generate heat or electricity. By converting biomass into biofuels or utilizing it directly in power plants, this technology provides a carbon-neutral alternative to fossil fuels. However, it

is important to ensure sustainable practices in biomass production to prevent deforestation and ecosystem degradation.

These renewable energy technologies offer immense potential for both environmental and economic benefits. They not only reduce greenhouse gas emissions and combat climate change but also create new job opportunities, stimulate local economies, and enhance energy security by diversifying the energy mix.

Sustainable Solutions

Apart from renewable energy technologies, various sustainable solutions complement the clean energy transition and facilitate long-term economic success. Let's explore some of these solutions:

1. Energy Storage: Energy storage technologies play a crucial role in the integration of renewable energy into the grid. As renewable sources like solar and wind are intermittent, energy storage systems allow excess energy to be stored and used during periods of low generation. Battery technologies, such as lithium-ion and flow batteries, are becoming more affordable and efficient, enabling grid stability and supporting the growth of renewable energy.

2. Smart Grids: Smart grids are modern electricity networks that utilize digital technology to optimize the generation, distribution, and consumption of electricity. These grids enable real-time communication between consumers, energy producers, and grid operators, allowing for efficient load management, demand response, and increased grid reliability. Smart grids also support the integration of renewable energy sources and enable the widespread adoption of electric vehicles (EVs).

3. Energy Efficiency: Energy efficiency measures focus on reducing energy consumption and wastage in buildings, industries, and transportation. This involves adopting energy-efficient technologies, improving insulation, implementing energy management systems, and promoting behavioral changes. Energy efficiency not only reduces carbon emissions but also lowers energy costs, increases productivity, and enhances the competitiveness of businesses.

4. Clean Transportation: The transportation sector is a major contributor to greenhouse gas emissions. Clean transportation solutions, such as electric

vehicles (EVs), fuel-cell vehicles, and sustainable biofuels, aim to decarbonize the sector and improve air quality. The widespread adoption of EVs, supported by the development of charging infrastructure, can significantly reduce the reliance on fossil fuels and mitigate the environmental impact of transportation.

By combining renewable energy technologies with sustainable solutions, countries and businesses can advance their economies while minimizing their environmental footprint. These clean and sustainable practices not only benefit society and the environment but also create new markets, spur innovation, and drive economic growth in the long run.

Case Studies: Clean Energy for Economic Success

Let's explore a few case studies that highlight the economic success achieved through the adoption of clean energy technologies and sustainable solutions:

1. Denmark's Wind Energy Revolution: Denmark is a global leader in wind energy, with wind power providing a significant share of the country's electricity needs. The Danish government's early investment in wind energy research, development, and subsidies paved the way for the growth of a competitive wind turbine industry. Today, Denmark's wind industry is a major economic driver, creating jobs, attracting investments, and exporting wind turbines around the world.

2. Germany's Energiewende: Germany's Energiewende, meaning "energy transition," is a comprehensive strategy to shift the country's energy system from fossil fuels to renewable sources. Through generous incentives for renewable energy investments, support for research and development, and innovative policy frameworks, Germany has transformed its energy sector. This transition not only reduced greenhouse gas emissions but also created a robust renewable energy industry, generating employment and driving economic growth.

3. China's Clean Energy Leadership: China's rapid economic growth and increasing energy demands have propelled the country to become a global leader in clean energy. Through substantial investments in renewable energy technologies, China has become the world's largest producer of solar panels, wind turbines, and electric vehicles. This ambitious embrace of clean energy has not only helped the country combat air pollution and reduce carbon

emissions but has also stimulated economic growth and created millions of jobs in the clean energy sector.

These case studies exemplify how clean energy technologies and sustainable solutions can drive economic success while addressing environmental challenges. By adopting and investing in clean energy, countries can cultivate new industries, enhance energy security, create employment opportunities, and foster innovation.

Conclusion

Clean energy technologies and sustainable solutions are indispensable for achieving economic success in a rapidly changing world. By transitioning to renewable energy sources, investing in energy storage and efficiency measures, and embracing sustainable practices, countries can pave the way for a greener and more prosperous future.

The clean energy revolution not only offers environmental benefits, such as mitigating climate change and improving air quality, but also presents immense economic opportunities. Through job creation, technological innovation, and enhanced energy security, clean energy technologies and sustainable solutions have the potential to drive long-term economic growth and ensure a sustainable future for generations to come.

Case Studies of Industry Transformations

Netflix and the Disruption of the Film Industry

The film industry has been a dominant force in entertainment for over a century. It has provided us with countless hours of entertainment, and its influence on popular culture cannot be overstated. However, with the rise of digital technology and the internet, the film industry has been undergoing a massive transformation. One company that has been at the forefront of this disruption is Netflix.

The Rise of Netflix

Netflix was founded in 1997 as a DVD-by-mail service, with the goal of bringing convenience and choice to movie lovers. By offering a large catalog of films available for rental, delivered right to your mailbox, Netflix soon became a popular alternative to traditional video rental stores. However, it was their decision to embrace streaming technology that would truly revolutionize the industry.

In 2007, Netflix introduced its streaming service, allowing subscribers to instantly stream movies and TV shows over the internet. This marked a significant shift in how people consumed media, as it eliminated the need for physical DVDs and offered a vast library of content at the click of a button. With the introduction of original programming in 2013, such as the critically acclaimed series "House of Cards," Netflix further solidified its position as a major player in the industry.

Disruption of the Film Industry

Netflix's streaming service has fundamentally disrupted the traditional film industry in several ways. Firstly, it has challenged the dominance of movie theaters as the primary distribution channel for new films. With the ability to stream movies directly to their homes, consumers now have more control over when and where they watch films. This has led to a decline in theater attendance and a shift towards online streaming platforms.

Secondly, Netflix's emphasis on producing original content has disrupted the traditional model of film production. In the past, major film studios held the power to greenlight projects and determine what content would be made available to the public. However, Netflix's entry into original programming has given filmmakers and creators a new avenue to bring their vision to life. This has resulted in a more diverse range of content being produced, catering to the specific interests and tastes of different audiences.

Finally, Netflix's data-driven approach has transformed the way films are marketed and distributed. By analyzing viewer data and preferences, Netflix is able to tailor its recommendations and promotional efforts to individual subscribers. This has allowed them to create a more personalized viewing experience and increase customer engagement. Additionally, their direct-to-consumer model has disrupted the traditional distribution system, bypassing intermediaries and allowing for greater control over the release and availability of content.

The Economics of Netflix

The success of Netflix can be attributed, in part, to its disruptive business model. By eliminating the need for physical stores and reducing distribution costs, Netflix has been able to offer its streaming service at a competitive price. This has allowed them to attract a large customer base, with over 200 million subscribers worldwide as of 2021.

Furthermore, Netflix's use of data analytics and recommendation algorithms has played a crucial role in their success. By collecting and analyzing user data, they can identify trends and preferences, which helps them make informed decisions about content production and acquisition. This data-driven approach has allowed Netflix to create a curated library of films and TV shows that appeals to a wide range of audiences.

In terms of revenue generation, Netflix relies predominantly on subscription fees. By offering different subscription tiers and pricing options, they are able to cater to different segments of the market and maximize their revenue potential. Additionally, their original content strategy has helped differentiate their service and justify the price to consumers.

Challenges and Future Outlook

While Netflix has enjoyed tremendous success, it also faces a number of challenges moving forward. One challenge is the increasing competition in the streaming market. With the entry of other major players such as Amazon Prime Video, Disney+, and HBO Max, the market has become more crowded, and customers now have more options to choose from. This puts pressure on Netflix to continue delivering high-quality content and maintaining its competitive edge.

Another challenge for Netflix is content production costs. As they continue to invest heavily in original programming, the cost of producing and acquiring content has risen significantly. This puts pressure on their profit margins and requires them to find a balance between creating compelling content and managing costs.

Looking to the future, Netflix is likely to continue investing in international markets as a key driver of growth. With expanding internet access and the rise of smartphones, there is a growing demand for streaming services in emerging economies. By expanding their global footprint, Netflix can tap into these new markets and reach a larger audience.

Additionally, technological advancements such as 5G and virtual reality present new opportunities for Netflix to enhance the viewing experience and explore innovative content formats. As these technologies become more widespread, Netflix will need to adapt and leverage them to stay ahead of the competition.

In conclusion, Netflix has disrupted the film industry through its streaming service, original content, and data-driven approach. It has challenged the traditional distribution model, empowered filmmakers, and revolutionized the way films are marketed. While it faces challenges and increased competition, Netflix's innovative business model and customer-centric approach position it as a key player in the future of entertainment.

Uber and the Ride-Sharing Revolution

The rise of Uber and the emergence of the ride-sharing industry have had a significant impact on transportation and the economy as a whole. This section explores the story behind Uber, the principles of the ride-sharing model, the benefits it brings, and the challenges it faces.

Background and Origins of Uber

Uber, founded in 2009, is a technology platform that connects riders with drivers through a smartphone app. It was started by Travis Kalanick and Garrett Camp, who aimed to revolutionize the taxi industry by introducing a more efficient and convenient way to book and pay for rides. The idea behind Uber was born out of frustration with the traditional taxi service and the desire to create a better experience for both riders and drivers.

Principles of the Ride-Sharing Model

The ride-sharing model operates on several key principles:

1. **Peer-to-peer (P2P) connectivity**: Uber facilitates direct connections between riders and drivers, eliminating the need for traditional taxi companies as intermediaries.

2. **Dynamic pricing**: Uber uses a dynamic pricing mechanism, known as surge pricing, which adjusts fares based on supply and demand. During periods of high demand, such as rush hour or bad weather, prices increase to incentivize more drivers to be available.

3. **Rating systems**: Both riders and drivers can rate each other after a trip, which helps maintain quality and safety standards. Ratings create a level of accountability and ensure a high level of service.

4. **Cashless transactions**: Payments are done electronically through the app, eliminating the need for cash transactions. This makes the process more seamless and convenient for both parties.

Benefits of Ride-Sharing

The ride-sharing revolution has brought numerous benefits to both riders and drivers, as well as to the economy as a whole:

1. **Convenience and accessibility**: Uber has made getting a ride more convenient than ever before. With just a few taps on the smartphone, customers can request a ride, track its progress, and even share their trip details with friends and family. Ride-sharing also provides increased accessibility, especially in areas with limited or inefficient public transportation options.

2. **Flexibility and earning opportunities**: One of the key advantages for drivers is the flexibility it offers. They can choose when and where to work, allowing them to balance their driving duties with other commitments. This is especially beneficial for those who want to earn extra income or have irregular schedules.

3. **Reduced transportation costs**: For riders, ride-sharing is often a more cost-effective option compared to traditional taxis. The various pricing tiers offered by Uber allow riders to choose the level of service that fits their budget, while still enjoying the benefits of convenience and reliability.

4. **Reduced traffic congestion and pollution**: By reducing the number of private vehicles on the road, ride-sharing can potentially help alleviate traffic congestion and reduce carbon emissions. Studies have shown that ride-sharing services contribute to a decrease in the number of vehicles, as well as a shift from personal car ownership to shared mobility.

Challenges and Controversies

While ride-sharing has been widely embraced, it has also faced several challenges and controversies:

1. **Regulatory issues**: The introduction of ride-sharing disrupted the traditional taxi industry, leading to conflicts with regulatory authorities. Taxi companies argue that ride-sharing services should be subject to the same regulations and licensing requirements as traditional taxis, while Uber maintains that it operates as a technology platform connecting independent drivers with passengers.

2. **Labor rights and worker classification**: Another contentious issue is the classification of drivers. Uber considers its drivers as independent contractors, which means they are not entitled to benefits and protections usually granted to traditional employees. This has led to legal battles and debates over labor rights and worker classification in the gig economy.

3. **Safety concerns:** Ride-sharing has raised concerns about passenger safety and driver screening. Uber has implemented safety measures such as driver background checks and vehicle inspections, but incidents involving drivers with criminal records have still occurred. The industry continues to address these challenges through enhanced safety protocols and regulations.

Case Study: Uber's Impact and Adaptation

Uber's success has propelled it to become one of the most valuable and influential tech companies in the world. However, its journey has not been without obstacles. One prime example of Uber's adaptive strategies is its gradual expansion into various markets and the evolution of its service offerings.

In the early stages, Uber focused on providing black car services to cater to a higher-end market. It then expanded to offer cheaper options like UberX and UberPOOL, targeting a broader customer base. This adaptability allowed Uber to appeal to a wide range of riders, making ride-sharing accessible to the masses and transforming the transportation landscape.

Additionally, Uber has ventured beyond ride-sharing by introducing new services such as UberEats, Uber Freight, and Uber for Business. These expansions demonstrate Uber's ability to identify growth opportunities and diversify its business, staying ahead of the competition and adapting to changing market dynamics.

Despite the controversies and challenges it has faced, Uber's success has served as inspiration for other ride-sharing companies globally. Its disruptive model has prompted traditional taxi services to innovate and adapt, ultimately benefiting consumers with improved transportation options.

Conclusion

Uber and the ride-sharing revolution have revolutionized the way people think about transportation, offering a convenient and efficient alternative to traditional taxis. The principles of the ride-sharing model, such as P2P connectivity, dynamic pricing, and cashless transactions, have redefined the industry.

Ride-sharing brings numerous benefits, including convenience, accessibility, and reduced transportation costs. It has also helped address issues like traffic congestion and pollution. However, challenges related to regulation, worker classification, and safety continue to be debated and addressed.

Uber's success story serves as a testament to the power of innovation and adaptation in the face of adversity. Its impact and influence have transformed the transportation industry globally, paving the way for a new era of mobility. As ride-sharing continues to evolve, it will be crucial to strike a balance between innovation, regulation, and ensuring the well-being of both riders and drivers.

Airbnb and the Sharing Economy

In this section, we will explore the success story of Airbnb and its impact on the sharing economy. Airbnb is an online platform that allows individuals to rent out their homes, apartments, or spare rooms to guests. It has revolutionized the travel and accommodation industry by enabling people to find unique and affordable lodging options worldwide. The rise of Airbnb is a testament to the transformative power of technology and the potential for collaborative consumption models to disrupt traditional industries.

The Sharing Economy and Collaborative Consumption

Before we delve into the Airbnb success story, it is important to understand the concept of the sharing economy and collaborative consumption. The sharing economy is an economic system in which assets or services are shared between individuals through online platforms. It is based on the idea of efficient resource utilization, where underutilized assets, such as spare rooms, cars, or even skills, can be shared with others for a fee.

Collaborative consumption refers to the peer-to-peer sharing of goods and services among individuals. It enables individuals to access resources without the need for ownership, leading to cost savings and environmental benefits. Airbnb is one of the most successful examples of collaborative consumption, as it allows homeowners to monetize their homes and travelers to find affordable and unique accommodations.

The Airbnb Story

Airbnb was founded in 2008 by Brian Chesky, Joe Gebbia, and Nathan Blecharczyk. The idea for Airbnb came about when the founders decided to rent out air mattresses in their living room to help pay their rent during a design conference in San Francisco, where hotels were fully booked. They quickly realized the potential for this innovative model and expanded their platform to include the renting of entire homes and apartments.

The initial growth of Airbnb was challenging, as convincing homeowners to rent out their properties to strangers was met with significant resistance. However, the founders implemented various strategies to build trust and ensure the safety of both hosts and guests. They introduced a user verification system, secure payment processing, and host/guest reviews to establish credibility within the Airbnb community.

As the number of users grew, so did the listings on the platform. Airbnb leveraged social media and various marketing techniques to attract new hosts and guests. They also partnered with influential organizations, such as the Democratic National Convention and the Maroon 5 band, to boost their brand visibility.

Impact on the Travel Industry

Airbnb has had a profound impact on the travel industry, disrupting the traditional hotel model and offering travelers alternative accommodation options. It has democratized travel by providing affordable and unique experiences in local neighborhoods that were previously inaccessible to tourists. This has resulted in a more authentic and localized travel experience, benefiting both guests and local communities.

From a financial perspective, Airbnb has allowed homeowners and renters to generate additional income by utilizing their unused or underutilized spaces. This has created economic opportunities and empowered individuals to become micro-entrepreneurs in the hospitality industry.

However, the rise of Airbnb has also raised concerns and regulatory challenges. Traditional hotel chains and industry associations argue that Airbnb operates without the same level of regulation and compliance, giving them an unfair advantage. Some cities have imposed restrictions on short-term rentals to address issues such as housing affordability and neighborhood disruptions.

Challenges and Solutions

Airbnb has faced various challenges and controversies throughout its growth. One of the main challenges is ensuring the safety and security of both hosts and guests. To address this, Airbnb has implemented safety standards, including a host/guest rating system, secure payment methods, and a 24/7 customer support team. They have also enhanced their identity verification procedures to minimize the risk of fraudulent activity.

Another challenge has been the issue of discrimination and bias among hosts. In response, Airbnb has implemented non-discrimination policies and developed initiatives, such as the Open Doors program, to promote inclusivity and address discriminatory behaviors.

In terms of regulatory challenges, Airbnb has engaged in dialogue with policymakers and sought to find common ground. They have collaborated with various cities to implement fair and responsible home-sharing regulations that balance the interests of hosts, guests, local communities, and the overall hospitality industry.

The Future of Airbnb and the Sharing Economy

Looking ahead, Airbnb continues to innovate and adapt to changing market conditions. They have expanded beyond traditional vacation rentals to include experiences and adventures, allowing hosts to offer immersive activities to guests. This diversification has positioned Airbnb as a comprehensive travel platform, further disrupting the tourism industry.

The success of Airbnb has influenced the growth of other sharing economy platforms, such as Uber and TaskRabbit. These platforms leverage technology to connect individuals and facilitate the sharing of resources, services, and skills. As the sharing economy continues to evolve, it will be crucial for businesses and policymakers to address any potential social, economic, and regulatory implications.

In conclusion, Airbnb has transformed the travel and accommodation industry through its innovative sharing economy model. By connecting hosts and guests through an online platform, Airbnb has enabled individuals to monetize their underutilized spaces and provided travelers with unique and affordable accommodations. However, the success of Airbnb has also presented challenges, such as safety concerns and regulatory issues. As the sharing economy expands, it will be important to strike a balance between innovation and responsible business practices to ensure its long-term success.

Chapter 4: Financial Market Innovations and Economic Success

Chapter 4: Financial Market Innovations and Economic Success

Chapter 4: Financial Market Innovations and Economic Success

In this chapter, we will explore the role of financial market innovations in driving economic success. Financial markets play a crucial role in facilitating the flow of funds between savers and borrowers, ensuring efficient allocation of resources, and promoting economic growth. Over the years, various financial market innovations have emerged, reshaping the way businesses and individuals access capital, invest, and manage risk.

The Evolution of Financial Markets

Financial markets have evolved significantly over time, adapting to changing economic conditions and technological advancements. Understanding the historical context is essential to appreciate the impact of financial market innovations on economic success.

Financial markets have been in existence for thousands of years, dating back to ancient civilizations. Some of the earliest forms of financial markets include the trade of goods and commodities, as well as rudimentary systems of lending and borrowing. As societies became more complex, the need for more sophisticated financial institutions and instruments grew.

The development of stock exchanges in the 17th century marked a significant milestone in the evolution of financial markets. These exchanges provided a centralized platform for trading shares of public companies, enabling investors to buy and sell ownership stakes. The establishment of stock exchanges facilitated the democratization of capital and allowed businesses to raise funds for expansion.

With the advent of modern banking in the 19th century, financial markets expanded further. Commercial banks emerged as intermediaries between depositors and borrowers, providing much-needed liquidity to the economy. The creation of central banks, such as the Federal Reserve System in the United States, introduced stability and regulation to the financial system.

Role of Financial Intermediaries

Financial intermediaries, including banks, insurance companies, and investment firms, play a crucial role in the functioning of financial markets. These institutions bridge the gap between savers and borrowers by accepting deposits and channeling them towards productive investments.

Banks, as the primary financial intermediaries, offer a range of services, including lending, deposit-taking, and payment systems. By accepting deposits from individuals and businesses, banks provide a safe place for savings and allocate capital to productive investments. The ability of banks to assess creditworthiness and manage risk is a key factor in the efficient functioning of financial markets.

Insurance companies, on the other hand, provide protection against various risks faced by individuals and businesses. Through the pooling of resources, insurance companies spread the financial burden of unexpected events, such as accidents or natural disasters. This promotes economic stability and enables individuals and businesses to undertake higher-risk activities.

Investment firms, including asset managers and mutual funds, facilitate investment in financial markets on behalf of individuals and institutions. These firms pool funds from multiple investors and allocate them across a diversified portfolio of assets. By doing so, they provide individuals with access to a wide range of investment opportunities and help optimize risk and return.

Financial Market Innovations

Financial market innovations have revolutionized the way capital is accessed, investments are made, and risks are managed. These innovations have transformed traditional financial markets and given rise to new forms of trading and investment.

Securitization and the Rise of Mortgage-Backed Securities: Securitization is a process by which financial assets, such as mortgages, auto loans, or credit card debt, are pooled together and transformed into tradable securities. Mortgage-backed securities (MBS) were one of the first widely adopted forms of securitization.

MBS enabled lenders to transfer the risk associated with mortgage loans to investors. By packaging multiple mortgages into a single security, lenders could sell these securities in the financial markets, thus replenishing their capital and allowing them to issue new loans. This innovation increased liquidity in the mortgage market and fueled lending, contributing to economic growth.

High-Frequency Trading and Algorithmic Strategies: High-frequency trading (HFT) refers to the use of powerful computers and algorithms to execute trades at incredibly fast speeds. HFT firms capitalize on tiny price discrepancies in financial instruments and engage in a large number of trades within a short period. This innovation has significantly increased trading volumes and liquidity in financial markets.

HFT has both advantages and drawbacks. On one hand, it improves market efficiency by reducing bid-ask spreads and enhancing price discovery. On the other hand, it raises concerns about market manipulation and the potential for systemic risks, as trades occur at lightning-fast speeds without human intervention.

Online Banking and Financial Inclusion: Online banking has transformed the way individuals and businesses conduct financial transactions. It has eliminated geographic barriers, allowing people to access banking services anytime, anywhere. Online banking also enables cost savings, as it reduces the need for physical branches.

Moreover, online banking has played a significant role in promoting financial inclusion. It has provided access to banking services for underserved populations, such as those in rural or remote areas. This innovation has empowered individuals and small businesses, enabling them to participate more fully in the economy.

Case Studies of Financial Market Success

Examining case studies of successful individuals in the financial market can provide valuable insights into how financial market innovations drive economic success.

Warren Buffett and Value Investing: Warren Buffett, one of the most successful investors of all time, is known for his value investing approach. Buffett seeks to identify undervalued companies with strong fundamentals and holds these investments for the long term. His disciplined investment strategy has earned him substantial returns and made him one of the wealthiest individuals in the world.

George Soros and the Theory of Reflexivity: George Soros, a renowned investor and philanthropist, is known for his theory of reflexivity. According to Soros, market prices are influenced not only by fundamental factors but also by the perceptions and biases of market participants. Soros's understanding of reflexivity has enabled him to capitalize on market inefficiencies and generate significant profits.

Ray Dalio and the Principles of Bridgewater Associates: Ray Dalio, the founder of Bridgewater Associates, one of the world's largest hedge funds, has gained recognition for his unique management philosophy. Dalio emphasizes radical transparency and the importance of embracing failure as a learning opportunity. These principles have fostered a culture of innovation and success at Bridgewater Associates.

Conclusion

Financial market innovations have played a vital role in driving economic success. They have enabled the efficient allocation of capital, facilitated investment in productive ventures, and managed risks. Understanding these innovations and their impact on the economy is essential for policymakers, investors, and individuals seeking to navigate the complex world of finance. By studying successful individuals and case studies, we can gain valuable insights into the strategies and principles that drive financial market success.

The Evolution of Financial Markets

Historical Overview of Financial Market Development

Financial markets have a long and rich history, evolving over centuries to become the complex and interconnected systems we see today. To understand the current state of financial markets, it is essential to take a journey back in time and explore their historical development.

Early Origins of Financial Markets

Financial markets can trace their origins back to ancient civilizations, where rudimentary forms of trading and lending emerged. For example, in ancient Mesopotamia, clay tablets served as records for commodities exchanged and loans provided. Similarly, in ancient Greece and Rome, moneylenders and bankers operated in marketplaces, facilitating trade and providing loans to individuals and businesses.

The medieval period witnessed the formation of early financial institutions and instruments. The Italian city-states, such as Venice and Florence, became hubs of commercial activity, with merchants and bankers playing a crucial role in financing ventures and facilitating international trade. To support these activities, institutions like the Bank of Venice and the Medici Bank were established, providing secure storage of money and facilitating remittances between different regions.

Development of Stock Exchanges

By the late medieval period, stock exchanges started to emerge in various European cities. These exchanges provided a centralized marketplace for the buying and selling of shares in companies. One of the earliest examples is the Amsterdam Stock Exchange, established in 1602, which facilitated the trading of shares of the Dutch East India Company. This marked a significant milestone in the development of financial markets, as it allowed individuals to invest in and profit from the success of commercial enterprises.

Over time, stock exchanges proliferated across Europe and later spread to other parts of the world. The London Stock Exchange, founded in 1801, became a prominent center of global finance, attracting investors from around the world. In the United States, the New York Stock Exchange, established in 1792, played a crucial role in the growth of American capitalism.

The Evolution of Financial Instruments

As financial markets developed, so too did the range of financial instruments available. In addition to stocks, new instruments emerged to meet the evolving needs of investors and businesses. Bonds, for example, became popular as a means for governments and corporations to raise capital. These fixed-income securities promised regular interest payments and the repayment of the principal amount at maturity.

Derivatives also played a significant role in the evolution of financial markets. Derivatives are financial contracts whose value is derived from an underlying asset or benchmark. Futures contracts, for instance, allowed participants to buy or sell commodities or financial assets at a predetermined price and date in the future. Options contracts provided the right, but not the obligation, to buy or sell an asset at a predetermined price within a specific time frame.

CHAPTER 4: FINANCIAL MARKET INNOVATIONS AND ECONOMIC SUCCESS

Globalization and Financial Market Integration

The 20th century witnessed the rapid globalization of financial markets, with advancements in technology and communication facilitating the seamless flow of capital across borders. Financial market integration was spurred by the establishment of international financial institutions, such as the International Monetary Fund (IMF) and the World Bank, which aimed to promote global economic stability and development.

The development of electronic trading platforms and the expansion of international financial networks further accelerated the pace of financial market globalization. Investors can now trade securities from anywhere in the world, and financial institutions can provide services spanning multiple jurisdictions.

Regulatory Frameworks and Challenges

Throughout history, the development of financial markets has been accompanied by the implementation of regulatory frameworks. These frameworks aim to ensure market integrity, protect investors, and maintain financial stability. Examples of regulatory measures include the establishment of securities commissions, central banks, and financial watchdogs.

However, financial markets have also faced numerous challenges and setbacks. Periodic financial crises, such as the Great Depression in the 1930s and the Global Financial Crisis in 2008, have highlighted the need for effective regulation and supervision. These crises have led to significant reforms in regulatory frameworks, aiming to prevent excessive risk-taking and ensure the stability of the financial system.

Emerging Trends and Future Outlook

Looking towards the future, financial markets continue to evolve in response to emerging trends and technologies. The rise of fintech companies and the proliferation of digital currencies, such as Bitcoin, have the potential to reshape the financial landscape. Additionally, environmental and sustainability concerns are increasingly influencing financial market development, with the promotion of green finance and the integration of environmental considerations into investment decisions.

As financial markets continue to evolve and adapt, the need for robust regulation and oversight remains crucial. Balancing innovation and stability will be one of the key challenges in the future of financial market development.

In conclusion, the historical development of financial markets is a testament to human ingenuity and the evolution of economic systems. From ancient civilizations to the digital age, financial markets have played a vital role in facilitating economic growth, enabling investment, and allocating capital efficiently. Understanding this historical journey provides valuable insights into the complex and interconnected nature of modern financial markets.

Role of Financial Intermediaries

In the world of finance, financial intermediaries play a crucial role in connecting lenders and borrowers, facilitating the smooth flow of funds in the economy. These intermediaries, including banks, credit unions, insurance companies, and investment firms, act as middlemen between those who have excess funds to lend and those who need to borrow. They perform a range of functions that contribute to the stability and efficiency of the financial system.

Functions of Financial Intermediaries

Financial intermediaries perform several key functions that are essential for the functioning of an economy. These functions can be grouped into three main categories: providing liquidity, managing risk, and minimizing transaction costs.

Providing Liquidity: One of the primary roles of financial intermediaries is to channel funds from savers to borrowers, helping to bridge the gap between those with surplus funds and those in need of funds. They do this by accepting deposits from individuals and institutions and using these funds to make loans to individuals, businesses, and other entities. This process transforms illiquid assets, such as deposits, into liquid ones, such as loans, that can be readily used by borrowers.

Managing Risk: Financial intermediaries also play a crucial role in managing and diversifying risk. They collect funds from a large number of savers and pool them together, allowing for the dispersion of risk across a broad range of investments. By diversifying their portfolios and investing in a variety of assets, intermediaries can mitigate the risk associated with individual investments. This reduces the exposure of individual savers and borrowers to specific risks and promotes overall financial stability.

Minimizing Transaction Costs: Financial intermediaries are also responsible for reducing transaction costs associated with borrowing and lending. They have the expertise and infrastructure to evaluate the creditworthiness of borrowers, screen potential investments, and monitor the performance of borrowers. By performing due diligence and credit assessments, intermediaries can reduce the information asymmetry between lenders and borrowers, making it easier for borrowers to access funds at lower costs. Additionally, intermediaries often benefit from economies of scale, allowing them to provide financial services more efficiently than individual lenders and borrowers could on their own.

Role of Banks as Financial Intermediaries

Among the various types of financial intermediaries, banks play a particularly critical role in the economy. They act as intermediaries between depositors, who provide funds, and borrowers, who need funds. Banks offer a wide range of financial services, including deposit accounts, loans, credit facilities, payment systems, and investment products.

Banks serve as the backbone of the financial system, performing several vital functions:

Facilitating Payments: Banks provide payment services that enable individuals, businesses, and governments to conduct transactions efficiently. These services include check clearing, electronic fund transfers, debit and credit card processing, and online banking. By facilitating secure and timely payments, banks support the smooth functioning of the economy.

Mobilizing Savings: Banks collect deposits from savers and use these funds to provide loans to borrowers. By offering attractive interest rates and assuring the safety of deposits through deposit insurance schemes, banks encourage individuals and organizations to save. These savings are then channeled into investments, stimulating economic growth.

Credit Intermediation: Banks play a crucial role in credit intermediation, connecting borrowers and lenders. They carefully assess the creditworthiness of borrowers to determine the terms and conditions for lending. By evaluating borrowers' financial positions, businesses, and investment prospects, banks help allocate credit efficiently, ensuring that funds are directed to the most promising and productive projects.

Risk Management: Banks manage various types of risk, including credit risk, market risk, and liquidity risk. They carefully evaluate the creditworthiness of borrowers, monitor the performance of loan portfolios, and implement risk management practices to protect depositors and shareholders. Banks also engage in hedging strategies to manage market and interest rate risks. By undertaking these risk-management activities, banks contribute to the stability and soundness of the financial system.

Regulation and Supervision of Financial Intermediaries

Given the critical role that financial intermediaries play in the economy, they are subject to stringent regulation and supervision by government authorities. The purpose of regulation is to ensure the stability, integrity, and transparency of the financial system, protect consumers, and guard against systemic risks.

Regulators set prudential standards for financial intermediaries, including capital adequacy requirements, risk management guidelines, and disclosure norms. They monitor the activities of intermediaries and enforce compliance with regulatory requirements. Supervision involves conducting regular audits, inspections, and stress tests to evaluate the financial health, risk management practices, and compliance of intermediaries.

The regulation and supervision of financial intermediaries help maintain public confidence and trust in the financial system, safeguard the interests of depositors and investors, and mitigate the potential adverse impact of financial crises.

Recent Trends and Challenges

The role of financial intermediaries has evolved over time, influenced by changes in technology, regulations, and market dynamics. In recent years, several trends and challenges have emerged that impact the functioning of financial intermediaries:

Digital Disruption: Technological advancements, such as the rise of fintech firms and the adoption of digital platforms, have disrupted traditional financial business models. These developments have led to increased competition, expanded access to financial services, and the emergence of new channels for lending and investment. Financial intermediaries must adapt to these changes and embrace technological innovations to remain relevant and competitive.

Regulatory Changes: The global financial crisis of 2008 highlighted the need for stronger regulation and supervision of financial intermediaries. As a result, regulatory frameworks have been tightened to enhance financial stability and protect consumers. Financial intermediaries must navigate a complex and evolving regulatory landscape, ensuring compliance with a multitude of rules and regulations.

Cybersecurity Risks: With the increasing reliance on digital platforms and technologies, financial intermediaries face heightened cybersecurity risks. Cyberattacks and data breaches pose significant threats to the security and privacy of customer information, as well as the operational resilience of intermediaries. Robust cybersecurity measures and the continuous monitoring of emerging threats are essential to safeguard financial systems.

Overall, financial intermediaries play a crucial role in the economy by mobilizing savings, facilitating the flow of funds, managing risk, and reducing transaction costs. By understanding their functions and the challenges they face, individuals and policymakers can navigate the complex world of finance and promote sustainable economic growth.

Financial Market Innovations

Securitization and the Rise of Mortgage-Backed Securities

Securitization is a financial process that involves pooling together various types of assets, such as mortgages, and transforming them into tradable securities. This process played a significant role in the financial industry, particularly in the late 20th century, and led to the rise of mortgage-backed securities (MBS).

Background

To understand securitization and MBS, it is essential to have a basic understanding of the mortgage market. Mortgages are long-term loans provided to individuals or families to purchase residential properties. These loans are typically large and extend over several decades. Banks and other financial institutions are the primary providers of mortgage loans.

Traditionally, banks would keep these loans on their balance sheets until the borrowers repaid them in full. However, this approach limited banks' ability to provide more loans, as it tied up their capital. In the 1970s, financial innovators sought to find a way to unlock the value of mortgages and enable banks to free up capital for new lending.

The Process of Securitization

Securitization involves several steps that transform individual mortgages into securities that can be bought and sold in the financial markets. Here's a simplified overview of the process:

1. Origination: Banks originate mortgages by lending money to borrowers for the purchase of homes. These mortgages form the underlying assets for securitization.

2. Pooling: The bank then bundles together a large number of mortgages with similar characteristics, such as interest rates and maturity dates, to create a mortgage pool. This pool spreads the risk associated with individual loans.

3. Creation of Special Purpose Vehicle (SPV): To isolate the mortgage pool from the originating bank, a separate legal entity called a Special Purpose Vehicle (SPV) is created. The SPV becomes the owner of the mortgage pool.

4. Transfer to the SPV: The bank transfers the mortgage pool to the SPV, removing the loans from its balance sheet. The SPV funds the purchase by issuing securities known as mortgage-backed securities (MBS).

5. Tranching: The MBS are structured into different tranches, each with different levels of risk and return. Senior tranches have priority in receiving interest and principal payments, while junior tranches have higher risk but potentially higher returns.

6. Sale to Investors: The tranches are sold to investors in the financial markets. These investors can be institutional investors, such as pension funds or insurance companies, or individual investors.

7. Cash Flows: The cash flows generated from the underlying mortgages are used to pay interest and principal to the investors in the MBS. The SPV acts as an intermediary, collecting the mortgage payments and distributing them to the MBS holders.

Benefits and Risks

The securitization of mortgages brought several benefits to the financial industry and the overall economy:

1. Increased Liquidity: By transforming illiquid assets like mortgages into tradable securities, securitization increased the liquidity of the mortgage market. This allowed banks to free up capital for new lending, stimulating economic activity.

2. Risk Spread: Pooling mortgages into MBS diversified the risk, reducing the exposure of individual investors to default by a single borrower. This made investing

in mortgages more attractive to a broader range of investors.

However, securitization also posed risks, particularly during the global financial crisis of 2008:

1. Information Asymmetry: The complex nature of MBS made it challenging for investors to assess the quality and underlying risks of the mortgages. This lack of transparency contributed to the underestimation of risk by investors.

2. Moral Hazard: The separation of mortgage originators from the ultimate owners of the loans created a moral hazard problem. Originators had less incentive to ensure that the borrowers were creditworthy since they were no longer exposed to the long-term risks associated with the loans.

3. Systemic Risk: The widespread use of securitization and the interconnectedness of financial institutions meant that a single event, such as a sharp decline in housing prices, could have a cascading effect on the entire financial system.

The 2008 financial crisis highlighted the need for better regulation and risk management in the securitization market. It led to a reevaluation of the securitization process and the implementation of stricter rules to enhance transparency and accountability.

Real-World Example: Subprime Mortgage Crisis

The subprime mortgage crisis, which began in 2007, provides a real-world example of the risks associated with securitization. During the housing boom leading up to the crisis, lenders provided mortgages to borrowers with low credit scores and high-risk profiles, known as subprime borrowers. These mortgages were bundled into MBS and sold to investors around the world.

As housing prices started to decline, many subprime borrowers defaulted on their mortgages, causing significant losses for investors holding the MBS. The complexity of the securitization process and the lack of transparency regarding the underlying risks magnified the impact of the crisis.

This example emphasizes the importance of proper risk assessment and due diligence in the securitization market. It also highlights the need for regulatory oversight and mechanisms to protect investors and the stability of the financial system.

Conclusion

Securitization and the rise of mortgage-backed securities transformed the mortgage market and had a profound impact on the financial industry. By pooling mortgages into tradable securities, securitization increased liquidity and spread risk. However, it also introduced complexities and risks, as highlighted by the subprime mortgage crisis.

To ensure the long-term success of securitization, proper risk management, transparency, and regulatory oversight are crucial. The lessons learned from past experiences can help guide future innovations in securitization and contribute to the overall stability and effectiveness of financial markets.

High-Frequency Trading and Algorithmic Strategies

In today's fast-paced financial markets, high-frequency trading (HFT) and algorithmic strategies play a crucial role in shaping trading activities. These innovative approaches have revolutionized the way financial transactions are executed, bringing both opportunities and challenges to market participants. In this section, we will explore the principles, benefits, and concerns associated with high-frequency trading and algorithmic strategies.

Principles of High-Frequency Trading

High-frequency trading (HFT) refers to the use of sophisticated algorithms and powerful computing systems to rapidly execute numerous trades within fractions of a second. The underlying principle of HFT is to exploit small price discrepancies and market inefficiencies that occur over very short time intervals.

One key principle of HFT is market microstructure. It focuses on understanding the dynamics of the order book, the collection of all outstanding buy and sell orders for a specific financial instrument. HFT systems analyze the order book to identify patterns and trends, allowing traders to make informed decisions based on market liquidity and price movements.

Another principle is statistical arbitrage. HFT strategies often seek to profit from deviations in the prices of related financial instruments. By simultaneously buying and selling correlated assets, HFT traders can capture small price differences and generate profits in a short period.

Benefits of High-Frequency Trading

High-frequency trading offers several benefits to market participants, including increased liquidity, improved market efficiency, and reduced transaction costs.

Firstly, HFT enhances market liquidity by constantly providing buy and sell orders, narrowing bid-ask spreads, and ensuring that a large volume of trades can be executed quickly. This liquidity is especially valuable during periods of market stress when traditional liquidity providers may withdraw from the market.

Secondly, HFT improves market efficiency by quickly incorporating new information into prices. HFT algorithms react to news and data releases almost instantaneously, ensuring that prices more accurately reflect available information. This efficiency benefits all market participants, as it reduces the risk of trading at stale prices.

Lastly, HFT can lower transaction costs for investors. By narrowing bid-ask spreads and reducing price discrepancies, HFT reduces the cost of executing trades. This is particularly important for institutional investors and fund managers who deal with large volumes of trades.

Concerns and Challenges

While HFT has its advantages, it also raises concerns and challenges that need to be addressed to ensure fair and stable markets.

One concern is market manipulation. Rapid and high-volume trades executed by HFT algorithms can disrupt market dynamics and create artificial price movements. Regulators closely monitor HFT activities to detect manipulative practices and maintain market integrity.

Another concern is systemic risk. The speed and interconnectedness of HFT systems can amplify market volatility and trigger cascading effects during periods of market stress. Regulators and market participants must be vigilant in managing systemic risks associated with HFT.

Challenges related to HFT include technological infrastructure, regulation, and market access. HFT requires robust and reliable technology to handle vast amounts of data and execute trades within microseconds. Regulators need to establish appropriate rules and oversight to prevent unfair practices and maintain a level playing field. Additionally, ensuring fair and equal access to markets is crucial to avoid market fragmentation and ensure transparency.

Real-world Example: Flash Crash of 2010

One notable example that highlights the challenges and risks of high-frequency trading is the Flash Crash of 2010. On May 6, 2010, U.S. stock markets experienced an unprecedented and rapid decline, with the Dow Jones Industrial Average plummeting nearly 1,000 points within minutes, only to recover a short time later.

The Flash Crash was triggered by a combination of economic factors and technical glitches involving high-frequency trading. HFT algorithms exacerbated the market decline by executing a high volume of sell orders, leading to a domino effect as other algorithms followed suit. This sudden and extreme market movement highlighted the potential dangers of relying heavily on automated trading systems without adequate safeguards in place.

Conclusion

High-frequency trading and algorithmic strategies have transformed the landscape of financial markets, offering increased liquidity, improved efficiency, and lower transaction costs. However, they also raise concerns regarding market manipulation, systemic risk, and fairness. Regulators and market participants must strike a balance between encouraging innovation and ensuring the stability and integrity of financial markets. By addressing these concerns and challenges, high-frequency trading can continue to play a vital role in the modern economy.

Here is an example of how the section "4.3.3 Online Banking and Financial Inclusion" could be written:

Online Banking and Financial Inclusion

In the digital age, technological advancements have transformed many aspects of our lives, including the way we handle financial transactions. Online banking has emerged as a convenient and accessible solution that allows individuals and businesses to manage their finances through internet-based platforms. In this section, we will explore the concept of online banking and its role in promoting financial inclusion.

Understanding Online Banking

Online banking, also known as internet banking or e-banking, refers to the provision of banking services through electronic channels such as websites and mobile applications. It allows users to perform various financial activities remotely, such as checking account balances, transferring funds, paying bills, and applying for loans or credit cards.

The advent of online banking has brought about significant benefits for individuals and businesses. One of the key advantages is the convenience it offers. Gone are the days of waiting in long queues at bank branches or adhering to limited operating hours. With online banking, customers can access their accounts and initiate transactions at any time, from anywhere in the world, as long as they have an internet connection.

Another important aspect of online banking is the enhanced security measures that have been put in place to protect users' financial information. Banks leverage encryption technologies and multifactor authentication methods to safeguard customer accounts and prevent unauthorized access.

Promoting Financial Inclusion

Financial inclusion, the availability and accessibility of financial services to all individuals and businesses, is crucial for economic development and reducing poverty. Online banking plays a vital role in promoting financial inclusion by breaking down barriers to entry and providing access to banking services for underserved populations.

One of the main barriers to financial inclusion is geographical distance. In many rural or remote areas, traditional banking infrastructure may be limited or nonexistent. Online banking bridges this gap by allowing individuals to access banking services regardless of their location. This is particularly beneficial for individuals who live far away from bank branches and face challenges in physically accessing financial services.

Furthermore, online banking promotes financial inclusion by offering services and products tailored to the needs of underserved populations. For example, digital wallets and mobile banking apps enable individuals with limited access to traditional banking services to conduct transactions, save money, and receive payments using their smartphones. This empowers marginalized groups, such as low-income individuals or those without a formal banking history, to participate in the financial system.

Challenges and Considerations

While online banking provides numerous benefits, it also presents some challenges and considerations. One of the main concerns is the digital divide, which refers to the gap between individuals who have access to digital technologies and those who do not. It is important to address this divide to ensure that financial inclusion efforts are comprehensive and inclusive.

Another challenge is cybersecurity. As online banking relies on digital platforms, there is a need to strengthen security measures and protect users' information from cyber threats. Banks and financial institutions continuously invest in robust security systems to mitigate risks and prevent fraud and data breaches.

Additionally, issues related to user awareness and digital literacy should be addressed to ensure that individuals are equipped with the necessary knowledge and skills to use online banking effectively and securely. Financial institutions can play a role in educating their customers about the benefits and risks associated with online banking, thereby enhancing user confidence and trust.

Real-world Example: M-Pesa in Kenya

A real-world example of the transformative potential of online banking and financial inclusion is M-Pesa in Kenya. Launched in 2007, M-Pesa is a mobile-based digital wallet that allows users to send, receive, and store money using their mobile phones. This innovative service has revolutionized the financial landscape in Kenya, where a significant portion of the population did not have access to traditional banking services.

Through M-Pesa, individuals in remote areas can conduct financial transactions and access basic banking services using their mobile phones. This has led to increased financial independence, improved livelihoods, and economic empowerment for millions of Kenyans who previously had limited access to formal financial services.

Conclusion

Online banking has emerged as a convenient and accessible solution that promotes financial inclusion. By leveraging the power of digital technology, it allows individuals and businesses to access and manage financial services remotely. However, it is important to address challenges such as the digital divide and cybersecurity to ensure that the benefits of online banking are accessible to all. Real-world examples, such as M-Pesa in Kenya, demonstrate the transformative potential of online banking in fostering economic empowerment and reducing poverty.

Case Studies of Financial Market Success

Warren Buffett and Value Investing

Warren Buffett, often referred to as the "Oracle of Omaha," is one of the most successful and influential investors in history. His investment philosophy, known as value investing, has earned him a reputation for consistently achieving high returns over the long term. In this section, we will explore the principles of value investing, the strategies employed by Warren Buffett, and the key lessons we can learn from his approach.

Principles of Value Investing

Value investing is a strategy based on the principle of buying assets that are undervalued by the market. The underlying concept is simple: identify companies with intrinsic values higher than their current market prices, and invest in them with a long-term perspective. Value investors believe that the market often misprices stocks, presenting opportunities to buy quality assets at a discount.

To implement value investing, investors should focus on the following principles:

- **Intrinsic Value:** Value investors analyze the underlying fundamentals of a company to estimate its intrinsic value. This involves assessing the company's financial statements, management team, competitive advantage, and growth prospects. The goal is to determine the true worth of the company and compare it to its current market price.

- **Margin of Safety:** Value investors seek a margin of safety by purchasing stocks at prices significantly below their estimated intrinsic values. This provides a cushion against potential errors in valuation or unexpected market fluctuations. The larger the margin of safety, the greater the potential for long-term gains.

- **Long-Term Perspective:** Value investing is not a short-term trading strategy. Instead, it requires patience and a focus on long-term value creation. Warren Buffett is famously quoted as saying, "Our favorite holding period is forever." By holding investments for extended periods, investors can benefit from compounding returns and give the market enough time to recognize the underlying value.

- **Contrarian Thinking:** Value investors are contrarians who are willing to swim against the tide. They look for opportunities in companies that are temporarily out of favor or experiencing short-term setbacks. By being patient and taking a contrarian stance, value investors can often acquire stocks at attractive prices before the market recognizes their true value.

Warren Buffett's Investment Strategies

Warren Buffett's success as an investor can be attributed to his disciplined application of the principles of value investing. While his approach has evolved over the years, certain key strategies have remained consistent throughout his career:

- **Focus on Quality Companies:** Buffett seeks to invest in companies with strong competitive advantages, enduring business models, and a history of consistent profitability. He looks for businesses that have a sustainable competitive moat, which protects them from competitors and allows them to generate high returns on capital.

- **Buy at a Discount:** Buffett is known for his ability to find undervalued stocks. He looks for companies trading below their intrinsic values, often due to temporary market conditions or negative investor sentiment. By buying at a discount, he maximizes the potential for future returns.

- **Long-Term Orientation:** Buffett takes a long-term approach to investing. He avoids short-term market speculation and focuses on the long-term fundamentals of the companies he invests in. His willingness to hold investments for years, sometimes even decades, allows him to capture the full potential of compounding returns.

- **Emphasis on Cash Flow:** Buffett puts a significant emphasis on a company's cash flow. He prefers businesses that generate consistent and predictable cash flows over those with volatile or uncertain earnings. By focusing on cash flow, he can assess the company's ability to generate profits and return value to shareholders.

- **Invest in What You Understand:** Buffett subscribes to the principle of investing in businesses that he understands well. He avoids complex financial instruments or industries outside his circle of competence. This approach allows him to make informed investment decisions based on his deep understanding of the underlying businesses.

Key Lessons From Warren Buffett

Warren Buffett's investment success provides valuable lessons for both novice and experienced investors. Here are some key takeaways from his approach:

- **Value Investing Works**: Buffett's track record proves that value investing can generate superior long-term returns. By focusing on intrinsic value, buying at a discount, and having a long-term perspective, investors can build wealth over time.

- **Patience is Key**: Buffett's success is a result of his patience and discipline. He does not succumb to short-term market fluctuations or chase after hot stocks. Instead, he waits for the right opportunities and takes a long-term view. Patience allows investors to avoid impulsive decisions and benefit from compounding returns.

- **Do Your Homework**: Buffett emphasizes the importance of thorough research and understanding before making investment decisions. Investors should analyze financial statements, study industry dynamics, and assess the management team. A well-informed investment decision is more likely to yield positive results.

- **Embrace Contrarian Thinking**: Buffett's ability to be contrarian and take positions when others are fearful has been a key factor in his success. Investors should not be swayed by market sentiment or short-term trends. Instead, they should focus on the intrinsic value of a company and have the conviction to go against the crowd when necessary.

- **Long-Term Thinking Pays Off**: Buffett's long-term orientation has allowed him to capitalize on the power of compounding returns. Investors should resist the urge to constantly buy and sell stocks, as this can lead to higher transaction costs and lower returns. Instead, they should adopt a patient and long-term mindset to achieve substantial wealth creation.

Learning Resources

To further explore Warren Buffett's investment philosophy and value investing principles, here are some recommended resources:

- *The Essays of Warren Buffett: Lessons for Corporate America* by Warren E. Buffett and Lawrence A. Cunningham.

- *The Intelligent Investor* by Benjamin Graham, the mentor and inspiration for Warren Buffett's investment approach.

- Annual shareholder letters written by Warren Buffett, available on Berkshire Hathaway's website.

- Various books and articles on value investing and Warren Buffett's investment strategies, available in libraries and online.

Exercise

As an exercise, consider the following scenario:

Company XYZ is a well-established manufacturing company that has recently faced declining sales due to increased competition. Its stock price has dropped significantly, and many investors have lost confidence in the company's future prospects. However, after conducting a thorough analysis, you believe that XYZ's intrinsic value is much higher than its current market price.

1. Estimate the intrinsic value of company XYZ based on its financial statements, industry analysis, and competitive position.

2. Determine the margin of safety you would require before investing in XYZ and justify your decision.

3. Analyze the risks associated with investing in XYZ and how you would manage them.

4. Develop a long-term investment strategy for XYZ, outlining your expected holding period and potential exit strategies.

By working through this exercise, you can apply the principles of value investing and gain a deeper understanding of Warren Buffett's approach.

In conclusion, Warren Buffett's success as an investor is a testament to the power of value investing. By focusing on intrinsic value, buying at a discount, and maintaining a long-term perspective, investors can improve their chances of achieving superior returns. Buffett's principles of quality investing, patience, thorough research, contrarian thinking, and long-term orientation provide valuable lessons for investors looking to build wealth over time.

George Soros and the Theory of Reflexivity

George Soros is a renowned investor, philanthropist, and author who has made significant contributions to the field of economics. One of Soros' key ideas is the theory of reflexivity, which challenges the traditional notion of market efficiency and rational decision-making.

CHAPTER 4: FINANCIAL MARKET INNOVATIONS AND ECONOMIC SUCCESS

Background

In traditional economic theory, markets are assumed to be efficient and participants are considered rational actors with perfect information. This implies that market prices reflect all available information, and investors make decisions based on this information. However, Soros argues that this view is overly simplistic and fails to capture the complexity of financial markets.

According to Soros, markets are influenced not only by fundamental economic factors but also by the beliefs and biases of market participants. These beliefs can create feedback loops that amplify market movements, leading to booms and busts that deviate from fundamental values. This is where the theory of reflexivity comes into play.

Principles of Reflexivity

The theory of reflexivity proposes that market prices do not simply reflect the objective reality of economic fundamentals but are also influenced by subjective perceptions and interpretations. Soros identifies two aspects of reflexivity: cognitive and manipulative.

The cognitive aspect refers to the relationship between market prices and the underlying fundamentals. Soros argues that market participants' perceptions of these fundamentals are subjective and can be biased. When market prices are rising, investors may develop positive sentiments and overestimate the value of an asset, leading to a self-reinforcing cycle of price appreciation. Similarly, when prices are falling, negative sentiments can lead to an excessive decline in prices.

The manipulative aspect refers to the fact that market participants can influence market prices through their actions. For example, if investors believe that a stock will increase in value, they may buy more, driving up the price. This increase in price can then attract more investors, creating a self-fulfilling prophecy.

Implications for Financial Markets

The theory of reflexivity challenges the efficient market hypothesis and has significant implications for financial markets. It suggests that market prices are not always an accurate reflection of underlying fundamentals and can deviate from their intrinsic values.

Soros argues that these deviations can create investment opportunities. By identifying instances where market prices are significantly diverging from fundamentals due to reflexivity, investors can position themselves to profit from the subsequent correction.

However, Soros also acknowledges that reflexivity can lead to market inefficiencies and bubbles. When market participants' beliefs are distorted or irrational, prices can become detached from reality, leading to speculative manias and asset bubbles. These bubbles can eventually burst, causing severe financial crises and economic downturns.

Real-World Examples

One well-known example of reflexivity is the dot-com bubble in the late 1990s. During this period, investors' perceptions of internet companies' potential for future growth led to a speculative frenzy. Stock prices of many dot-com companies soared to excessive levels, detached from their actual earnings and valuations. Eventually, the bubble burst, resulting in substantial losses for investors.

Another example is the 2008 financial crisis. Housing prices in the United States were driven up by speculative buying and lax lending practices. As prices continued to rise, investors believed that they would keep increasing indefinitely. However, when the housing bubble burst, triggering a wave of mortgage defaults, it led to a severe financial crisis and a global recession.

Caveats and Limitations

While the theory of reflexivity provides valuable insights into the dynamics of financial markets, it has some limitations. Firstly, the reflexive nature of markets does not imply that prices are always irrational or detached from fundamentals. Markets can be both efficient and reflexive, with prices reflecting both fundamental values and subjective beliefs.

Secondly, reflexivity theories can be challenging to test empirically due to the subjective nature of beliefs and perceptions. It is difficult to quantify and measure these factors accurately.

Finally, Soros himself acknowledges that reflexivity is not a foolproof investment strategy. Identifying market distortions and timing their corrections is a complex task that requires careful analysis and judgment.

Conclusion

George Soros' theory of reflexivity provides a valuable framework for understanding the dynamics of financial markets. By recognizing the influence of subjective beliefs and biases on market prices, investors can gain insights into market inefficiencies and potentially profit from them. However, reflexivity also highlights the potential for market bubbles and crises when beliefs become distorted. Understanding the theory of reflexivity can contribute to a more nuanced understanding of market behavior and enhance investment decision-making.

Ray Dalio and the Principles of Bridgewater Associates

Ray Dalio, the founder of Bridgewater Associates, is widely recognized as one of the most successful investors and influential figures in the finance industry. His investment firm, Bridgewater Associates, is known for its unique investment philosophy and approach, which is based on a set of principles that Dalio developed throughout his career. In this section, we will explore the principles of Bridgewater Associates, their significance in the financial world, and the lessons we can learn from them.

Background

Before delving into the principles of Bridgewater Associates, it's important to understand the background that shaped Ray Dalio's thinking and approach to investing. Dalio started his career in finance in the 1970s and experienced both successes and failures along the way. These experiences led him to realize the importance of understanding the economic machine and developing principles to navigate the financial markets successfully.

Dalio's belief in the power of principles as guiding forces in decision-making formed the foundation of Bridgewater Associates. He recognized that markets are driven by predictable patterns and that understanding these patterns could lead to greater investment success. With this mindset, he developed an extensive set of principles that provide a framework for decision-making and risk management.

Principles of Bridgewater Associates

The principles of Bridgewater Associates can be broadly categorized into three areas: radical transparency, meritocracy, and a systematic approach to decision-making.

Radical Transparency One of the core principles of Bridgewater Associates is radical transparency. This principle emphasizes open and honest communication among team members and encourages the sharing of thoughts, ideas, and concerns. It aims to create an environment where everyone is comfortable challenging each other's ideas and fostering intellectual curiosity. By embracing diverse viewpoints and encouraging constructive feedback, the firm aims to make better decisions and avoid costly mistakes.

Radical transparency extends beyond interpersonal communication and also applies to the relationships with clients and external stakeholders. Bridgewater Associates believes in providing transparent and clear explanations for its investment decisions, ensuring that clients understand the rationale behind each move.

Meritocracy Meritocracy is another fundamental principle of Bridgewater Associates. Dalio believes that the best ideas should win, regardless of rank or tenure. The firm values intellectual rigor, expertise, and evidence-based decision-making. This principle encourages a culture of continuous learning and self-improvement, where employees are rewarded based on the quality of their contributions and the accuracy of their decision-making rather than their seniority or position.

By promoting a meritocratic environment, Bridgewater Associates aims to foster a culture of excellence, where individuals are motivated to improve their skills continually and generate innovative ideas. This approach ensures that decisions are made based on sound reasoning and thorough analysis, leading to better investment outcomes.

Systematic Approach to Decision-Making Bridgewater Associates is known for its systematic approach to decision-making, driven by data and algorithms. The firm uses a combination of quantitative models and qualitative analysis to make investment decisions. This systematic approach allows for consistent evaluation of investment opportunities and helps remove biases that can cloud judgment.

Dalio believes that by relying on well-defined processes and models, the firm can minimize the influence of emotions and personal biases on investment decisions. This approach reduces the potential for irrational behavior and improves the overall effectiveness of the investment process.

Lessons Learned

The principles of Bridgewater Associates provide valuable lessons for investors and individuals in the finance industry. Here are some key takeaways:

Importance of Transparency and Open Communication The principle of radical transparency highlights the importance of open communication and constructive feedback. Embracing diverse viewpoints and encouraging intellectual debate can lead to better decision-making and improved outcomes. Investors and individuals in the finance industry can apply this principle by fostering a culture of open communication, promoting transparency in investment decisions, and seeking diverse perspectives.

Value of Meritocracy Promoting a meritocratic culture can drive excellence and innovation. By rewarding individuals based on their contributions and the quality of their ideas, rather than external factors, organizations can create an environment that encourages continuous learning and improvement. Investors can adopt this principle by focusing on the quality of investment ideas and considering the expertise and track record of investment managers.

Benefits of a Systematic Approach A systematic approach to decision-making can help investors avoid biases and emotion-driven decisions. By relying on data, models, and well-defined processes, investors can make more objective and consistent decisions. Developing a systematic approach to investment analysis and decision-making can lead to more robust and successful investment strategies.

Continual Learning and Adaptation One of the underlying themes of Bridgewater Associates' principles is the importance of continual learning and adaptation. Dalio's belief in the ongoing pursuit of knowledge and improvement has been instrumental in his success. Investors can benefit from adopting a similar mindset by continuously seeking new insights, embracing new technologies and methodologies, and adapting their investment strategies to changing market conditions.

Conclusion

Ray Dalio and the principles of Bridgewater Associates have had a significant impact on the investment industry. The principles of radical transparency, meritocracy, and a systematic approach to decision-making provide valuable insights and lessons for investors. By embracing these principles, investors can enhance their decision-making processes, improve investment outcomes, and navigate the complexities of the financial markets more effectively. The legacy of Ray Dalio and Bridgewater Associates serves as a reminder of the power of principles in achieving economic success.

Chapter 5: Globalization and Economic Success

Chapter 5: Globalization and Economic Success

Chapter 5: Globalization and Economic Success

Globalization has become a defining characteristic of the modern world, shaping economies, societies, and cultures across the globe. In this chapter, we will explore the relationship between globalization and economic success, examining its definition, historical context, drivers, and the various ways in which it impacts economic growth and development.

Defining Globalization

Globalization refers to the increasing interconnectedness and interdependence of countries through the exchange of goods, services, capital, information, and ideas. It is driven by advancements in technology, communication, transportation, and the liberalization of trade and investment. Globalization has transformed the world into a more integrated and interrelated global economy, enabling the flow of goods, services, and capital across national borders.

Historical Context of Globalization

Globalization is not a recent phenomenon but has evolved over centuries. The modern era of globalization can be traced back to the Industrial Revolution in the 18th century when technological advancements and international trade led to increased economic integration between countries. However, the pace and scale of globalization accelerated significantly in the late 20th century with the removal of trade barriers and the advent of digital technologies.

Drivers of Globalization

Several factors have contributed to the rise of globalization. One key driver is the liberalization of trade and investment, as countries have lowered trade barriers and embraced free trade policies. Multilateral agreements such as the General Agreement on Tariffs and Trade (GATT) and its successor, the World Trade Organization (WTO), have played a crucial role in promoting global trade.

Technological advancements in transportation and communication have also been major drivers of globalization. The development of container shipping, air travel, and the internet has made it easier and faster to transport goods, travel between countries, and communicate across borders. These technologies have reduced the cost and time associated with international trade and have facilitated the global exchange of ideas and information.

Additionally, factors such as the outsourcing of production, foreign direct investment (FDI), global supply chains, and the growth of multinational corporations (MNCs) have contributed to the deepening of economic integration on a global scale.

Economic Success in the Globalized World

Globalization has brought about significant economic benefits for countries that have actively participated in the global economy. It has created opportunities for economic growth, increased competitiveness, and improved living standards. Some of the key economic benefits of globalization include:

1. **Access to larger markets**: Globalization allows countries to access larger markets for their goods and services, expanding their customer base and export opportunities. This can lead to increased production, economies of scale, and higher profits for businesses.

2. **Efficient allocation of resources**: Globalization promotes the efficient allocation of resources by allowing countries to specialize in the production of goods and services for which they have a comparative advantage. This leads to increased productivity, improved efficiency, and higher economic output.

3. **Innovation and technological progress**: Globalization facilitates the transfer of knowledge, technology, and innovation across borders. Through international collaboration and competition, countries can learn from each other, adopt best practices, and drive technological advancements that can spur economic growth.

CHAPTER 5: GLOBALIZATION AND ECONOMIC SUCCESS 115

4. **Foreign direct investment (FDI):** Globalization attracts foreign direct investment, which can provide countries with access to capital, technology, managerial expertise, and market opportunities. FDI can stimulate economic development, create jobs, and enhance productivity in host countries.

5. **Skills and knowledge transfer:** Globalization enables the mobility of labor, allowing individuals to seek employment and educational opportunities in different countries. This facilitates the transfer of skills, knowledge, and expertise, contributing to human capital development and economic success.

Case Studies of Global Economic Success

To illustrate the impact of globalization on economic success, let's explore three case studies of countries that have experienced significant economic growth and development through their engagement with the global economy.

    South Korea's Economic Miracle: South Korea's transformation from a war-torn agrarian economy to a global economic powerhouse is widely regarded as one of the most remarkable success stories of the 20th century. The country embraced export-oriented industrialization, focusing on sectors such as electronics, automobiles, and shipbuilding. By actively participating in global trade and attracting foreign direct investment, South Korea achieved rapid economic growth, technological advancement, and improved living standards.

    Singapore and the Transformation into a Global Financial Hub: Singapore, a small city-state with limited natural resources, has become a global financial center and a hub for international trade. Through its open and business-friendly policies, Singapore has attracted multinational corporations, financial institutions, and skilled professionals from around the world. The country's strategic location, efficient infrastructure, and strong governance have made it a preferred destination for global businesses, contributing to its economic success.

    China's Rise as an Economic Superpower: China's economic rise is arguably one of the most significant outcomes of globalization. By embracing market-oriented reforms and opening up its economy to foreign investment and trade, China has experienced extraordinary economic growth over the past few decades. The country has leveraged its abundant labor force, manufacturing capabilities, and export-oriented industries to become the world's largest exporter and a major player in the global economy.

Conclusion

Globalization has reshaped the global economy, leading to increased economic interdependence and integration. It has provided countries with opportunities for economic growth, innovation, and development. However, globalization also presents challenges, including economic inequality, social disruption, and environmental concerns. As economies become more interconnected, it is crucial for governments, businesses, and individuals to navigate the complexities of globalization while striving for inclusive and sustainable economic success. By embracing the potential of globalization and addressing its challenges, countries can position themselves for long-term prosperity in the globalized world.

The Rise of Globalization

Definition and Historical Context

In this section, we will explore the definition and historical context of globalization, a phenomenon that has significantly impacted the modern economy. Globalization refers to the increasing interconnectedness and interdependence of countries through the exchange of goods, services, capital, and information on a global scale. It has been facilitated by advancements in technology, transportation, and communication, allowing for the rapid flow of ideas, capital, and people across borders.

Historically, globalization can be traced back to ancient times when trade routes such as the Silk Road between Asia and Europe facilitated the exchange of goods and ideas. However, the pace and scale of globalization have accelerated in recent centuries. The industrial revolution, which began in the 18th century, marked a significant turning point, as advancements in manufacturing and transportation technologies spurred global trade and investment.

The 20th century witnessed further integration of economies through the establishment of international organizations and agreements. The Bretton Woods system, created after World War II, aimed to foster economic stability and cooperation by establishing a fixed exchange rate system and facilitating international trade. The General Agreement on Tariffs and Trade (GATT), which later evolved into the World Trade Organization (WTO), was established to promote free trade and reduce barriers to international commerce.

In the late 20th century, advancements in information and communication technologies, such as the internet, revolutionized global connectivity. The emergence of multinational corporations and global supply chains further deepened economic interdependence among countries. As a result, goods and services are now produced and consumed globally, with companies sourcing inputs and customers from different parts of the world.

Globalization has also been propelled by the liberalization of trade and investment policies. Many countries have reduced tariffs and other trade barriers to attract foreign direct investment and stimulate economic growth. Additionally, improvements in transportation and logistics have made it easier and cheaper to transport goods across borders, further facilitating global trade.

However, globalization has not been without challenges. Critics argue that it has contributed to income inequality, as the benefits of globalization have not been evenly distributed. Additionally, concerns have been raised about the impact of globalization on the environment and cultural diversity. The ongoing debates surrounding globalization highlight the need for careful policy considerations to ensure its benefits are shared equitably.

Understanding the definition and historical context of globalization provides the groundwork for exploring its impact on economic success. In the following sections, we will delve into the drivers of globalization and examine the ways in which it has shaped economic growth, trade, and foreign direct investment. We will also discuss the challenges and opportunities that arise in a globalized world and explore the case studies of countries that have achieved economic success through embracing globalization.

To enhance your understanding of the concept of globalization, let's consider a real-world example. Imagine a company called TechConnect, based in the United States, that manufactures smartphone components. In the past, TechConnect sourced all its raw materials domestically and only sold their products within the country.

However, in response to increased global demand and competition, TechConnect decided to expand its operations globally. It established production facilities in countries with lower production costs, such as China and Vietnam, to take advantage of their skilled labor and cost-effective resources. By doing so, TechConnect was able to lower its production costs and offer competitive prices to its customers worldwide.

To distribute its products globally, TechConnect entered into strategic partnerships with logistics companies that specialized in international shipping. This allowed them to efficiently transport their products to various markets, such as Europe and Asia. Furthermore, TechConnect used digital platforms to market and sell its products globally, leveraging the power of e-commerce.

This example illustrates how globalization has enabled companies like TechConnect to expand their reach, access new markets, and optimize their production processes. By embracing globalization, TechConnect was able to achieve economic success by tapping into the opportunities presented by the interconnected global economy.

In the next section, we will explore the drivers of globalization and how they have shaped the economic landscape of nations around the world.

Drivers of Globalization

Globalization is a complex and multifaceted process that has transformed the world economy over the past few decades. It refers to the increasing interconnectedness and interdependence of countries through the flow of goods, services, capital, and ideas. There are several key drivers that have contributed to the rise of globalization, each playing a significant role in shaping the current global economic landscape.

Technological Advancements

One of the primary drivers of globalization is the rapid advancement of technology, particularly in the fields of communication and transportation. The development and widespread adoption of the internet, mobile telecommunications, and containerization have significantly reduced the cost of information exchange and transportation of goods across geographic borders.

The internet, in particular, has revolutionized the way businesses operate. It has transformed the global marketplace by enabling instant communication and facilitating the exchange of ideas, information, and services. E-commerce platforms such as Amazon and Alibaba have emerged as global giants, allowing businesses to reach customers around the world with ease.

Furthermore, advances in transportation technology, such as containerization, have greatly facilitated global trade. Containers standardized the shipping process and made it more efficient, reducing the time and cost of transporting goods internationally. This has led to a substantial increase in the volume of trade between countries.

Trade Liberalization

Another crucial driver of globalization is the liberalization of trade policies across the world. Countries have recognized the benefits of international trade, including access to a wider range of goods and services, economies of scale, and increased competition, which spurs innovation and efficiency improvements.

Trade liberalization has been facilitated through a variety of mechanisms, such as multilateral trade agreements like the World Trade Organization (WTO) and regional trade agreements like the European Union (EU) and the North American Free Trade Agreement (NAFTA). These agreements aim to reduce barriers to trade by eliminating tariffs, quotas, and other restrictions on the movement of goods and services.

Additionally, countries have undertaken unilateral trade liberalization measures to attract foreign investment and promote economic growth. By lowering import tariffs and easing regulatory barriers, nations create a more favorable environment for international trade.

Financial Flows

The globalization of financial markets has also been a significant driver of globalization. Advances in technology and deregulation of financial markets have facilitated the flow of capital across borders, enabling businesses and governments to access funds from international sources.

Financial globalization allows firms to raise capital from the most efficient sources, increasing their competitiveness. It also provides countries with access to foreign investment, supporting economic growth and development. Global financial markets enable investors to diversify their portfolios and take advantage of investment opportunities worldwide.

The development of complex financial instruments, such as derivatives and securitization, has further facilitated the mobility of capital. These financial innovations have made it easier for investors to manage risks and allocate capital efficiently.

Globalization of Production

The globalization of production is another significant driver of globalization. Many companies now operate globally, spreading their production activities across different countries to take advantage of various factors, such as lower labor costs, access to resources, and proximity to markets.

Multinational corporations (MNCs) play a crucial role in driving the global economy. They establish subsidiaries and production facilities in different countries, creating global supply chains. This fragmentation of production allows companies to specialize in specific tasks and achieve cost efficiencies through economies of scale.

Furthermore, advancements in transportation and communication technology have made it easier for firms to coordinate and manage production activities across borders. Supply chain management systems and real-time communication tools enable companies to coordinate with suppliers and partners globally, ensuring the smooth flow of goods and services.

Conclusion

The drivers of globalization, such as technological advancements, trade liberalization, financial flows, and the globalization of production, have transformed the global economic landscape. These drivers have connected countries and facilitated the exchange of goods, services, and ideas on an unprecedented scale.

However, it is important to acknowledge that globalization has not been without challenges. It has led to economic dislocation, income inequality, and environmental concerns. Governments and policymakers need to address these issues and ensure that the benefits of globalization are shared more widely.

Moreover, the future of globalization is likely to be influenced by emerging trends such as technological disruptions, climate change, and the need for global economic cooperation. Adapting to these challenges and leveraging the opportunities they present will be crucial for future economic success in a globalized world.

Key Takeaways

- Technological advancements, such as the internet and containerization, have significantly reduced the cost of communication and transportation, enabling the globalization of trade.

- Trade liberalization through multilateral and regional trade agreements has facilitated the flow of goods and services across borders.

- Financial globalization has allowed for the efficient allocation of capital and increased access to international investment.

- The globalization of production has led to the establishment of global supply chains, enabling firms to take advantage of cost efficiencies and specialized skills.

- Globalization presents both opportunities and challenges, and policymakers need to address the issues of economic dislocation, income inequality, and environmental sustainability.

Discussion Questions

1. How have technological advancements, such as the internet and containerization, changed the dynamics of global trade?

2. What are the potential benefits and drawbacks of trade liberalization?

3. How has financial globalization impacted the movement of capital and investment opportunities?

4. What are the main drivers behind the globalization of production? How has this affected the global economy?

5. What are some of the challenges associated with globalization, and how can policymakers address them?

6. What emerging trends do you think will shape the future of globalization? How can countries adapt to these trends to ensure future economic success?

Economic Success in the Globalized World

Advanced Manufacturing and Supply Chain Integration

In today's globalized economy, advanced manufacturing and supply chain integration play a crucial role in driving economic success. Advanced manufacturing refers to the use of innovative technologies and processes to enhance productivity, improve product quality, and reduce production costs. It encompasses various disciplines such as robotics, automation, additive manufacturing, and artificial intelligence. On the other hand, supply chain integration focuses on streamlining the movement of goods and services from raw material suppliers to end consumers, ensuring efficient coordination and collaboration among different stakeholders in the supply chain. In this section, we will explore the importance of advanced manufacturing and supply chain integration and discuss their impact on economic success.

The Benefits of Advanced Manufacturing

Advanced manufacturing technologies have revolutionized traditional manufacturing processes, enabling companies to produce goods faster, with higher precision, and at a lower cost. This has resulted in numerous benefits for both businesses and consumers.

Increased productivity : Advanced manufacturing technologies, such as robotics and automation, have significantly increased productivity levels in manufacturing operations. By automating repetitive tasks, companies can reduce human error, optimize production flow, and achieve higher output rates. This leads to improved efficiency and cost savings.

Enhanced product quality : Advanced manufacturing techniques, such as additive manufacturing (3D printing), allow for greater customization and precision in product development. This results in higher product quality, reduced defects, and increased customer satisfaction. Furthermore, advanced manufacturing technologies enable real-time monitoring and quality control, ensuring consistent product standards.

Reduced production costs : By leveraging advanced manufacturing technologies, companies can achieve cost savings through various means. For example, automation reduces labor costs, while additive manufacturing eliminates the need for expensive tooling and molds. Furthermore, advanced manufacturing techniques enable just-in-time production and inventory optimization, minimizing storage costs and waste.

The Role of Supply Chain Integration

Supply chain integration involves the seamless coordination and collaboration of various stakeholders in the supply chain, including suppliers, manufacturers, distributors, and retailers. An integrated supply chain helps to improve operational efficiency, reduce lead times, and enhance customer satisfaction.

Improved visibility and transparency : Supply chain integration enables real-time visibility into inventory levels, production schedules, and transportation logistics. This visibility allows for better demand forecasting, inventory management, and coordination among supply chain partners. By having access to accurate and timely information, companies can make more informed decisions and respond quickly to market changes.

Enhanced operational efficiency : Integrated supply chains facilitate the smooth flow of materials, information, and funds across different stages of production and distribution. This reduces disruptions, minimizes bottlenecks, and optimizes resource allocation. By streamlining processes and reducing inefficiencies, companies can improve operational performance and reduce costs.

Faster time to market : Supply chain integration enables faster product development and delivery cycles. By collaborating closely with suppliers and customers, companies can shorten lead times and respond more quickly to market demands. This agility is particularly crucial in industries with rapidly changing consumer preferences and short product life cycles.

Case Studies and Examples

To further illustrate the importance of advanced manufacturing and supply chain integration, let's explore two case studies of companies that have succeeded in leveraging these principles to achieve economic success.

Tesla: Revolutionizing the Automotive Industry Tesla, the electric vehicle manufacturer, has revolutionized the automotive industry through advanced manufacturing and supply chain integration. The company utilizes advanced manufacturing technologies, such as robotics and automation, to produce electric vehicles with high precision and efficiency. Tesla's vertically integrated supply chain enables seamless coordination of component production, vehicle assembly, and distribution. By integrating suppliers, manufacturing processes, and logistics, Tesla has been able to streamline its operations, reduce costs, and deliver innovative products to the market faster.

Zara: Fast Fashion through Efficient Supply Chain Zara, the Spanish fast-fashion retailer, has achieved remarkable success through its efficient supply chain integration. Zara's vertically integrated supply chain allows for quick decision-making and a fast response to changing fashion trends. The company leverages advanced manufacturing techniques, such as just-in-time production and agile manufacturing, to minimize inventory holding and reduce lead times. Zara's close collaboration with suppliers and its ability to quickly incorporate customer feedback into its product design and production processes have enabled the company to stay ahead in the highly competitive fashion industry.

Challenges and Future Trends

While advanced manufacturing and supply chain integration offer significant advantages, they also present challenges that need to be addressed for sustained economic success.

Skilled workforce : The implementation of advanced manufacturing technologies requires a highly skilled workforce capable of operating, maintaining, and optimizing complex systems. Companies need to invest in workforce training and development to ensure that employees have the necessary skills to leverage advanced technologies effectively.

Cybersecurity risks : As manufacturing processes become increasingly interconnected and reliant on digital systems, the risk of cyber threats and data breaches becomes more prominent. Companies must implement robust cybersecurity measures to protect intellectual property, sensitive information, and the integrity of their supply chains.

Sustainability and ethical considerations : In the pursuit of economic success, it is crucial to consider the environmental and social impact of advanced manufacturing and global supply chains. Companies need to adopt sustainable practices, such as reducing waste, minimizing carbon emissions, and ensuring ethical sourcing, to create long-term value and maintain stakeholder trust.

Conclusion

Advanced manufacturing and supply chain integration are vital drivers of economic success in today's globalized economy. By leveraging innovative technologies and optimizing supply chain processes, companies can achieve increased productivity, enhanced product quality, and reduced production costs. The case studies of Tesla and Zara demonstrate the transformative power of these principles in achieving market success. However, challenges such as the need for a skilled workforce, cybersecurity risks, and sustainability considerations must be addressed to ensure long-term prosperity. As we look to the future, advanced manufacturing and supply chain integration will continue to evolve, enabling companies to navigate emerging trends, embrace new opportunities, and drive economic growth.

Global Trade and Export-Led Growth

Global trade plays a crucial role in driving economic growth and promoting prosperity. It refers to the exchange of goods and services between countries, facilitated by international markets and trade agreements. Export-led growth, on the other hand, focuses on increasing exports as a primary driver of economic development. In this section, we will explore the importance of global trade and its impact on economic success, with a specific focus on export-led growth strategies.

The Benefits of Global Trade

Global trade offers numerous benefits to countries, which contribute to their economic success. These benefits include:

- **Economic growth:** Global trade allows countries to expand their markets beyond their domestic boundaries, leading to increased demand for goods and services. This, in turn, stimulates economic growth and creates employment opportunities.

- **Efficiency gains:** Trade enables countries to specialize in the production of goods and services in which they have a comparative advantage. By focusing on producing what they can produce most efficiently, countries can achieve economies of scale and improve productivity.

- **Access to resources:** Global trade provides countries with access to resources that are not available or are limited domestically. This includes both natural resources and intermediate goods needed for production. Access to resources from other countries allows countries to expand their production possibilities and enhances their competitiveness.

- **Technological progress:** Trade promotes the diffusion of technology across countries. Through trade, countries can adopt and adapt technological advancements developed elsewhere, accelerating their own technological progress. This technology transfer enhances productivity and innovation, leading to economic success.

- **Enhanced consumer choice:** Trade enables consumers to access a wide variety of goods and services from different countries, enhancing their choices and improving their living standards. It also encourages competition, leading to lower prices and higher quality products.

Export-Led Growth Strategies

Export-led growth strategies focus on boosting exports as a key driver of economic development. They involve developing a competitive advantage in specific industries and increasing the share of exports in the overall economy. Here are some key elements of export-led growth strategies:

- **Identifying export opportunities:** Countries need to identify the most promising export opportunities based on their resource endowments, comparative advantages, and market demand. This requires thorough market research and analysis to determine the industries and products with the highest export potential.

- **Investing in export-oriented industries:** To support export-led growth, countries need to invest in the development of industries with export potential. This includes providing infrastructure, promoting research and development, and facilitating access to finance for export-oriented businesses. Governments can also offer incentives such as tax breaks and subsidies to encourage the growth of export industries.

- **Promoting trade facilitation:** Export-led growth requires efficient trade facilitation measures to reduce trade barriers, streamline customs procedures, and improve logistics and transportation infrastructure. Simplified and transparent trade procedures can enhance the competitiveness of export-oriented industries by reducing transaction costs and time.

- **Investing in human capital:** A skilled workforce is crucial for the success of export-oriented industries. Countries should invest in education and vocational training programs to equip their workforce with the necessary skills and knowledge. This will enable them to adapt to changing market demands and compete effectively in global trade.

- **Diversifying export markets:** Relying on a single market for exports can be risky. Countries should aim to diversify their export markets to reduce vulnerability to economic shocks. This involves actively seeking new trading partners and exploring emerging markets with growing demand for their products.

Challenges and Caveats

While global trade and export-led growth strategies offer numerous benefits, there are also challenges and caveats that countries need to consider:

- **Trade imbalances:** Pursuing export-led growth can lead to trade imbalances, where a country's exports significantly exceed its imports. Persistent trade imbalances can pose risks to the stability of the economy and may require policy interventions to address.

- **Market volatility:** Global trade is subject to market volatility, including fluctuations in exchange rates, changes in global demand, and trade policy uncertainties. Countries need to be prepared to deal with these volatilities and develop strategies to mitigate their impact on export-led growth.

- **Competition and protectionism:** Increasing participation in global trade exposes countries to intense competition from other exporters. It is essential to develop strategies to maintain competitiveness and adapt to changing market conditions. Additionally, protectionist measures in other countries can limit access to markets and hinder export-led growth.

- **Sustainable development:** While export-led growth can drive economic success, it is crucial to ensure that it aligns with sustainable development goals. Countries should consider the social and environmental impacts of their export-oriented industries and adopt measures to mitigate any negative consequences.

Real-World Example: China's Export-Led Growth

China's remarkable economic success over the past few decades can be attributed, in large part, to its export-led growth strategy. By focusing on manufacturing and becoming the "factory of the world," China has achieved significant economic growth and lifted millions of people out of poverty.

China's export-led growth strategy involved several key elements. The country identified labor-intensive industries with high export potential, such as textiles, electronics, and toys. It invested heavily in infrastructure, created special economic zones, and provided tax breaks and subsidies to attract foreign direct investment in these industries. The government also implemented policies to promote export-oriented businesses, including trade facilitation measures and currency management to maintain export competitiveness.

China's export-led growth strategy not only led to remarkable economic growth but also contributed to global trade dynamics. The country became the world's largest exporter and a key player in global supply chains. However, it also faced challenges such as trade imbalances with other countries and criticisms of unfair trade practices.

In recent years, China has been transitioning its economic model towards a more balanced and sustainable growth path, with a focus on domestic consumption and innovation. This transition reflects the challenges and caveats associated with long-term reliance on export-led growth.

Conclusion

Global trade and export-led growth strategies are essential drivers of economic success. They provide countries with opportunities to benefit from comparative advantages, expand their markets, and create jobs. However, countries need to carefully consider their specific circumstances and address the challenges and risks associated with global trade. By implementing effective export-led growth strategies, countries can boost their economic development and create a path towards long-term prosperity.

Key Takeaways:

- Global trade promotes economic growth, efficiency gains, access to resources, technological progress, and enhanced consumer choice.

- Export-led growth strategies focus on increasing exports as a key driver of economic development.

- Export-led growth strategies involve identifying export opportunities, investing in export-oriented industries, promoting trade facilitation, investing in human capital, and diversifying export markets.

- Challenges and caveats of global trade and export-led growth include trade imbalances, market volatility, competition and protectionism, and the need for sustainable development.

Foreign Direct Investment and Economic Development

Foreign direct investment (FDI) plays a crucial role in driving economic development and growth in countries around the world. It involves the investment of capital by a company or individual from one country into a business enterprise located in another country. FDI can take various forms, including the establishment of new businesses, the expansion of existing operations, or the acquisition of local companies.

The Importance of FDI

FDI brings numerous economic benefits to both the host country and the investing country. For the host country, FDI can result in job creation, technology transfer, and increased access to capital and resources. It can boost productivity, stimulate domestic industries, and enhance export competitiveness. FDI also contributes to the development of infrastructure and the improvement of local skills and expertise.

From the perspective of the investing country, FDI provides opportunities for market expansion, diversification of operations, and access to new resources or technologies. It can help companies gain a competitive advantage in global markets and foster innovation through collaborations and knowledge sharing. Additionally, FDI allows firms to tap into the growth potential and consumer markets of other countries.

Determinants of FDI

Several factors influence the decision of multinational corporations (MNCs) to invest in a particular country. These factors include market size and growth, political stability, regulatory environment, labor costs and skills, infrastructure availability, and potential returns on investment. Governments often use policies and incentives to attract FDI, such as tax breaks, streamlined business regulations, and investment protection measures.

It is important to note that FDI does not flow evenly across countries and sectors. Some countries, known as FDI destinations, are more successful in attracting FDI due to their favorable investment conditions, while others struggle to attract significant inflows. Additionally, certain industries, such as manufacturing, services, and natural resources sectors, are more likely to attract FDI due to their characteristics and growth potential.

Benefits and Challenges of FDI

FDI can bring notable benefits to the host country's economy. It often leads to technology transfers, knowledge spillovers, and skill development through interactions with foreign investors. This can enhance the productivity and competitiveness of local firms, contributing to the overall economic growth. FDI also facilitates the integration of the host country into global value chains, enabling it to participate in international trade and gain a share of global markets.

However, FDI also poses challenges and risks that need to be managed. One major concern is the potential for exploitation and dependency, where multinational corporations extract natural resources or exploit cheap labor without contributing to the broader development of the host country. Additionally, there may be cultural and social challenges associated with foreign investment that need to be addressed to ensure positive social impacts.

Policy Implications of FDI

Governments play a crucial role in shaping the impact of FDI on economic development. They design policies and frameworks to attract and regulate FDI inflows, aiming to maximize the benefits and minimize the potential risks. Key policy areas include investment promotion, investor protection, intellectual property rights, labor standards, and environmental regulations.

To promote FDI inflows, governments often implement investment facilitation measures, such as streamlined administrative processes, investment incentives, and the establishment of special economic zones. They also focus on improving the regulatory and legal environment to attract and retain foreign investors. Additionally, governments can play a role in enhancing the absorptive capacity of the local economy through investment in education, infrastructure, and research and development.

Case Studies: FDI and Economic Development

To illustrate the impact of FDI on economic development, let's consider two case studies: China and Ireland.

China has been successful in attracting significant FDI inflows, which have played a crucial role in its economic transformation. FDI has helped China develop a competitive manufacturing sector, create millions of jobs, and upgrade its technology and production capabilities. Through joint ventures and technology transfers, China has been able to acquire knowledge and advanced manufacturing techniques, contributing to its rapid industrialization and export growth.

In contrast, Ireland has leveraged FDI to become an attractive location for foreign investors, particularly in the technology and pharmaceutical sectors. FDI has been a key driver of Ireland's economic growth, contributing to high-value job creation, innovation, and export-oriented industries. The country's favorable business environment, skilled workforce, and investment promotion strategies have positioned it as a hub for multinational corporations seeking a European base.

Innovative Approaches to FDI Promotion

In today's rapidly changing global landscape, countries are adopting innovative approaches to attract and benefit from FDI. One example is the focus on sustainable investment and responsible business practices. Governments are increasingly encouraging foreign investors to adhere to environmental, social, and governance (ESG) standards and promote sustainable development. This includes incorporating sustainability criteria into investment promotion strategies and providing incentives for green and socially responsible investments.

Another innovative approach is the promotion of strategic partnerships between foreign investors and local companies or institutions. By fostering collaboration and knowledge sharing, these partnerships can enhance the capacity and competitiveness of local firms, driving economic development. This approach also helps address the concerns of dependency and exploitation by ensuring a more balanced relationship between foreign investors and the host country.

Conclusion

Foreign direct investment is a critical driver of economic development, bringing valuable benefits to both host and investing countries. It provides access to capital, technology, and markets, fostering economic growth, job creation, and innovation. However, careful management and policy considerations are necessary to maximize the positive impacts of FDI and ensure that host countries can reap the full benefits. By adopting innovative approaches and fostering responsible investment, countries can leverage FDI to achieve sustainable and inclusive economic success.

Case Studies of Global Economic Success

South Korea's Economic Miracle

South Korea's economic miracle is a captivating story of how a nation transformed itself from a war-torn country to one of the world's most vibrant and prosperous economies. This section explores the key factors and strategies that contributed to South Korea's remarkable economic success.

Historical Context

To truly understand South Korea's economic miracle, it is essential to delve into its historical context. After the Korean War (1950-1953), the country was devastated, with its infrastructure in ruins and its economy in shambles. However, the determination of its people and the visionary leadership that emerged played a vital role in rebuilding the nation.

Export-Oriented Industrialization

One of the crucial strategies that propelled South Korea's economic success is export-oriented industrialization. The government recognized the potential of exporting goods to fuel economic growth and promote industrial development. Policies were implemented to support and incentivize exports, such as providing financial assistance to export-oriented industries, creating export processing zones, and negotiating favorable trade agreements.

The focus on exports allowed South Korea to tap into global markets and attract foreign investment. Key industries, such as electronics, automobiles, shipbuilding, and petrochemicals, flourished, contributing significantly to the country's economic growth.

Investment in Education and Human Capital

South Korea's commitment to education and human capital development also played a pivotal role in its economic miracle. Recognizing that knowledge and skills are crucial for economic competitiveness, the government heavily invested in education at all levels.

The emphasis on education, particularly in STEM (science, technology, engineering, and mathematics) fields, laid the foundation for a highly skilled and innovative workforce. South Korean students consistently excel in global assessments, and the country has become a hub for technological advancements.

Innovation and Technological Advancements

South Korea's economic success can be attributed to its remarkable drive for innovation and technological advancements. The country is known for its continuous efforts to stay at the forefront of technological developments. It has successfully fostered a culture of innovation and entrepreneurship, encouraging creativity and risk-taking.

South Korean companies, such as Samsung, LG, and Hyundai, have been leaders in technological innovation, introducing groundbreaking products and revolutionizing various industries. The government has provided support through incentives for research and development, the establishment of innovation centers, and collaboration between academia and industry.

Government-led Industrial Policies

Another key factor in South Korea's economic miracle is the government's proactive industrial policies. The government played an active role in shaping the industrial structure and supporting strategic industries. It implemented policies to nurture promising sectors, provided financial assistance and tax incentives, and facilitated partnerships between large corporations and smaller firms.

The government's support and guidance helped facilitate rapid industrialization and create globally competitive industries. Examples of successful government-led initiatives include the promotion of the automobile industry through the "Automobile Industry Development Policy" and the establishment of the Korea Aerospace Industries to develop the country's aerospace capabilities.

Infrastructure Development

South Korea's economic miracle was made possible by its robust infrastructure development. The government invested heavily in building a world-class infrastructure, including roads, ports, airports, railways, and power generation facilities. These investments not only supported industrial growth but also laid the foundation for South Korea to become a global hub for trade and logistics.

The country's advanced infrastructure has been a critical factor in attracting foreign direct investment, facilitating the efficient movement of goods and people, and ensuring connectivity across regions.

Caveat: Rising Income Inequality

While South Korea's economic transformation has brought significant prosperity, it has also led to rising income inequality. The benefits of economic growth have not been evenly distributed, resulting in a wealth gap between different segments of society. This issue poses a challenge for the country's continued development and requires a concerted effort to address.

Conclusion

South Korea's economic miracle is a testament to the power of proactive government policies, investment in education and human capital, a focus on innovation and technological advancements, and robust infrastructure. The combination of these factors transformed a war-torn country into a global economic powerhouse.

The lessons learned from South Korea's experience can serve as an inspiration for other nations aspiring to achieve economic success. However, it is crucial to adapt these strategies to each country's unique context and challenges. By embracing innovation, investing in education, and pursuing sustainable development, countries can chart their own path towards economic prosperity.

Singapore and the Transformation into a Global Financial Hub

Singapore's remarkable transformation into a global financial hub is a testament to its strategic economic planning, sound governance, and proactive policies. This section explores the key factors that have contributed to Singapore's success, including its regulatory framework, financial infrastructure, and innovation-driven approach. We will also discuss the challenges faced by Singapore and its future prospects in maintaining its position as a leading global financial center.

Regulatory Framework

One of the cornerstones of Singapore's success as a financial center is its robust regulatory framework. The Monetary Authority of Singapore (MAS) is the central bank and financial regulatory authority responsible for ensuring the stability and integrity of the financial sector. MAS adopts a risk-based approach in its supervision, focusing on the soundness of financial institutions and the effectiveness of risk management practices.

Singapore's regulatory framework is known for its transparency, strong legal framework, and strict enforcement of regulations. The country has implemented measures to combat money laundering, terrorist financing, and corruption, which have helped to build trust and confidence in its financial system. The strong regulatory environment has attracted international banks, asset managers, and other financial institutions to set up operations in Singapore.

Financial Infrastructure

Singapore boasts a world-class financial infrastructure that supports its role as a global financial hub. The country has a sophisticated payment and settlement system, efficient clearing and settlement processes, and a comprehensive network of financial intermediaries. The establishment of the Singapore Exchange (SGX) has provided a platform for trading equities, bonds, derivatives, and other financial instruments.

In recent years, Singapore has also developed as a hub for wealth management and private banking. The country offers a conducive environment for high-net-worth individuals to manage their wealth and access a wide range of investment opportunities. The presence of global banks and asset managers, coupled with a strong legal framework for asset protection and wealth preservation, has contributed to the growth of Singapore's wealth management industry.

Innovation-driven Approach

Another key factor in Singapore's success as a financial hub is its emphasis on innovation and technology. The country has been at the forefront of fintech development, embracing new technologies such as blockchain, artificial intelligence, and data analytics. The establishment of an innovative regulatory sandbox by MAS has supported experimentation and adoption of fintech solutions.

Singapore's focus on innovation has attracted fintech startups and multinational corporations to establish their presence in the country. The government has also introduced initiatives to promote collaboration between financial institutions, technology companies, and research institutions. This collaborative ecosystem has fostered the development of innovative financial services and solutions, positioning Singapore as a global leader in fintech.

Challenges and Future Prospects

While Singapore has achieved remarkable success as a global financial hub, it faces several challenges in maintaining its position in the future. One of the challenges is increasing competition from other financial centers, particularly in the Asia-Pacific region. Cities like Hong Kong, Shanghai, and Tokyo are vying to attract international businesses and investors, posing a competitive threat to Singapore.

Another challenge is the evolving regulatory landscape and the need to keep pace with technological advancements. As financial services become increasingly digital and interconnected, regulators need to strike a balance between fostering innovation and maintaining financial stability. Singapore will need to continue adapting its regulatory framework to address emerging risks and promote the responsible use of technology in the financial sector.

Looking ahead, Singapore's prospects as a global financial hub remain promising. The country's strategic location, political stability, and business-friendly environment continue to attract multinational corporations, financial institutions, and skilled professionals. Singapore also has a strong pipeline of initiatives to enhance its financial ecosystem, including enhancing connectivity with other financial centers, expanding its fintech ecosystem, and promoting sustainable finance.

In conclusion, Singapore's transformation into a global financial hub is a remarkable success story. Its strong regulatory framework, world-class financial infrastructure, and innovation-driven approach have positioned it as a leading global financial center. While it faces challenges in an increasingly competitive and complex environment, Singapore's proactive policies and commitment to innovation provide a solid foundation for its future success in the global financial landscape.

China's Rise as an Economic Superpower

In recent decades, China has emerged as a global economic powerhouse and has been widely recognized as an economic superpower. Its remarkable economic growth and transformation have caught the attention of policymakers, economists, and business leaders worldwide. In this section, we will delve into the key factors that have contributed to China's rise and explore the implications of its economic success.

Historical Context

To understand China's economic success, it is crucial to examine its historical context. China has a rich history of economic development and trade, dating back thousands of years. However, it experienced significant challenges in the 20th century, including political instability, social upheaval, and economic stagnation.

The turning point for China came in 1978 with the initiation of economic reforms led by Deng Xiaoping. These reforms aimed to transition China from a centrally planned economy to a more market-oriented system, emphasizing the role of the private sector and opening up to international trade and investment. Deng's policy of "reform and opening up" laid the foundation for China's economic rise.

Market-Oriented Reforms

One of the critical drivers of China's economic success has been its market-oriented reforms. These reforms encompassed several key areas, including rural decollectivization, the establishment of special economic zones, and the liberalization of foreign trade and investment.

Rural decollectivization allowed farmers to have greater control over agricultural production and sales, leading to increased productivity and income growth in rural areas. This, in turn, stimulated domestic demand and provided a solid foundation for China's industrialization and urbanization.

The establishment of special economic zones, starting with Shenzhen in 1980, created pockets of openness and experimentation where market forces were given more freedom to operate. These zones attracted foreign direct investment (FDI) and facilitated technology transfer, contributing to the rapid growth of export-oriented industries.

Liberalizing foreign trade and investment was instrumental in integrating China into the global economy. China joined the World Trade Organization (WTO) in 2001 and committed to gradually reducing tariff barriers and removing trade restrictions. This move not only increased China's access to international markets but also encouraged foreign companies to establish operations in China.

Investment in Infrastructure

China's rise as an economic superpower has been accompanied by massive investments in infrastructure. The government recognized the importance of building a solid foundation for economic development through the construction of transportation networks, energy systems, and communication networks.

China's infrastructure projects are often large-scale and ambitious, such as the impressive high-speed rail network that connects major cities across the country. These investments have not only improved connectivity within China but have also enhanced its integration into the global economy.

The development of state-of-the-art ports, airports, and logistics hubs has facilitated international trade and made China a crucial player in global supply chains. These infrastructure investments have also contributed to regional development by connecting previously isolated regions to the national and global markets.

Export-Led Growth

China's economic success has been greatly influenced by its export-led growth strategy. By leveraging its competitive advantage in manufacturing and low-cost labor, China became the "factory of the world" and a global exporter of various goods and services.

Foreign companies were attracted to China's abundant labor force, which offered lower production costs compared to developed countries. Multinational corporations set up manufacturing facilities in China to take advantage of its large consumer market and gain access to global supply chains.

China's export-oriented industries, such as electronics, textiles, and machinery, grew rapidly, driving economic expansion and job creation. This export-led growth played a vital role in lifting millions of people out of poverty and fueling the country's economic rise.

Technology and Innovation

While initially known for its manufacturing prowess, China has made significant strides in technology and innovation in recent years. It has invested heavily in research and development (R&D), aiming to position itself as a global leader in emerging technologies.

China's focus on innovation has resulted in advancements in areas such as artificial intelligence, biotechnology, renewable energy, and telecommunications. Companies like Huawei, Alibaba, and Tencent have gained international recognition for their technological achievements and have become major players in their respective industries.

To foster innovation, the Chinese government has implemented policies and provided incentives to support research and development activities. It has also encouraged collaborations between academia, industry, and government agencies to drive technological advancements.

Challenges and Implications

Despite China's remarkable economic success, it faces several challenges and implications. One significant challenge is the need to transition from an export-driven economy to one driven by domestic consumption and services. This shift requires addressing income inequality, improving social safety nets, and promoting inclusive growth.

Another challenge is managing the environmental impact of rapid industrialization and urbanization. China has faced air and water pollution as well as resource depletion. However, the government has made efforts to combat environmental degradation, including setting targets for renewable energy and introducing strict emission standards.

China's economic rise also has geopolitical implications. It has increased its influence on global trade and investment flows, leading to concerns about fair competition, intellectual property rights, and national security. Balancing these concerns with cooperation and collaboration will be critical for maintaining a stable global economic order.

In conclusion, China's rise as an economic superpower stems from a combination of market-oriented reforms, infrastructure investments, export-led growth, and a focus on technology and innovation. Its remarkable journey from an agrarian society to an economic powerhouse holds valuable lessons for other developing countries. However, China's ongoing economic transformation brings challenges that need to be addressed to ensure long-term sustainable growth and social prosperity.

Chapter 6: Sustainable Development and Economic Success

Chapter 6: Sustainable Development and Economic Success

Chapter 6: Sustainable Development and Economic Success

In this chapter, we explore the concept of sustainable development and its relationship to economic success. Sustainable development refers to the idea of meeting the needs of the present generation without compromising the ability of future generations to meet their own needs. It encompasses three main dimensions: environmental, social, and economic. Achieving sustainable development requires a balance between these dimensions, ensuring the preservation and enhancement of natural resources, addressing social inequalities, and promoting economic prosperity.

Understanding Sustainable Development

Sustainable development recognizes that economic progress is intertwined with environmental and social considerations. It rejects the notion that economic growth at the expense of the environment and social well-being is a viable long-term strategy. Instead, it advocates for a holistic approach that considers the interactions between the economy, society, and the environment.

At the core of sustainable development is the idea that economic activities should be conducted in a way that minimizes environmental impacts. This involves adopting cleaner and more efficient production processes, reducing waste and pollution, and promoting the use of renewable resources. By doing so, we can ensure the long-term availability of natural resources and mitigate the adverse effects of climate change.

In addition to environmental sustainability, sustainable development also recognizes the importance of social equity. It emphasizes the need to address poverty, inequality, and social exclusion. This involves providing access to basic necessities such as education, healthcare, and housing for all individuals, regardless of their socio-economic background. Moreover, it seeks to empower marginalized groups and promote inclusive economic and social systems.

The Role of Sustainable Business Practices

Corporate social responsibility (CSR) plays a crucial role in achieving sustainable development. Businesses are increasingly expected to take responsibility for their social, environmental, and economic impacts. By integrating sustainable practices into their operations, businesses can contribute to the achievement of sustainable development goals.

One key aspect of sustainable business practices is environmental stewardship. This involves reducing carbon emissions, minimizing waste generation, and adopting sustainable resource management strategies. For example, companies can invest in renewable energy sources, implement recycling programs, and promote energy and water conservation.

Another important component of sustainable business practices is social responsibility. Companies can contribute to society by fostering inclusive workplaces, promoting fair labor practices, and supporting community development initiatives. This includes providing employees with fair wages, safe working conditions, and opportunities for advancement. Additionally, companies can engage in philanthropic activities and support local communities through partnerships and investments.

Moreover, sustainable business practices can also lead to economic benefits. By embracing sustainability, companies can improve operational efficiency, reduce costs, and enhance their reputation. Consumers are increasingly choosing to support environmentally and socially responsible businesses, which can translate into increased market share and customer loyalty. Furthermore, sustainable practices can spur innovation and drive the development of new products and services, leading to long-term business growth and profitability.

CHAPTER 6: SUSTAINABLE DEVELOPMENT AND ECONOMIC SUCCESS

Case Studies of Sustainable Economic Success

To illustrate the link between sustainable development and economic success, let's examine three case studies of companies that have embraced sustainable practices and achieved remarkable results:

Case Study 1: Patagonia and the Triple Bottom Line

Patagonia, an outdoor clothing company, is renowned for its commitment to environmental and social responsibility. The company has implemented a range of sustainability initiatives, including using recycled materials in its products, reducing water and energy consumption in its manufacturing processes, and promoting fair labor practices throughout its supply chain.

By aligning its business practices with sustainable principles, Patagonia has not only minimized its environmental footprint but also achieved significant economic success. The company's revenue has consistently grown over the years, demonstrating that sustainability and profitability can go hand in hand. Patagonia's success highlights the potential for businesses to thrive by prioritizing social and environmental considerations.

Case Study 2: Novozymes and the Biotech Revolution in Sustainable Industrial Processes

Novozymes, a Danish biotech company, specializes in the development of enzymes and microorganisms for industrial applications. The company's innovative solutions enable industries to improve their production processes while reducing environmental impacts. For example, Novozymes has developed enzymes that enable the production of biofuels from agricultural waste, reducing reliance on fossil fuels and contributing to climate change mitigation.

By addressing pressing environmental challenges through biotech innovations, Novozymes has positioned itself as a leader in sustainable industrial practices. The company's success demonstrates the potential for technological advancements to drive sustainable economic development.

Case Study 3: Costa Rica's Environmental Leadership and Sustainable Tourism

Costa Rica, a small Central American country, has gained international recognition for its commitment to environmental conservation and sustainable tourism. The country boasts diverse ecosystems and has implemented various policies and initiatives to protect its natural resources.

By leveraging its natural capital and promoting sustainable tourism, Costa Rica has achieved considerable economic success. The tourism industry contributes significantly to the country's GDP and provides employment opportunities to local communities. Furthermore, Costa Rica's environmental reputation attracts environmentally conscious tourists, creating a competitive advantage in the global tourism market.

These case studies demonstrate that sustainable development can be a driver of economic success. By embracing sustainable practices, businesses and countries can create value, promote social well-being, and safeguard the environment for future generations.

Conclusion

Sustainable development is a critical pathway to economic success. By adopting sustainable business practices, companies can reduce their environmental impact, improve their social responsibility, and enhance their economic performance. Moreover, sustainable development is not limited to individual businesses; it requires collaboration between governments, businesses, and civil society to create an enabling environment for sustainable economic growth.

Achieving sustainable development requires a shift in mindset and the willingness to embrace innovative approaches. It calls for a departure from the traditional notion of economic growth at any cost and emphasizes the need to build a more inclusive, resilient, and environmentally conscious economy.

In the next chapter, we will explore the role of government policies in driving economic success. We will examine how governments can promote sustainable development through regulations, incentives, and strategic interventions.

The Concept of Sustainable Development

Environmental, Social, and Economic Dimensions

In order to understand the concept of sustainable development, it is essential to consider the interplay between environmental, social, and economic dimensions. These three dimensions are interconnected and influence one another in complex ways. In this section, we will explore each dimension and examine how they contribute to economic success.

Environmental Dimension

The environmental dimension focuses on the natural resources, ecosystems, and environmental quality that sustain human life and economic activities. It recognizes that economic development should not come at the expense of the environment, but rather strive for its conservation and preservation.

One of the key principles in the environmental dimension is ecological sustainability. This principle emphasizes the need to use natural resources in a way that allows them to replenish and regenerate over time. It involves adopting practices that minimize waste, promote recycling and reuse, and reduce pollution. By embracing ecological sustainability, businesses can ensure the long-term availability of resources and contribute to the overall health of the planet.

Additionally, environmental regulations and policies play a crucial role in promoting sustainable development. These regulations aim to prevent or minimize negative environmental impacts caused by economic activities. They set standards for emissions, waste disposal, and resource management, and hold businesses accountable for their environmental performance. Compliance with these regulations not only protects the environment but also enhances the reputation and credibility of businesses.

For example, the automotive industry has been heavily regulated to reduce the emissions of greenhouse gases and air pollutants. This has led to the development of cleaner and more fuel-efficient vehicles, contributing to the overall reduction in environmental impact.

Social Dimension

The social dimension of sustainable development focuses on the well-being of individuals, communities, and society as a whole. It recognizes that economic success should not be measured solely in terms of material wealth, but also in terms of social progress, equity, and inclusivity.

One of the key principles in the social dimension is social justice. This principle emphasizes the need to create a society where all individuals have equal opportunities to fulfill their potential and enjoy a decent quality of life. It involves promoting equal access to education, healthcare, and basic services, as well as eliminating discrimination and inequality.

Social responsibility is another important aspect of the social dimension. It refers to the ethical behavior and actions of individuals and organizations that benefit society as a whole. Businesses that embrace social responsibility prioritize the well-being of their employees, customers, and communities. They engage in philanthropic activities, support local initiatives, and contribute to the overall social welfare.

For example, companies may implement fair labor practices, provide safe and healthy working conditions, and support diversity and inclusion. These actions not only enhance the reputation of businesses but also contribute to the well-being of employees and society.

Economic Dimension

The economic dimension of sustainable development focuses on achieving economic growth, prosperity, and stability while considering the environmental and social implications of economic activities. It recognizes that economic success should be achieved in a way that is sustainable and inclusive.

One of the key principles in the economic dimension is resource efficiency. This principle emphasizes the need to use resources efficiently and minimize waste generation. It involves adopting technologies and practices that optimize resource use, reduce energy consumption, and minimize environmental impact. By maximizing resource efficiency, businesses can reduce costs, increase productivity, and enhance competitiveness.

Another important aspect of the economic dimension is inclusive economic growth. This refers to the equitable distribution of economic benefits and opportunities across the population. Inclusive economic growth aims to reduce poverty, inequality, and social exclusion, and promote shared prosperity. It involves creating an enabling environment for entrepreneurship, job creation, and innovation, as well as providing access to finance, infrastructure, and markets for all.

For example, microfinance institutions provide financial services to low-income individuals and small businesses that have limited access to traditional banking services. By providing loans, savings, and insurance products, microfinance institutions empower individuals and contribute to poverty reduction and economic development.

Integration of Environmental, Social, and Economic Dimensions

The integration of the environmental, social, and economic dimensions is the cornerstone of sustainable development. It requires a holistic and integrated approach to decision-making and policy formulation.

One approach to integrating these dimensions is through the concept of the triple bottom line. The triple bottom line framework expands the traditional focus on financial performance (the "bottom line") to include environmental and social performance. It encourages businesses and organizations to assess their impact and success in terms of economic, environmental, and social measures.

Another approach is through the adoption of sustainability reporting and performance measurement. Many businesses and organizations now produce sustainability reports that disclose their environmental and social performance alongside their financial performance. This enables stakeholders to evaluate their overall sustainability and provides a basis for accountability and transparency.

In conclusion, the environmental, social, and economic dimensions are interconnected and essential for achieving sustainable development. By considering and addressing the environmental and social implications of economic activities, businesses and organizations can contribute to long-term economic success while ensuring the well-being of people and the planet.

Sustainable Development Goals and Targets

In recent years, the concept of sustainable development has gained significant attention, both in academic circles and in policy discussions. It recognizes the interconnectedness of social, economic, and environmental factors and aims to promote long-term well-being for current and future generations. The United Nations has taken a leading role in advancing the agenda of sustainable development through the adoption of the Sustainable Development Goals (SDGs) in 2015. These goals, along with their specific targets, provide a roadmap for countries to address key global challenges and promote sustainable development worldwide.

The SDGs consist of 17 goals and 169 targets that cover a wide range of social, economic, and environmental issues. They address critical areas such as poverty eradication, health and well-being, quality education, clean energy, sustainable cities, responsible consumption and production, climate action, and biodiversity conservation. Each goal and target represents a specific area of focus and provides a set of measurable objectives to guide policy actions and monitor progress.

One of the key principles underlying the SDGs is the principle of universality. This means that all countries, regardless of their level of development, have a shared responsibility to achieve the goals and targets. The SDGs recognize that sustainable development is a global challenge that requires collective action and cooperation among all stakeholders, including governments, international organizations, civil society, and the private sector.

To illustrate the importance of the SDGs, let's take a closer look at one of the goals and its targets: Goal 7 - Affordable and Clean Energy. This goal aims to ensure access to affordable, reliable, sustainable, and modern energy for all. It recognizes that energy is central to nearly all aspects of sustainable development and is crucial for eradicating poverty, improving health and education, and promoting economic growth.

Target 7.2 specifically focuses on increasing the share of renewable energy in the global energy mix. It sets a target of doubling the global share of renewable energy by 2030. This target reflects the need to shift away from fossil fuel-based energy systems, which contribute to climate change and have serious environmental and health impacts. Increasing the use of renewable energy sources, such as solar and wind power, not only helps reduce greenhouse gas emissions but also provides opportunities for job creation, economic growth, and energy access in remote and underserved areas.

Target 7.3 complements this by calling for improvements in energy efficiency. It aims to double the global rate of improvement in energy efficiency by 2030. Energy efficiency is a crucial aspect of sustainable development as it helps reduce energy consumption, lower greenhouse gas emissions, and enhance energy security. Improving energy efficiency in buildings, transportation, industry, and appliances can significantly contribute to achieving multiple SDGs, including those related to climate action, clean air, and economic productivity.

Achieving the targets under Goal 7 requires concerted efforts from governments, businesses, and individuals. It involves the development and implementation of policies and regulations that support renewable energy deployment and energy efficiency measures. It also requires investment in research and development, infrastructure, and capacity building to enable the transition to a sustainable energy system.

Furthermore, the SDGs emphasize the importance of partnerships and collaboration among different actors. They recognize that no single stakeholder can address the complex challenges of sustainable development on their own. Partnerships between governments, businesses, civil society organizations, and local communities are essential for mobilizing resources, sharing knowledge and expertise, and implementing effective solutions.

To monitor progress towards the SDGs, a set of global indicators has been developed. These indicators provide a framework for tracking the implementation of the goals and targets and assessing the impact of policies and interventions. Regular reporting and review mechanisms help identify gaps and bottlenecks and inform decision-making processes at the national and international levels.

In conclusion, the Sustainable Development Goals and Targets represent a comprehensive framework for addressing the world's most pressing social, economic, and environmental challenges. They provide a clear vision for a more sustainable and inclusive future and offer guidance to countries and stakeholders on how to achieve it. By working collectively and taking concrete actions, we can make significant progress towards realizing the goals and building a better world for current and future generations.

Sustainable Business Practices

Corporate Social Responsibility and Ethical Business Models

In today's globalized and interconnected world, there is an increasing recognition of the need for businesses to go beyond profit-making and contribute positively to society and the environment. Corporate Social Responsibility (CSR) is a concept that encompasses the voluntary actions taken by businesses to address social, environmental, and ethical concerns. Ethical business models refer to approaches and strategies that prioritize moral principles and values in conducting business operations.

Definition and Importance of Corporate Social Responsibility

CSR can be defined as the integration of ethical, social, and environmental considerations into the core business strategy of a company. It involves taking responsibility for the company's impact on stakeholders, such as employees, customers, suppliers, communities, and the natural environment. CSR encompasses a wide range of activities, including philanthropy, sustainability initiatives, ethical sourcing, employee well-being programs, and community development projects.

The importance of CSR lies in its potential to create a positive impact on both society and business performance. By addressing social and environmental issues, companies can enhance their reputation, attract and retain talented employees, strengthen customer loyalty, foster innovation, and mitigate risks. Moreover, as consumers and investors increasingly prioritize sustainability and ethical practices, companies that embrace CSR are better positioned to thrive in the long run.

Principles of Corporate Social Responsibility

Several guiding principles underpin the implementation of CSR:

1. **Triple Bottom Line:** The concept of the triple bottom line emphasizes the need for businesses to consider not only their financial performance but also their social and environmental impacts. It entails measuring success based on three dimensions: profit, people, and planet.

2. **Stakeholder Engagement:** Effective CSR involves engaging with stakeholders to identify their concerns, priorities, and expectations. By actively involving stakeholders, companies can gain insights, build trust, and

ensure that their CSR initiatives align with the needs of the communities they operate in.

3. **Sustainability:** A key aspect of CSR is promoting sustainable practices. This involves minimizing environmental footprints, conserving resources, reducing waste, and supporting the transition to a low-carbon economy. Sustainable business models aim to create value while preserving the natural environment for future generations.

4. **Ethics and Transparency:** CSR requires businesses to uphold high ethical standards in their operations. This includes fair treatment of employees, responsible marketing practices, ethical sourcing, and transparent reporting on social and environmental impacts. Ethical business models prioritize honesty, integrity, and accountability.

Examples of Corporate Social Responsibility Initiatives

Numerous companies have implemented impressive CSR initiatives, setting examples for others to follow. Here are three prominent examples:

1. **Patagonia:** The outdoor clothing company Patagonia is renowned for its commitment to environmental sustainability. It invests in renewable energy, promotes fair labor practices, and advocates for the protection of natural resources. Patagonia's "Worn Wear" program encourages customers to repair and reuse their clothing items, reducing waste and prolonging the lifespan of its products.

2. **Unilever:** Unilever, a multinational consumer goods company, has made sustainability a core component of its business strategy. It has set ambitious targets to reduce its environmental impact, improve the well-being of one billion people, and enhance the livelihoods of its workers and suppliers. Unilever's Sustainable Living Brands, such as Dove and Ben & Jerry's, promote social and environmental causes.

3. **Interface:** Interface, a global modular flooring company, is known for its mission to achieve sustainability by 2020. It has implemented innovative practices like closed-loop manufacturing, where used carpets are recycled into new products. Interface's commitment to sustainability has not only reduced its environmental footprint but also enhanced its brand reputation and attracted environmentally conscious customers.

Challenges and Strategies for Implementing CSR

Implementing CSR initiatives can present challenges to businesses. Some common obstacles include:

- **Lack of Awareness and Commitment:** Many companies may lack awareness of the benefits of CSR or may not be fully committed to integrating it into their business operations. Overcoming this challenge requires leadership buy-in, education, and effective communication to foster a culture of corporate responsibility.

- **Resource Constraints:** Implementing CSR initiatives can require substantial investments of time, money, and expertise. Small and medium-sized enterprises, in particular, may face resource constraints that make it challenging to prioritize and implement CSR practices. Collaboration and partnerships with stakeholders can help overcome resource limitations.

- **Measuring Impact:** Assessing and measuring the impact of CSR initiatives can be complex. Companies need to develop appropriate metrics and indicators to track progress, evaluate outcomes, and communicate their impact effectively. Strategic monitoring and evaluation frameworks can help demonstrate the long-term value of CSR investments.

To overcome these challenges, businesses can adopt various strategies:

- **Integration into Business Strategy:** Embedding CSR into the core business strategy ensures that it becomes an integral part of day-to-day operations rather than a peripheral activity. Companies can align CSR goals with their overall mission and values, creating a shared sense of purpose among employees.

- **Partnerships and Collaboration:** Collaboration with stakeholders, including non-governmental organizations, governments, and local communities, can enhance the effectiveness of CSR initiatives. Partnerships can leverage expertise, resources, and networks to address complex social and environmental challenges more comprehensively.

- **Transparency and Reporting:** Transparent reporting allows stakeholders to assess a company's CSR performance, enabling accountability and trust-building. Companies should communicate their CSR activities, goals, and progress through sustainability reports, websites, and public disclosures. Engaging in dialogue with stakeholders and responding to their feedback is also crucial.

Conclusion

Corporate Social Responsibility and ethical business models have gained significant importance in today's business landscape. By integrating social, environmental, and ethical considerations into their operations, businesses can contribute to sustainable development while also achieving long-term success. Embracing CSR not only benefits society and the environment but also enhances a company's reputation, attracts stakeholders, and fosters innovation. Through responsible business practices, companies can create shared value and help build a more inclusive and sustainable future.

Circular Economy and Waste Reduction

In recent years, the concept of a circular economy has gained significant attention as a means to address the environmental challenges associated with traditional linear economic models. A circular economy aims to decouple economic growth from resource consumption and waste generation by promoting a more sustainable and efficient use of resources. This section explores the principles and strategies of the circular economy, with a specific focus on waste reduction.

Principles of the Circular Economy

The circular economy is based on three fundamental principles: reduce, reuse, and recycle. These principles guide the transition from a linear model of production and consumption to a closed-loop system that maximizes resource efficiency and minimizes waste.

1. **Reduce:** The first principle of the circular economy is to reduce the consumption of resources. This involves eliminating unnecessary waste by designing products and processes that use fewer raw materials and minimize energy and water consumption. It also involves promoting sustainable consumption patterns, such as choosing products with longer lifespans and reducing the overall demand for goods and services.

2. **Reuse:** The second principle focuses on the reuse of products and materials. Instead of disposing of items after a single use, the circular economy

promotes the reutilization of products through repair, refurbishment, and remanufacturing. By extending the lifespan of products, the need for new production and the associated resource extraction and waste generation are reduced.

3. **Recycle:** The third principle emphasizes the recycling and recovery of materials at the end of their life cycle. Recycling involves the collection and processing of waste materials to produce raw materials for the production of new goods. It helps conserve resources, reduce pollution, and decrease the reliance on virgin materials. Recycling can be facilitated through effective waste management systems and the implementation of appropriate infrastructure and technologies.

Strategies for Waste Reduction

To achieve waste reduction within a circular economy, various strategies can be implemented at different stages of the product life cycle. These strategies aim to minimize waste generation and maximize resource recovery.

- **Design for Disassembly:** To enable the efficient recovery of materials from products, designing for disassembly is crucial. This involves the consideration of how products can be easily taken apart at the end of their life cycle, allowing for the recovery of valuable components and materials. Design choices, such as the use of standardized connectors, labeling of materials, and modular design, can facilitate disassembly and enhance recycling rates.

- **Extended Producer Responsibility (EPR):** EPR is a policy approach that holds manufacturers responsible for the entire life cycle of their products, including their disposal. By imposing financial and operational obligations on producers, EPR encourages them to adopt environmentally friendly design practices and implement take-back systems. This approach incentivizes producers to incorporate recycling and waste reduction strategies into their business models.

- **Industrial Symbiosis:** Industrial symbiosis promotes the collaboration between different industries to utilize waste materials and by-products as inputs for other production processes. This approach aims to create closed-loop systems where one company's waste becomes another company's resource. By fostering resource exchange and sharing, industrial symbiosis reduces waste generation and promotes resource efficiency.

- **Product-Service Systems (PSS):** PSS involves shifting from the traditional model of product ownership to the provision of services. Instead of selling products, companies provide access to the functionality of products, enabling customers to use them on a pay-per-use or subscription basis. PSS encourages manufacturers to design products for long service life, as well as facilitating repair, maintenance, and end-of-life management.

Case Studies and Examples

Several real-world examples demonstrate the effectiveness of circular economy principles and waste reduction strategies in achieving sustainable economic success.

- **The Ellen MacArthur Foundation:** The Ellen MacArthur Foundation is a global leader in promoting the transition to a circular economy. It collaborates with businesses, governments, and academia to develop innovative solutions and strategies. The foundation's circular economy program showcases successful case studies, such as H&M's recycling initiative for textiles and Philips' shift to a circular business model in the lighting industry.

- **Interface's Mission Zero:** Interface, a global modular flooring company, implemented its Mission Zero initiative, which aims to eliminate any negative impact the company may have on the environment by 2020. Through innovative design approaches, resource-efficient manufacturing processes, and the integration of recycled materials, Interface has achieved significant waste reduction and resource conservation while maintaining profitable operations.

- **The Waste Electrical and Electronic Equipment (WEEE) Directive:** The WEEE Directive is an example of legislation aimed at reducing electronic waste and promoting its proper disposal and recycling. It requires producers to take responsibility for the entire life cycle of their electrical and electronic products, including collection, recycling, and environmentally sound treatment. The directive has resulted in increased recycling rates and the recovery of valuable materials from electronic waste.

Benefits and Challenges

The circular economy and waste reduction strategies offer various benefits, including:

- **Resource Efficiency:** By minimizing waste and maximizing resource utilization, the circular economy promotes resource efficiency and reduces the consumption of raw materials and energy.

- **Environmental Protection:** Waste reduction and resource recovery contribute to the protection of ecosystems, reduce pollution, and mitigate the environmental impact of economic activities.

- **Economic Opportunities:** The circular economy presents economic opportunities by fostering innovation, creating new business models, and generating employment in sectors such as recycling, remanufacturing, and repair.

However, the implementation of circular economy principles and waste reduction strategies also presents challenges, including:

- **Technological and Infrastructural Barriers:** The adoption of circular economy practices may require technological advancements and the development of appropriate infrastructure for waste collection, sorting, and recycling.

- **Behavioral Change:** Changing consumption patterns and promoting sustainable behaviors among individuals and businesses can be challenging and may require education, awareness campaigns, and incentives.

- **Policy and Regulatory Frameworks:** The successful implementation of the circular economy relies on supportive policy and regulatory frameworks that incentivize waste reduction, encourage resource recovery, and promote collaboration among stakeholders.

Overall, the circular economy and effective waste reduction strategies offer a promising pathway towards achieving sustainable economic success by decoupling economic growth from resource consumption and waste generation. By embracing the reduce, reuse, and recycle principles and implementing innovative solutions, businesses, governments, and individuals can contribute to a more sustainable and prosperous future.

Green Technologies and Renewable Energy

Introduction

In recent years, the importance of green technologies and renewable energy has become increasingly evident. As the world faces the challenges of climate change and resource scarcity, the need for sustainable energy solutions has become more urgent than ever. In this section, we will explore the role of green technologies in driving economic success and promoting environmental sustainability. We will discuss the various types of renewable energy sources, their benefits, and their potential for transforming industries. Additionally, we will delve into the challenges and opportunities associated with the widespread adoption of green technologies.

Types of Renewable Energy

Renewable energy refers to energy that is derived from sources that naturally replenish themselves over time. Unlike fossil fuels, which are finite and contribute to greenhouse gas emissions, renewable energy sources offer a sustainable and environmentally friendly alternative. Some of the most common types of renewable energy include:

1. Solar Energy: Solar energy harnesses the power of the sun to generate electricity or heat. Photovoltaic (PV) cells convert sunlight into electricity, while solar thermal systems use mirrors or lenses to concentrate solar energy for heating purposes.

2. Wind Energy: Wind turbines capture the kinetic energy of wind and convert it into electricity. Wind farms, consisting of multiple turbines, are often deployed in areas with strong and consistent wind patterns.

3. Hydropower: Hydropower utilizes the energy of flowing or falling water to generate electricity. It is primarily derived from dams and reservoirs, where water is released through turbines to produce power.

4. Biomass: Biomass refers to organic materials, such as wood, crop residues, and animal waste, that can be burned or processed to produce heat or electricity. It is a renewable energy source as long as the biomass is sustainably harvested.

5. Geothermal Energy: Geothermal energy taps into the heat stored beneath the Earth's surface. It involves extracting hot water or steam from geothermal reservoirs to generate electricity or provide direct heating.

Each type of renewable energy has its own unique advantages and limitations. Solar and wind energy, for example, are abundant and widely available, while hydropower offers the advantage of storage and dispatchability. Biomass can provide a continuous and reliable energy supply, while geothermal energy is relatively constant and unaffected by weather conditions.

Benefits of Green Technologies

The adoption of green technologies and the transition to renewable energy systems offer numerous benefits for both the economy and the environment. Some of the key advantages include:

1. Environmental Sustainability: Green technologies help reduce greenhouse gas emissions, mitigate climate change impacts, and preserve natural resources. By shifting away from fossil fuels, we can decrease air pollution, improve overall air quality, and protect biodiversity.

2. Economic Growth: The deployment of green technologies stimulates economic growth and creates job opportunities. The renewable energy sector has seen significant job growth in recent years, with a focus on manufacturing, installation, operation, and maintenance.

3. Energy Security: Investing in renewable energy reduces reliance on imported fossil fuels, enhancing energy security and reducing geopolitical risks. By diversifying the energy mix, countries can strengthen their resilience to price fluctuations and supply disruptions.

4. Price Stability: Renewable energy resources, such as wind and sunlight, are freely available and do not experience price volatility like fossil fuels. This stability in energy costs benefits consumers and businesses alike, providing long-term price predictability.

5. Technological Innovation: The development and implementation of green technologies drive innovation, leading to advancements in energy storage, grid integration, and energy efficiency. These innovations have spillover effects across various sectors of the economy, contributing to overall technological progress.

Challenges and Opportunities

While the benefits of green technologies are significant, their widespread adoption also presents challenges and opportunities. Some of the key considerations include:

1. Intermittency and Storage: Renewable energy sources, such as solar and wind, are intermittent in nature, meaning their availability fluctuates depending on weather conditions. This intermittency creates challenges for grid integration and necessitates the development of efficient energy storage systems.

2. Infrastructure and Grid Upgrades: The transition to a renewable energy system requires substantial investments in infrastructure and grid upgrades. The

existing electrical grid may not be equipped to handle the decentralized nature of renewable energy generation, necessitating modifications and enhancements.

3. Cost Competitiveness: While the cost of renewable energy has significantly decreased in recent years, it still faces competition from conventional fossil fuel-based energy sources. Continued advancements in technology, economies of scale, and supportive policy frameworks are needed to improve the cost competitiveness of renewable energy.

4. Policy and Regulatory Frameworks: The success of green technologies heavily relies on the presence of supportive policy and regulatory frameworks. Governments need to establish clear and consistent policies that incentivize renewable energy adoption and create a level playing field for all stakeholders.

5. Public Acceptance and Community Engagement: The successful deployment of green technologies requires public acceptance and community engagement. Educating the public about the benefits of renewable energy and addressing concerns related to aesthetics, noise, and land use are crucial for widespread acceptance and adoption.

Case Studies of Successful Green Technologies

Let us now explore some case studies that highlight the transformative potential of green technologies:

1. Tesla and Electric Vehicles: Tesla, led by Elon Musk, has revolutionized the automotive industry with its electric vehicles (EVs). By combining advanced battery technology, cutting-edge design, and a robust charging infrastructure, Tesla has successfully accelerated the adoption of EVs and paved the way for a future of sustainable transportation.

2. Denmark's Wind Power Success: Denmark has emerged as a global leader in wind energy, with more than 50% of its electricity consumption being generated from wind power. Through strong government support, favorable policies, and collaborative partnerships, Denmark has created an enabling environment for wind energy development, leading to economic growth and reduced carbon emissions.

3. Germany's Energiewende: Germany's Energiewende, or energy transition, aims to achieve a sustainable energy system by phasing out nuclear power and transitioning to renewable energy sources. This ambitious project has made Germany a trailblazer in renewable energy adoption, with significant investments in solar and wind power, energy efficiency, and grid infrastructure.

Conclusion

Green technologies and renewable energy have the power to drive economic success while addressing the urgent challenge of environmental sustainability. By embracing renewable energy sources and investing in technological innovation, societies can achieve a transition towards a greener and more prosperous future. However, the successful integration of green technologies requires concerted efforts from governments, businesses, and individuals. It is through collaboration and commitment that we can build a sustainable and resilient economy for generations to come.

Case Studies of Sustainable Economic Success

Patagonia and the Triple Bottom Line

In this section, we will explore the case study of Patagonia, an outdoor clothing company that has become a pioneer in sustainable business practices. Patagonia's commitment to the triple bottom line - people, planet, and profit - has set it apart as a leader in environmental and social responsibility within the business world.

Background

Patagonia was founded in 1973 by Yvon Chouinard, a passionate rock climber and environmentalist. The company initially focused on producing high-quality climbing gear, but it soon expanded its product line to include outdoor clothing and accessories. Throughout its history, Patagonia has maintained a strong ethos of environmental stewardship, guided by the belief that businesses have a responsibility to protect and preserve the natural world.

The Triple Bottom Line

The concept of the triple bottom line refers to the idea that businesses should consider their impact on three dimensions: people, planet, and profit. Traditional business models tend to prioritize financial success above all else, but Patagonia believes that it is essential to balance economic gains with social and environmental considerations. Let's explore each dimension of the triple bottom line in more detail:

1. **People:** Patagonia places a strong emphasis on the well-being of its employees, customers, and communities. The company provides fair wages, safe working conditions, and opportunities for personal and professional development. It also actively supports grassroots environmental organizations and encourages employee activism.

2. **Planet:** As an outdoor clothing company, Patagonia recognizes its significant impact on the environment. The company has taken bold steps to minimize its ecological footprint. It uses organic and recycled materials in its products, reduces waste through recycling and repair programs, and invests in renewable energy sources. Patagonia is also a vocal advocate for environmental causes and engages in activism to protect natural resources.

3. **Profit:** While prioritizing people and the planet, Patagonia has also achieved remarkable financial success. The company's commitment to sustainability has resonated with consumers who value ethically produced goods. By aligning its values with those of its customer base, Patagonia has built a loyal and engaged customer community, leading to increased sales and profitability.

The Impact of Patagonia's Triple Bottom Line Approach

Patagonia's triple bottom line approach has had a profound impact on various stakeholders and the broader business community. Here are some examples:

1. **Customer Loyalty and Brand Reputation:** Patagonia's strong commitment to social and environmental responsibility has earned it a loyal customer base that values ethical and sustainable business practices. By consistently demonstrating its commitment to the triple bottom line, Patagonia has built a strong brand reputation as a company that cares about people and the planet.

2. **Employee Engagement and Satisfaction:** Patagonia's unique approach to business has attracted and retained passionate employees who align with the company's values. The company's focus on personal development, work-life balance, and social activism creates a positive work environment. This, in turn, leads to higher employee engagement, satisfaction, and productivity.

3. **Industry Leadership and Influence:** Patagonia's success has inspired other companies to adopt more sustainable practices. The company actively shares its knowledge and experiences to encourage other organizations to prioritize social and environmental responsibility. By leading by example, Patagonia has become a powerful advocate for change within the business community.

Challenges and Future Opportunities

While Patagonia has achieved remarkable success in integrating the triple bottom line into its business model, it continues to face challenges and identifies future opportunities. Some of these include:

1. **Supply Chain Transparency:** Patagonia recognizes the importance of knowing and improving the social and environmental impacts of its entire supply chain. The company continues to invest in traceability and

transparency, working closely with suppliers to improve labor practices and reduce environmental harm.

2. **Circular Economy and Extended Producer Responsibility**: Patagonia aims to further reduce waste and create a more sustainable business model. The company has introduced initiatives such as its Worn Wear program, which promotes clothing repair and recycling. Patagonia is exploring innovative solutions to design products that can be easily repaired, recycled, or upcycled.

3. **Policy Advocacy and Systemic Change**: Recognizing that individual business efforts alone cannot solve large-scale social and environmental challenges, Patagonia actively engages in policy advocacy and supports organizations working for systemic change. The company believes that collaboration between business, government, and civil society is essential for creating a more sustainable and just future.

Conclusion

Patagonia's success as a sustainable business driven by the triple bottom line demonstrates that aligning profitability with social and environmental responsibility is not only possible but also highly beneficial. By prioritizing the well-being of people and the planet alongside financial gains, Patagonia has built a business model that sets the standard for others to follow. As the company continues to innovate and advocate for change, it inspires a new generation of entrepreneurs to embrace the triple bottom line and strive for economic success with a positive impact on society and the environment.

Exercises

1. Explore the website of Patagonia and identify three specific initiatives or programs the company has implemented to support each dimension of the triple bottom line (people, planet, and profit).

2. Research and discuss another company or organization that embodies the principles of the triple bottom line. Explain how they have integrated the triple bottom line into their business model and highlight their impact on people, the planet, and profit.

3. Reflect on your own beliefs and values regarding the triple bottom line. How does this influence your consumer behavior and decision-making

process? Share a personal example of a product or service you have chosen based on its social or environmental attributes.

Additional Resources

1. *Let My People Go Surfing: The Education of a Reluctant Businessman* by Yvon Chouinard.

2. Patagonia's website: `https://www.patagonia.com/`

3. TED Talk: "The Business Case for Working with Your 'Enemy'" - Yvon Chouinard (`https://www.ted.com/talks/yvon_chouinard_the_business_case_for_working_with_your_enemy?language=en`)

Novozymes and the Biotech Revolution in Sustainable Industrial Processes

Novozymes, a Danish biotech company, has been at the forefront of the biotech revolution, leading the way in sustainable industrial processes. With its innovative approach and commitment to environmental sustainability, Novozymes has become a global leader in developing biotechnological solutions for various industries.

Background and Overview

Novozymes was founded in 2000 as a spin-off from the pharmaceutical company Novo Nordisk. The company specializes in the development of enzymes and microorganisms for a wide range of industries, including agriculture, detergents, biofuels, and food production. By harnessing the power of nature's own catalysts, Novozymes has revolutionized industrial processes, making them more efficient, cost-effective, and environmentally friendly.

Principles of Biotechnology

Biotechnology is the application of biological processes, organisms, or systems to produce products or technologies that improve human lives and the health of the planet. The core principles of biotechnology involve the use of living organisms, such as enzymes and microorganisms, to perform specific tasks, such as breaking down complex organic materials or producing valuable compounds.

In the case of Novozymes, the company utilizes enzymes, which are natural proteins that act as catalysts to speed up chemical reactions. Enzymes can be tailored to perform specific functions, making them highly effective in a variety of industrial processes. By using enzymes instead of traditional chemical methods, Novozymes reduces the need for harsh chemicals, energy consumption, and waste generation, resulting in more sustainable and efficient production processes.

Applications in Sustainable Industrial Processes

Novozymes' biotechnological solutions have a wide range of applications in sustainable industrial processes. Here are a few notable examples:

- **Biofuels:** Novozymes has played a crucial role in the development of second-generation biofuels, such as cellulosic ethanol. By breaking down plant biomass into fermentable sugars using enzymes, Novozymes enables the production of biofuels from non-food sources, reducing reliance on fossil fuels and mitigating the environmental impact of transportation.

- **Detergents:** Enzymes produced by Novozymes are used in laundry and dishwashing detergents to enhance their cleaning power. Enzymes break down stains and dirt more effectively than traditional chemical detergents, allowing consumers to wash their clothes at lower temperatures, saving energy, and reducing their carbon footprint.

- **Agriculture:** Novozymes' agricultural solutions focus on improving crop yields while minimizing the use of chemical fertilizers and pesticides. Enzymes and microorganisms developed by the company enhance soil health, promote nutrient absorption, and reduce the environmental impact of agricultural practices.

- **Food Production:** Novozymes' enzymes are used in various stages of food production, such as the processing of dairy products, baking, and brewing. These enzymes optimize production processes, improve product quality, and reduce waste, making food production more sustainable.

Challenges and Innovations

While Novozymes has achieved significant success in sustainable industrial processes, there are challenges that the company has faced and continues to address:

- **Economic Viability:** The cost of enzymes and biotechnological solutions can be a barrier to their widespread adoption. Novozymes continues to invest in research and development to optimize enzyme production processes, reduce production costs, and make their products more economically viable for various industries.

- **Regulatory Environment:** The use of genetically modified organisms (GMOs) and the release of enzymes into the environment are subject to strict regulations. Novozymes works closely with regulatory bodies, ensuring compliance with safety standards and advocating for policies that support the use of biotechnological solutions.

Despite these challenges, Novozymes remains dedicated to innovation and strives to develop more efficient enzymes, expand their product portfolio, and explore new applications of biotechnology to further drive sustainable industrial processes.

Examples and Impact

Novozymes' biotechnological solutions have had a significant impact on various industries, driving sustainability and efficiency. Here are a few examples of their impact:

- **Reduced Environmental Footprint:** By replacing traditional chemical processes with enzymatic processes, Novozymes' solutions have helped reduce the use of hazardous chemicals, minimize waste generation, and lower energy consumption in industries such as biofuels, detergent manufacturing, and food production.

- **Increased Efficiency:** Enzymes developed by Novozymes improve the efficiency of industrial processes, leading to higher productivity, reduced production costs, and improved product quality. For example, their enzymes used in the production of biofuels enable higher ethanol yields and more efficient conversion of biomass into renewable energy.

- **Sustainable Agriculture:** Novozymes' agricultural solutions have contributed to sustainable farming practices by reducing chemical inputs, improving soil health, and increasing crop yields. This has a positive impact on food security, environmental conservation, and the livelihoods of farmers.

Resources for Further Learning

To delve deeper into the topic of Novozymes and the biotech revolution in sustainable industrial processes, here are some resources for further learning:

- **Novozymes' Official Website:** The official website of Novozymes provides comprehensive information about the company's products, technologies, and sustainability initiatives.

- **Scientific Publications:** Numerous scientific articles and publications explore the applications of biotechnology in sustainable industrial processes. These publications provide in-depth insights into the scientific principles, innovations, and challenges of this field.

- **Industry Conferences and Events:** Attending conferences and events focused on biotechnology and sustainable industrial processes can offer valuable networking opportunities and the chance to stay updated on the latest advancements in the field.

Conclusion

Novozymes' journey in the biotech revolution in sustainable industrial processes exemplifies the power of biotechnology in driving environmental sustainability, efficiency, and economic prosperity. By harnessing the potential of enzymes and microorganisms, Novozymes has brought forth innovative solutions that have transformed a wide range of industries. Through ongoing research, development, and collaboration, Novozymes continues to pave the way for a more sustainable and prosperous future.

Costa Rica's Environmental Leadership and Sustainable Tourism

Costa Rica, a small country in Central America, has gained worldwide recognition for its environmental leadership and commitment to sustainable tourism. In recent decades, Costa Rica has become a global example of how a country can successfully preserve its natural resources while promoting economic growth through sustainable practices. This section will explore the key factors that have contributed to Costa Rica's environmental success and how sustainable tourism has played a vital role in driving economic development.

Protecting Biodiversity and Ecosystems

Costa Rica is known for its incredible biodiversity, boasting around 6% of the world's species despite covering less than 0.03% of the Earth's surface. The country has made significant efforts to protect its natural habitats and ecosystems, establishing a vast network of protected areas such as national parks, biological reserves, and wildlife refuges. These protected areas cover over 25% of the country's land and are crucial in preserving Costa Rica's rich biodiversity.

One of the standout examples is Corcovado National Park, located on the Osa Peninsula. It is renowned for its dense rainforests, mangroves, and vast array of wildlife, including endangered species like jaguars and Baird's tapirs. The government's commitment to conserving such areas has not only preserved valuable ecosystems but has also attracted tourists from around the world, contributing to the country's economy.

In addition to protected areas, Costa Rica has taken steps to promote sustainable land use and forestry practices. The country has implemented reforestation programs to restore degraded lands and combat deforestation. It has also recognized the rights of indigenous communities and involved them in forest management, enhancing their livelihoods while ensuring the conservation of these valuable resources.

Promoting Sustainable Tourism

Sustainable tourism has played a pivotal role in Costa Rica's economic growth while ensuring the preservation of its natural environment. The country has embraced a "green" approach to tourism, focusing on responsible practices that minimize negative environmental impacts and benefit local communities. This has allowed Costa Rica to attract a growing number of eco-tourists seeking unique experiences in an environmentally conscious destination.

One example of sustainable tourism in Costa Rica is its eco-lodges and ecolodges. These accommodations are designed to blend in with the natural surroundings, using renewable energy sources, implementing water-saving measures, and employing local staff. Such initiatives not only minimize the ecological footprint but also contribute to the local economy, providing employment opportunities and supporting small businesses.

Furthermore, Costa Rica has actively promoted adventure tourism and ecotourism activities that offer visitors the chance to explore its diverse landscapes responsibly. Activities such as hiking, birdwatching, zip-lining, and nature tours contribute to the local economy while raising awareness about the importance of conserving the country's ecological heritage.

Public-Private Partnerships for Sustainability

Costa Rica's environmental leadership is not solely reliant on government initiatives but also on successful public-private partnerships. These partnerships bring together various stakeholders, including government agencies, businesses, local communities, and non-governmental organizations (NGOs), to collaborate on sustainable development projects.

One remarkable example is the partnership between the government and the Certification for Sustainable Tourism (CST) program. The CST program encourages tourism businesses to adopt sustainable practices and provides them with certification based on their environmental, social, and economic performance. This initiative has not only raised awareness about sustainable tourism but has also rewarded businesses that prioritize environmental conservation and social responsibility.

Additionally, the government has implemented economic incentives and policies that promote sustainability. It offers tax breaks and grants to businesses that adopt sustainable practices, such as energy efficiency and waste reduction. These incentives encourage companies to invest in environmentally friendly technologies while making a positive impact on the environment.

Challenges and Future Outlook

Despite its remarkable achievements, Costa Rica still faces challenges in maintaining its environmental leadership and ensuring the long-term sustainability of its tourism industry. One of the main challenges is balancing the increasing demand for tourism with the need to preserve fragile ecosystems. Managing visitor numbers and implementing sustainable tourism practices will be essential in preventing overtourism and minimizing negative impacts on the environment.

Furthermore, climate change poses a significant threat to Costa Rica's natural resources, including its forests, coastal areas, and water sources. Rising temperatures, changing precipitation patterns, and sea-level rise can disrupt ecosystems and impact biodiversity. To address these challenges, Costa Rica must continue to invest in climate change mitigation and adaptation strategies, such as promoting renewable energy and implementing resilient infrastructure.

In conclusion, Costa Rica's environmental leadership and sustainable tourism efforts have not only protected its exceptional biodiversity and ecosystems but also stimulated economic growth. By embracing sustainable practices, promoting responsible tourism, and fostering public-private partnerships, Costa Rica serves as an inspiring model for countries around the world. However, ongoing efforts are necessary to address evolving challenges and ensure a sustainable future for Costa Rica's environment and tourism industry.

Chapter 7: Government Policies and Economic Success

Chapter 7: Government Policies and Economic Success

Chapter 7: Government Policies and Economic Success

Government policies play a crucial role in shaping the economic success of a country. In this chapter, we will examine the importance of government intervention in promoting economic growth, reducing market failures, and ensuring equitable distribution of resources. We will explore various fiscal and monetary policy tools used by governments, as well as the role of taxation, central banking, and government debt management. Additionally, we will discuss the Nordic Model, Singapore's economic planning, and Brazil's social welfare program as case studies of government-led economic success.

The Role of Government in Economic Development

Governments have a fundamental role in fostering economic development and addressing market failures. While free markets are efficient, they are not always able to allocate resources optimally. Market failures, such as externalities, public goods, and information asymmetry, require government intervention to overcome inefficiencies and achieve a desirable outcome.

One of the key roles of the government is to provide public goods. Public goods, such as national defense and infrastructure, are non-excludable and non-rivalrous, meaning that their consumption by one individual does not diminish their availability to others. Because of their unique characteristics, the private sector may not have sufficient incentives to produce public goods, leading to underinvestment. Governments step in to provide and finance the production of public goods, ensuring their provision for the benefit of society as a whole.

Furthermore, governments play a crucial role in addressing externalities, which are costs or benefits imposed on third parties as a result of economic activities. Externalities can be positive, such as education spillovers, or negative, such as pollution. Without government intervention, individuals and firms may not take into account the full social costs or benefits associated with their actions, leading to an inefficient allocation of resources. Through regulation and the imposition of taxes or subsidies, governments can internalize external costs or benefits, promoting efficiency and sustainability.

Fiscal and Monetary Policy

Governments use fiscal and monetary policy tools to influence the overall performance of the economy. Fiscal policy refers to the use of government spending and taxation to achieve macroeconomic objectives, such as controlling inflation, promoting economic growth, and reducing inequality. Monetary policy, on the other hand, focuses on the control of money supply and interest rates to influence aggregate demand and stabilize the economy.

Taxation is a key component of fiscal policy. Governments raise revenue through various taxes, such as income tax, sales tax, and corporate tax. The distribution of the tax burden can have significant effects on income inequality and economic growth. Progressive taxation, where higher-income individuals are taxed at a higher rate, can help redistribute income and reduce inequality. However, excessive taxation can create disincentives for work, saving, and investment, leading to lower economic growth. Finding the right balance between income redistribution and economic incentives is crucial for effective tax policy.

Central banks play a crucial role in implementing monetary policy. They control the money supply and influence interest rates to manage inflation and stabilize the economy. By increasing or decreasing the money supply, central banks can affect the cost of borrowing, investment decisions, and overall aggregate demand. Through open market operations, discount rate changes, and reserve requirements, central banks can stimulate or restrain economic activity. However, monetary policy effectiveness depends on the credibility and independence of the central bank, as well as its ability to accurately assess economic conditions.

Government Debt and Deficit Management

Another important aspect of government policies is managing government debt and deficits. Governments often resort to borrowing when tax revenues are insufficient to cover expenses. However, excessive government borrowing can lead to an accumulation of debt, which can have adverse effects on the economy.

Government debt is typically issued in the form of bonds, which are purchased by individuals, financial institutions, and foreign governments. The sustainability of government debt is measured by the debt-to-GDP ratio, which compares the size of the debt to the size of the economy. High levels of government debt can impede economic growth by crowding out private investment, increasing interest rates, and reducing fiscal flexibility.

To ensure the sustainability of government debt, governments must effectively manage their budgets and control deficits. Deficits occur when government spending exceeds tax revenues. While deficits may be necessary during economic downturns to stimulate demand, persistent and large deficits can lead to an accumulation of debt. Governments must strike a balance between stimulating the economy and maintaining fiscal discipline to prevent excessive debt levels.

Case Studies of Government-led Economic Success

To illustrate the impact of government policies on economic success, we will review three case studies: the Nordic Model, Singapore's economic planning, and Brazil's Bolsa Família program.

The Nordic Model refers to the socio-economic policies adopted by the Nordic countries, including Denmark, Finland, Iceland, Norway, and Sweden. These countries have experienced high levels of economic growth, low income inequality, and strong social welfare systems. The Nordic Model combines market capitalism with an extensive welfare state, providing universal healthcare, education, and social support. Through progressive taxation, strong labor market regulations, and active labor market policies, the Nordic countries have achieved high levels of social mobility and economic prosperity.

Singapore is often regarded as a model of successful economic planning. With limited natural resources, Singapore has transformed itself into a global financial and trading hub. The government has played a central role in guiding economic development through long-term planning, industrial policies, and strategic investments in education and infrastructure. Singapore has attracted foreign direct investment, developed a skilled workforce, and fostered an innovation-driven economy. The country's success can be attributed to effective government policies, a business-friendly environment, and strong governance.

Brazil's Bolsa Família program is a social welfare program aimed at reducing poverty and inequality. It provides conditional cash transfers to low-income families in exchange for specific behaviors, such as keeping children in school and ensuring they receive regular health check-ups. The program has been successful in reducing poverty and improving education and health outcomes. By addressing income inequality and investing in human capital, Brazil has achieved inclusive economic growth and social development.

In conclusion, government policies play a crucial role in promoting economic success. Through addressing market failures, implementing fiscal and monetary policies, managing government debt, and designing effective social welfare programs, governments can create an enabling environment for economic growth, reduce inequality, and ensure sustainable development. The case studies of the Nordic Model, Singapore's economic planning, and Brazil's Bolsa Família program illustrate the positive impact of government-led initiatives on achieving economic success. It is essential for governments to strike a balance between market forces and government intervention to foster sustainable economic growth and prosperity.

The Role of Government in Economic Development

Market Failures and the Need for Government Intervention

In a market economy, the allocation of resources and the determination of prices are primarily driven by supply and demand. This system, known as the price mechanism, is often effective in promoting efficiency and encouraging economic growth. However, there are situations where the market fails to achieve desirable outcomes and there is a need for government intervention. This section explores the concept of market failures and the role of the government in addressing them.

Definition of Market Failures

Market failures occur when the price mechanism fails to allocate resources efficiently or results in undesirable outcomes. These failures can be classified into several categories:

1. **Externalities:** Externalities occur when the production or consumption of a good or service affects third parties who are not involved in the transaction.

Externalities can be positive (e.g., the provision of education leading to a more skilled workforce) or negative (e.g., pollution from industrial activities). In the presence of externalities, the market fails to account for the social costs or benefits associated with the activity, leading to an inefficient allocation of resources.

2. **Public Goods:** Public goods are non-excludable and non-rivalrous in consumption. This means that once a public good is provided, it is difficult to exclude anyone from consuming it, and one person's consumption does not diminish its availability to others. Examples of public goods include national defense and public parks. Because individuals cannot be excluded from enjoying the benefits of public goods, the market tends to underprovide them due to the free-rider problem.

3. **Market Power:** Market power exists when a firm or a group of firms has the ability to influence the market price by controlling the quantity of goods or services supplied. Market power can lead to higher prices, reduced consumer choice, and decreased economic welfare. Monopoly power, oligopoly power, and monopolistic competition are examples of market power situations where the market fails to achieve competitive outcomes.

4. **Information Asymmetry:** Information asymmetry occurs when one party in an economic transaction has more information than the other party. This imbalance of information can lead to market failures. In situations of adverse selection, one party has more information about the quality of a product than the other, resulting in a market failure. Moral hazard, on the other hand, refers to situations where one party has an incentive to take on excessive risk after entering into a transaction.

Consequences of Market Failures

Market failures can have significant consequences for the overall economy and society as a whole. Some of the key consequences include:

- **Inefficient Allocation of Resources:** Market failures can lead to an inefficient allocation of resources. For example, negative externalities such as pollution may result in the overproduction of goods with harmful side effects, while positive externalities, such as education, may be underprovided. In the absence of government intervention, resources may be misallocated, leading to a suboptimal use of society's scarce resources.

- **Reduced Economic Welfare:** Market failures can lead to a reduction in economic welfare. For instance, market power can result in higher prices and reduced consumer surplus. Externalities can impose costs on society that are not reflected in market prices. The underprovision of public goods can limit the ability of individuals to enjoy their benefits. All these factors can result in a decrease in overall economic well-being.

- **Social Inequality:** Market failures can contribute to social inequality. For example, adverse selection in the insurance market can result in higher premiums for low-risk individuals, making it unaffordable for some segments of the population. Similarly, the underprovision of public goods such as education and healthcare can limit opportunities for disadvantaged individuals and perpetuate inequality.

Government Intervention to Address Market Failures

Given the negative consequences of market failures, governments play a crucial role in addressing these failures and promoting economic efficiency and equity. Government intervention can take various forms:

1. **Correcting Externalities:** Governments can intervene to internalize externalities by imposing taxes or subsidies. For example, a carbon tax can be imposed to account for the environmental costs associated with pollution. Subsidies can be provided for activities with positive externalities, such as research and development or education.

2. **Providing Public Goods:** Governments are responsible for providing public goods that are underprovided by the market. Public goods like infrastructure, defense, and basic research are essential for the functioning of the economy, and their provision can lead to positive spillover effects.

3. **Regulating Market Power:** Governments regulate markets with significant market power to promote competition and prevent abuse of market dominance. Antitrust laws and regulations are put in place to prevent anti-competitive practices and ensure fair market outcomes.

4. **Addressing Information Asymmetry:** Governments can address information asymmetry through regulations that require the disclosure of relevant information to consumers. For instance, laws requiring product labeling or mandatory disclosures in the financial industry aim to reduce information asymmetry.

Critiques and Challenges of Government Intervention

While government intervention is essential in addressing market failures, it is not without its challenges and criticisms. Some of the key critiques include:

- **Government Failure:** Similar to market failures, government failures can occur when government interventions result in unintended consequences or inefficiencies. Examples of government failure include regulatory capture, rent-seeking behavior, and bureaucratic inefficiencies.

- **Balancing Efficiency and Equity:** Balancing economic efficiency and equity is a challenge for policymakers. While government intervention can address market failures and promote equity, excessive intervention may hinder economic growth and limit individual freedom.

- **Political Considerations:** Government intervention is influenced by political considerations. Policies may be influenced by special interest groups or short-term political goals rather than long-term economic objectives. This can lead to suboptimal policy outcomes.

Real-World Example: Government Intervention in Healthcare

One of the most notable examples of government intervention to address market failures is the provision of healthcare. The healthcare industry has several characteristics that can lead to market failures, including information asymmetry, high costs, and unequal access to care.

Governments around the world intervene in healthcare through various means. In many countries, governments play a direct role in the provision of healthcare services, often through public healthcare systems. These systems aim to ensure access to quality healthcare for all citizens, regardless of their ability to pay. Government intervention in healthcare also includes regulations to ensure patient safety, control prices of pharmaceuticals, and promote equity in access to healthcare.

However, the provision of healthcare involves complex trade-offs, and finding the right balance between efficiency and equity remains a challenge. Healthcare systems vary across countries, reflecting different approaches and priorities. The ongoing debate on the optimal level of government intervention in healthcare highlights the complexity of addressing market failures in this sector.

Conclusion

Market failures are a significant challenge in modern economies, and addressing them requires government intervention. Externalities, public goods, market power, and information asymmetry are common sources of market failures. Government intervention can help correct these failures and lead to a more efficient and equitable allocation of resources. However, government intervention is not without challenges, and careful consideration is needed to strike a balance between economic efficiency and equity. Real-world examples, such as government intervention in healthcare, highlight the complexities involved in addressing market failures.

Economic Planning and Industrial Policies

Economic planning and industrial policies play a crucial role in shaping a country's economic development. These policies are designed to guide the allocation of resources, promote industrial growth, and address market failures. In this section, we will explore the objectives, principles, and tools of economic planning, as well as the key considerations and challenges associated with industrial policies.

Objectives of Economic Planning

The main objective of economic planning is to achieve sustainable and inclusive economic growth. It involves setting targets and formulating policies to enhance productivity, increase employment opportunities, reduce poverty, and promote equitable distribution of resources and wealth. In addition to economic growth, economic planning also aims to achieve social and environmental goals, such as improving education, healthcare, and environmental sustainability.

Principles of Economic Planning

Economic planning is based on a few key principles that guide the formulation and implementation of policies. These principles include:

1. **Long-term perspective:** Economic planning takes into account the long-term needs and goals of a country, rather than focusing solely on short-term considerations. It involves setting objectives and implementing policies that will have a sustained impact on the economy over time.

2. **Holistic approach:** Economic planning considers the interdependence of various sectors and factors of production in the economy. It takes into

account the relationships and linkages among different industries, as well as the social and environmental implications of economic activities.

3. **Stakeholder engagement:** Economic planning involves engaging relevant stakeholders, including government agencies, businesses, labor unions, civil society organizations, and local communities. Stakeholder participation ensures that diverse perspectives and interests are taken into account during the planning process.

4. **Evidence-based decision-making:** Economic planning relies on empirical data, economic analysis, and rigorous research to inform policy decisions. It involves conducting feasibility studies, cost-benefit analysis, and impact assessments to evaluate the potential outcomes of different policy options.

5. **Flexibility and adaptability:** Economic planning recognizes the dynamic nature of the economy and the need for flexibility in policy implementation. It allows for adjustments and fine-tuning of policies based on changing economic conditions, emerging challenges, and new opportunities.

6. **Coordination and collaboration:** Economic planning requires coordination and collaboration among different government agencies, as well as between the public and private sectors. Effective coordination ensures coherent policy implementation and avoids duplication of efforts.

Tools of Economic Planning

Economic planning utilizes a range of tools and instruments to achieve its objectives. These tools include:

1. **Development plans:** Development plans outline the goals, strategies, and policies for a specified period, such as five or ten years. These plans provide a roadmap for achieving economic objectives and serve as a basis for policy formulation and implementation.

2. **Fiscal policies:** Fiscal policies involve the use of government spending, taxation, and borrowing to influence the level and composition of aggregate demand in the economy. These policies aim to stabilize the economy, promote investment, and address income inequality.

3. **Monetary policies:** Monetary policies are implemented by central banks to manage the money supply, interest rates, and credit conditions in the

economy. These policies influence the cost of borrowing, inflation, and exchange rates, and thereby impact investment, consumption, and economic growth.

4. **Regulatory frameworks:** Regulatory frameworks establish rules and regulations to govern economic activities and ensure fair competition, consumer protection, and environmental sustainability. These frameworks provide a predictable and transparent business environment, which is essential for attracting investment and promoting industrial growth.

5. **Public investment:** Public investment in infrastructure, education, healthcare, and research and development is a key tool of economic planning. These investments create the necessary enabling conditions for private sector development, improve productivity, and enhance the competitiveness of industries.

6. **Industrial policies:** Industrial policies are aimed at promoting the growth and competitiveness of specific industries or sectors. These policies may include targeted financial incentives, supportive infrastructure, research and development support, and skills development programs. Industrial policies are particularly important for countries seeking to develop strategic sectors or move up the value chain in global production networks.

Considerations and Challenges

While economic planning and industrial policies offer opportunities for economic development, they also face certain considerations and challenges. Some of these include:

1. **Market distortions:** In some cases, economic planning and industrial policies may create market distortions, such as preferential treatment for certain industries or protectionist measures that limit competition. Balancing the need for targeted support with ensuring a level playing field for all market participants is a key challenge.

2. **Policy coordination:** Coordinating different policies across various sectors and levels of government can be challenging, especially in countries with decentralized governance structures. Ensuring policy coherence and avoiding conflicting objectives require effective coordination mechanisms and inter-agency collaboration.

3. **Political economy considerations:** Economic planning and industrial policies can be influenced by political considerations, vested interests, and rent-seeking behavior. It is important to safeguard against corrupt practices and ensure that policies are designed and implemented in the best interest of the overall economy and society.

4. **External shocks and global dynamics:** Economic planning needs to take into account external shocks, such as global financial crises, commodity price fluctuations, and geopolitical uncertainties. Global trade dynamics, technological advancements, and changing consumer preferences also pose challenges and opportunities for economic planning.

5. **Monitoring and evaluation:** Monitoring and evaluating the impact of economic planning and industrial policies is essential to assess their effectiveness, identify areas for improvement, and ensure accountability. Developing robust monitoring and evaluation frameworks can be challenging, particularly in collecting reliable data and measuring complex and long-term impacts.

Conclusion

Economic planning and industrial policies are important tools for shaping economic development and achieving sustainable growth. By setting long-term objectives, utilizing evidence-based decision-making, and implementing a range of policy instruments, countries can effectively promote industrial growth, address market failures, and achieve inclusive economic success. However, careful considerations and continuous monitoring are required to overcome challenges and ensure policy coherence and effectiveness. Through effective economic planning and industrial policies, countries can create an enabling environment for businesses, generate employment opportunities, and improve the well-being of their citizens.

Note: The remaining sections of the book continue the exploration of different aspects of economic success stories, including the role of entrepreneurs, technological innovations, financial market developments, globalization, sustainable development, government policies, education, inclusive growth, and future perspectives. Each chapter provides in-depth analysis, case studies, and valuable insights into these topics.

Fiscal and Monetary Policy

Taxation and Government Revenue Generation

Taxation plays a critical role in government revenue generation, providing the necessary funds for public spending on various services and programs. In this section, we will explore the principles of taxation, different types of taxes, and the challenges and implications of taxation on economic success.

Principles of Taxation

Taxation is guided by several principles that aim to ensure fairness, efficiency, and effectiveness. These principles include:

1. **Ability-to-Pay Principle:** This principle suggests that individuals with higher incomes should contribute a larger proportion of their income in taxes. The idea is rooted in the concept of progressive taxation, where tax rates increase as income levels rise. Progressive taxation helps redistribute wealth and reduce income inequality.

2. **Benefit Principle:** According to this principle, individuals should pay taxes in proportion to the benefits they receive from public goods and services. For example, those who use public infrastructure, such as roads and bridges, more frequently should contribute more through taxes.

3. **Simplicity and Transparency:** Tax systems should be easy to understand and administer, minimizing compliance costs for individuals and businesses. Transparent tax systems build trust among taxpayers and encourage voluntary compliance.

4. **Neutrality:** Tax systems should avoid distorting economic decisions and behaviors. Neutrality ensures that taxes do not influence individuals' choices, such as whether to save or spend, invest or consume.

5. **Efficiency:** Tax systems should be designed to minimize efficiency losses and deadweight burden. High tax rates and complex tax structures can create disincentives for work, investment, and entrepreneurship, reducing overall economic productivity.

Types of Taxes

Governments levy various types of taxes to generate revenue. Let's explore the most common ones:

1. **Income Tax:** Income tax is levied on individuals and businesses' earnings. It can be progressive, where tax rates increase with income levels, or flat, with a fixed rate for all income levels. Income tax is a significant revenue source for governments and often fuels wealth redistribution efforts.

2. **Sales Tax:** Sales tax is imposed on the purchase of goods and services. It is usually calculated as a percentage of the transaction value and varies across different jurisdictions. Sales tax can be regressive, as lower-income individuals may spend a larger portion of their income on taxable goods.

3. **Corporate Tax:** Corporate tax is levied on businesses' profits. It aims to ensure that businesses contribute their fair share of taxes based on their earnings. Corporate tax rates can vary depending on the size and type of business.

4. **Property Tax:** Property tax is based on the assessed value of real estate properties, including land, buildings, and structures. Property taxes provide a stable source of revenue for local governments and are often used to fund public education, infrastructure, and local services.

5. **Value-added Tax (VAT):** VAT is a consumption tax levied at each stage of the production and distribution process. It applies to the value added at each stage, ensuring that tax is paid on the final goods or services consumed. VAT is prevalent in many countries and is considered a more efficient way of raising revenue.

6. **Import and Export Duties:** Import and export duties are imposed on goods and services traded internationally. These taxes are often used to protect domestic industries, regulate trade, and generate revenue. Tariffs and customs duties are examples of import and export duties.

Challenges and Implications of Taxation

Taxation is not without challenges and implications that can impact economic success. Some of these include:

1. **Tax Evasion and Avoidance:** Individuals and businesses may try to evade or avoid taxes to reduce their tax burden. This can lead to lost revenue for governments, increased inequality, and a burden shift onto compliant taxpayers. Governments need to implement effective enforcement measures to combat illegal tax activities.

2. **Tax Incidence:** Tax incidence refers to the distribution of the tax burden among individuals or groups. Depending on factors such as elasticity of demand and supply, taxes can be passed onto consumers in the form of higher prices or borne by producers, impacting their profitability and competitiveness.

3. **Competitiveness and Investment:** High tax rates can reduce the attractiveness of a country for investment and entrepreneurship. Businesses may seek jurisdictions with lower tax rates, resulting in a loss of economic activity and job opportunities. Governments need to strike a balance between revenue generation and maintaining a favorable business environment.

4. **Tax System Complexity:** Complex tax systems can be difficult to understand and comply with, leading to increased compliance costs for individuals and businesses. Simplifying tax systems can enhance voluntary compliance and reduce the administrative burden on taxpayers.

Example: The Impact of Taxation on Economic Growth

To better understand the implications of taxation on economic success, let's consider an example. Suppose a government decides to increase the income tax rate for high-income individuals. This can lead to several outcomes:

- Higher-income individuals may experience a reduction in disposable income. This could lead to a decrease in consumption and investment, as individuals have less money available for spending and saving.

- Wealth redistribution may occur, as the increased tax revenue can be used to fund social programs and provide public goods. This can help reduce income inequality and provide opportunities for the less fortunate.

- High-income individuals may alter their behavior to mitigate the impact of higher taxes. They may invest in tax shelters, seek tax deductions, or relocate to jurisdictions with more favorable tax regimes. This could lead to unintended consequences, such as reduced investment and job creation.

This example highlights the complex relationship between taxation, economic behavior, and outcomes. It underscores the importance of carefully designing tax policies that balance revenue generation, equity, and economic growth.

Resources and Further Reading

To delve deeper into the topic of taxation and government revenue generation, here are some recommended resources:

- "Public Finance" by Harvey S. Rosen and Ted Gayer provides a comprehensive overview of taxation principles, public spending, and fiscal policy.

- "The Benefit and The Burden: Tax Reform–Why We Need it and What It Will Take" by Bruce Bartlett explores the various aspects of taxation, its effects on the economy, and the need for tax reform.

- The World Bank's "Taxation and State-Building in Developing Countries: Capacity and Consent" offers insights into taxation challenges faced by developing countries and the role of taxation in state-building.

Conclusion

Taxation is a crucial aspect of government finance and plays a significant role in economic success. By understanding the principles of taxation, different types of taxes, and the challenges and implications they entail, policymakers can design tax systems that promote economic growth, fairness, and sustainability. Balancing revenue generation with economic efficiency and social considerations is key to achieving long-term prosperity and a well-functioning society.

Central Banking and Monetary Policy Tools

Central banks play a crucial role in a country's economy by managing monetary policy. They are responsible for maintaining price stability, controlling inflation, promoting economic growth, and ensuring financial stability. In this section, we will explore the key functions of central banks and the various tools they use to implement monetary policy.

Functions of Central Banks

Central banks serve as the primary authority for monetary policy in a country. They perform several key functions:

- **Controlling the money supply**: Central banks have the authority to control the money supply, which is the total amount of money circulating in the economy. They can increase or decrease the money supply through various policy tools.

- **Managing interest rates**: Central banks have the power to influence interest rates, which play a vital role in the economy. By adjusting interest rates, central banks can impact borrowing costs, investment decisions, and overall economic activity.

- **Ensuring financial stability**: Central banks monitor the stability and health of financial institutions and markets. They implement measures to prevent financial crises and maintain the stability of the banking system.

- **Acting as a lender of last resort**: Central banks provide emergency liquidity support to banks and financial institutions during times of financial stress. This helps maintain the stability of the financial system and prevents widespread panic.

- **Conducting foreign exchange operations**: Central banks manage a country's foreign exchange reserves and intervene in foreign exchange markets to stabilize the exchange rate. This helps support international trade and ensure currency stability.

Now that we understand the functions of central banks, let's delve into the various tools they use to implement monetary policy.

Monetary Policy Tools

Central banks employ a range of tools to influence the money supply, interest rates, and overall economic conditions. These tools include:

1. **Open Market Operations (OMO)**: This is one of the most commonly used tools by central banks. In OMO, central banks buy or sell government securities (bonds) in the open market. When the central bank purchases government securities, it injects money into the economy, increasing the

money supply. Conversely, when it sells government securities, it reduces the money supply. OMOs help control short-term interest rates and manage liquidity in the banking system.

2. **Reserve Requirements:** Central banks require commercial banks to hold a certain percentage of their deposits as reserves. By increasing or decreasing reserve requirements, central banks can influence the amount of money banks can lend. Higher reserve requirements reduce the lending capacity of banks, reducing the money supply. Conversely, lower reserve requirements increase lending capacity and expand the money supply.

3. **Discount Window Lending:** Central banks act as lenders of last resort by providing short-term loans to commercial banks through the discount window. Banks can borrow funds from the central bank when they face temporary liquidity shortages. By adjusting the interest rate charged on these loans, central banks can influence borrowing costs for banks.

4. **Interest Rate Policy:** Central banks set key interest rates, such as the benchmark interest rate (also known as the policy rate or the repo rate). By raising or lowering interest rates, central banks can affect borrowing costs for banks and consumers. Higher interest rates discourage borrowing and spending, leading to reduced money supply, while lower interest rates encourage borrowing and stimulate economic activity, increasing the money supply.

5. **Forward Guidance:** Central banks provide forward guidance on their future policy intentions. This communication helps shape expectations and influence market interest rates. By signaling their future monetary policy actions, central banks can influence borrowing costs and economic decisions in the present.

6. **Quantitative Easing (QE):** In times of economic crisis or recession, central banks may engage in QE. This involves the purchase of long-term government bonds or other financial assets from the market. QE injects money into the economy and aims to lower long-term interest rates, stimulate lending, and boost economic activity.

It is important to note that central banks use a combination of these tools to achieve their policy objectives. The specific tools and strategies employed can vary depending on the central bank's goals, economic conditions, and the unique challenges it faces.

Challenges and Limitations

While central banks have significant influence over the economy, they also face challenges and limitations in implementing monetary policy effectively. Some of these challenges include:

- **Unpredictable Economic Factors:** Central banks must navigate unpredictable economic factors that can impact their policy decisions and outcomes. Factors such as changes in global economic conditions, geopolitical risks, and natural disasters can complicate decision-making.

- **Time Lags:** Implementing monetary policy changes takes time to have an impact on the economy. There are often significant time lags between policy adjustments and their effects on inflation, economic growth, or unemployment. Central banks must anticipate future economic conditions and make policy decisions accordingly.

- **Effective Communication:** Central banks must effectively communicate their policy decisions, goals, and strategies to the public and market participants. Miscommunication or ambiguity can lead to uncertainty and market volatility.

- **Conflicting Objectives:** Central banks may face conflicting objectives, such as managing inflation and promoting economic growth simultaneously. Balancing these objectives is challenging and requires careful consideration of economic trade-offs.

- **Limited Policy Tools:** Central banks' policy effectiveness can be limited in certain situations, especially during periods of near-zero or negative interest rates. This can restrict their ability to stimulate the economy through conventional policy measures alone, leading to the exploration of unconventional policy tools like QE.

It is worth noting that the effectiveness of central bank policy tools can vary across different economic conditions and countries. Central banks closely monitor economic indicators, conduct research, and employ sophisticated models to inform their decision-making processes.

Real-World Example: The European Central Bank

To illustrate the practical application of central banking and monetary policy tools, let's consider the case of the European Central Bank (ECB). The ECB is responsible for formulating and implementing monetary policy for the Eurozone countries.

During the global financial crisis of 2008, the ECB faced unprecedented challenges in maintaining financial stability and promoting economic growth. To combat the crisis, the ECB employed a range of policy tools, including:

- Conducting large-scale OMOs to inject liquidity into the banking system and address funding shortages in financial markets.

- Implementing unconventional measures like QE to stimulate lending and support economic activity. The ECB purchased government bonds and private sector assets to increase the money supply and lower borrowing costs.

- Providing long-term loans to banks through targeted longer-term refinancing operations (TLTROs) to enhance liquidity conditions and encourage lending to businesses and households.

- Lowering the benchmark interest rate to near-zero levels to encourage borrowing and investment.

These measures helped restore stability to financial markets, stimulate economic growth, and mitigate the effects of the crisis. The ECB continues to use a combination of these tools to address new challenges and foster economic recovery in the Eurozone.

In conclusion, central banks play a crucial role in shaping economic conditions through their monetary policy decisions. By implementing various tools such as open market operations, reserve requirements, and interest rate policies, central banks can influence money supply, interest rates, and overall economic activity. However, central banks face challenges and limitations, ranging from unpredictable economic factors to time lags and conflicting objectives. Understanding the functions and tools of central banks provides valuable insights into the mechanisms driving monetary policy and its impact on the economy.

Exercises

1. Explain how open market operations (OMO) work and their impact on the money supply.

2. Discuss the role of central banks as lenders of last resort and the importance of this function for maintaining financial stability.

3. Compare and contrast the tools of conventional monetary policy (such as interest rate policy) with unconventional policy tools (such as quantitative easing).

4. Analyze the challenges central banks face in implementing effective monetary policy in a globalized and interconnected world.

5. Research and discuss a recent monetary policy decision made by a central bank. Evaluate the effectiveness of the policy and its impact on the economy.

Resources

1. Federal Reserve Bank of St. Louis: https://www.stlouisfed.org/

2. European Central Bank: https://www.ecb.europa.eu/home/html/index.en.html

3. Bank of Japan: https://www.boj.or.jp/en/index.htm/

4. Bank of England: https://www.bankofengland.co.uk/

Further Reading

1. Mishkin, F. S. (2018). *The Economics of Money, Banking and Financial Markets*. Pearson.

2. Blinder, A. S. (2017). *Central Banking in Theory and Practice*. MIT Press.

3. Caruana, J. (2018). *Central Banking and Monetary Policy: What Will be the New Normal?* Banque de France Financial Stability Review.

Government Debt and Deficit Management

In this section, we will explore the important topic of government debt and deficit management. Governments play a crucial role in the economy by providing essential public goods and services, such as infrastructure, education, healthcare, and defense. However, these expenditures often exceed the revenue collected through taxes and other sources. As a result, governments resort to borrowing and accumulating debt to finance their spending.

Understanding Government Debt

Government debt, also known as public debt, refers to the total amount borrowed by the government to cover its deficits over time. It is composed of two components: external debt and domestic debt. External debt represents the amount owed to foreign entities, such as other governments or international financial institutions. Domestic debt, on the other hand, refers to the amount borrowed from within the country, typically from individuals, businesses, and financial institutions.

Government debt is typically issued in the form of bonds, which are fixed-income securities that pay periodic interest and return the principal amount upon maturity. Investors, including individuals, institutional investors, and even other governments, purchase these bonds as a way to lend money to the government in exchange for interest income and eventual repayment.

The Role of Deficits

Deficits occur when government expenditures exceed its revenue in a given fiscal year. These deficits contribute to the accumulation of government debt. Governments often implement fiscal policies, such as taxation and government spending, to manage the level of deficits and debt.

Deficits can be caused by various factors, including economic downturns, increased government spending on welfare programs or infrastructure projects, or inadequate revenue collection. During recessions or periods of economic instability, governments may increase spending to stimulate the economy, resulting in larger deficits and higher debt levels. Conversely, during periods of economic growth, governments may aim to reduce deficits and pay down debt.

Implications of Government Debt and Deficits

While government debt is a common financing tool, excessive levels of debt and persistent deficits can have several negative implications for the economy:

1. **Interest Payments**: As government debt increases, so do the interest payments required to service that debt. These interest payments represent a significant portion of government expenditures, diverting resources that could have been used for productive investments or social programs.
2. **Crowding Out**: Large government borrowing can compete with private investment for available funds in the financial markets. This "crowding out" effect can lead to higher interest rates, making it more expensive for businesses and individuals to borrow for investment purposes.

3. **Inflation and Currency Devaluation:** If a government resorts to excessive borrowing to finance its spending, it may result in an increase in the money supply. This increase in the money supply can lead to inflation and devalue the currency, eroding purchasing power and creating economic instability.

4. **Reduced Confidence and Investment:** High levels of debt and deficits can undermine investor confidence in the long-term fiscal sustainability of a country. This lack of confidence can lead to a decrease in foreign investments and capital outflows, negatively impacting economic growth and development.

Debt and Deficit Management Strategies

To manage government debt and deficits effectively, policymakers employ several strategies:

1. **Fiscal Discipline:** Governments need to maintain fiscal discipline by adopting prudent budgetary practices. This includes careful planning, setting realistic revenue targets, and controlling expenditures to avoid excessive deficits and debt accumulation.

2. **Debt Management Strategies:** Governments utilize effective debt management strategies to optimize their borrowing costs and minimize risks. This may include refinancing debt at lower interest rates, managing the maturity structure of debt to avoid excessive repayment obligations in a single year, and diversifying the investor base to reduce dependence on specific lenders.

3. **Revenue Generation:** Governments can enhance revenue generation through various means, such as implementing fair and efficient tax systems, broadening the tax base, reducing tax evasion, and exploring alternative sources of revenue, such as royalties from natural resources or public-private partnerships.

4. **Expenditure Control:** Governments need to carefully control expenditures by prioritizing essential services and investments, reducing wasteful spending, and implementing efficient public financial management systems to prevent corruption and leakage.

5. **Structural Reforms:** Structural reforms can address the root causes of fiscal imbalances and promote sustainable economic growth. These reforms may include improving governance and transparency, enhancing productivity through innovation and technology adoption, and promoting competition in markets.

Case Study: Japan's Debt and Deficit Challenges

One notable case study in government debt and deficit management is Japan. The country has experienced high levels of debt and persistent deficits for several decades.

As of 2021, Japan's public debt-to-GDP ratio stands at around 250%, one of the highest in the world.

Despite the high levels of debt, Japan has managed to maintain low borrowing costs due to factors such as strong domestic savings and the Bank of Japan's monetary policy measures. However, the country continues to face challenges posed by its aging population, slow economic growth, and the need for sustainable fiscal policies.

To address these challenges, Japan has implemented various strategies, including a mix of monetary and fiscal policies. The government aims to achieve a primary fiscal surplus by a specific target year and has introduced consumption tax hikes to generate additional revenue. Additionally, Japan has focused on structural reforms to promote growth, such as deregulation, labor market reforms, and opening up to foreign investment.

The case of Japan illustrates the complexities and trade-offs involved in managing government debt and deficits. It highlights the importance of long-term planning, policy coordination, and a multifaceted approach to addressing fiscal challenges.

Conclusion

Government debt and deficit management are critical aspects of fiscal policy. Governments must carefully balance their spending and revenue collection to avoid excessive debt accumulation and persistent deficits. Effective management strategies involving fiscal discipline, debt optimization, revenue generation, expenditure control, and structural reforms can contribute to sustainable economic growth and long-term prosperity.

Understanding the implications of government debt and deficits is essential for policymakers, economists, and citizens alike. By analyzing past experiences, learning from case studies, and implementing sound fiscal policies, countries can navigate the challenges associated with debt and deficits and pave the way for economic success.

Case Studies of Government-led Economic Success

The Nordic Model and Social Welfare Policies

The Nordic Model refers to the unique economic and social system practiced in the Nordic countries: Denmark, Finland, Iceland, Norway, and Sweden. This model is characterized by a combination of free-market capitalism and a comprehensive welfare state. In this section, we will explore the key principles and policies of the Nordic Model, focusing on its social welfare aspects.

Principles of the Nordic Model

The Nordic Model is built on a set of principles that aim to promote social equality, economic prosperity, and a high quality of life for citizens. These principles include:

1. Universal welfare: The Nordic countries provide citizens with a wide range of universal welfare benefits, including healthcare, education, childcare, and social security. These benefits are accessible to all residents, regardless of income or social status.

2. High taxation: To fund their welfare programs, the Nordic countries have implemented progressive tax systems. High-income individuals and corporations are taxed at higher rates, ensuring that the burden of financing the welfare state is shared fairly among the population.

3. Active labor market policies: The Nordic countries emphasize the importance of employment and have implemented policies that promote labor market participation. These policies include job training programs, active labor market measures, and support for entrepreneurship.

4. Strong social safety nets: The Nordic Model aims to protect individuals from economic risks and social hardships. Robust social safety nets, such as unemployment benefits and income support programs, provide a safety net for those facing temporary or long-term financial difficulties.

Social Welfare Policies

The Nordic countries have developed a comprehensive set of social welfare policies to support their citizens and promote social cohesion. These policies cover various aspects of social welfare, including healthcare, education, childcare, and elderly care.

1. Universal healthcare: The Nordic countries offer universal healthcare systems that provide comprehensive medical care to all residents. These systems are primarily funded through taxes and provide high-quality healthcare services, including preventive care, hospital treatment, and specialist care.

2. Education and childcare: The Nordic countries place a strong emphasis on education, providing free or highly subsidized education from early childhood to higher education. Additionally, they offer affordable and accessible childcare services, allowing parents to work and pursue education while ensuring the well-being of their children.

3. Elderly care: The Nordic countries have developed robust elderly care systems to support their aging populations. These systems provide a range of services, including home care, nursing homes, and rehabilitation programs, with the aim of promoting a dignified and comfortable life for seniors.

4. Gender equality: The Nordic countries are known for their strong commitment to gender equality. They have implemented policies and programs to promote women's participation in the labor market, close the gender pay gap, and ensure equal opportunities for men and women in all aspects of life.

Success and Challenges

The Nordic Model has been successful in achieving high levels of social well-being, economic prosperity, and equality. The countries that practice this model consistently rank highly in global measures of happiness, life satisfaction, and social progress.

Some of the key factors contributing to the success of the Nordic Model include:

1. Strong social cohesion: The emphasis on social welfare and equality fosters a sense of social cohesion and solidarity among citizens. This helps to create a harmonious society with low levels of social unrest and inequality.

2. Investment in human capital: The Nordic countries have invested heavily in education and skills development, creating a highly skilled workforce. This has contributed to their economic competitiveness and innovation capabilities.

3. High trust in institutions: The Nordic Model is underpinned by a high level of trust in institutions, including government, public services, and the rule of law. This trust enables effective implementation and governance of welfare policies.

However, the Nordic Model also faces challenges that need to be addressed to ensure its long-term sustainability:

1. Aging population: The Nordic countries, like many developed nations, are experiencing an aging population. This puts pressure on public resources, particularly in areas like elderly care and pensions. Efforts are needed to ensure the sustainability of welfare systems in the face of demographic changes.

2. Integration of immigrants: The Nordic countries have experienced a growing influx of immigrants in recent decades. Ensuring their successful integration into society and the labor market is a complex challenge that requires adaptability and an inclusive approach.

3. Economic competitiveness: While the Nordic countries have achieved remarkable social outcomes, they also need to maintain their economic competitiveness in a rapidly changing global economy. Balancing the welfare state with economic growth and innovation is crucial to ensure long-term success.

In conclusion, the Nordic Model's social welfare policies have been instrumental in creating societies characterized by social equality, economic prosperity, and high levels of well-being. By providing universal welfare benefits and prioritizing social cohesion, these countries have achieved remarkable success. However, they also face ongoing challenges that require continuous adaptation and innovation to ensure the sustainability of their welfare systems in a changing world.

Singapore's Economic Planning and Industrial Policies

Singapore is widely regarded as one of the world's most successful economies, and its success can be attributed in large part to its effective economic planning and industrial policies. In this section, we will explore the strategies and initiatives that Singapore has implemented to achieve sustainable economic growth and development.

Historical Background

To understand Singapore's economic planning and industrial policies, it is important to recognize the historical context in which these policies were formulated. Singapore gained independence in 1965 and faced numerous challenges, including high unemployment, limited natural resources, and a small domestic market. The government recognized the need to transform Singapore into a competitive and innovative economy, which led to the formulation of long-term development plans.

Strategic Economic Planning

One key aspect of Singapore's economic planning is the development of strategic long-term plans. The government formulated a series of economic development plans, starting with the First Industrial Master Plan in 1965 and followed by subsequent plans such as the Industrial Structure Improvement Programme and the Economic Structure and Strategies Committee Report.

These plans outlined specific goals and strategies to diversify the economy, attract foreign direct investment (FDI), and build up key industries. The government's approach emphasized forward-looking strategies and proactive government intervention to guide economic development.

Industrial Policies

Singapore's industrial policies played a crucial role in supporting economic growth and development. The government identified and supported key industries that had the potential for growth and global competitiveness. Some of the main industrial policies implemented in Singapore include:

- **Export-Oriented Manufacturing:** Singapore focused on developing a robust manufacturing sector that could compete internationally. The government provided incentives such as tax breaks, grants, and loans to attract multinational corporations (MNCs) and encourage the establishment of export-oriented industries.

- **Attracting Foreign Direct Investment (FDI):** Singapore actively pursued FDI to supplement its limited domestic resources. The government created an attractive business environment by offering tax incentives, providing excellent infrastructure, and ensuring a reliable legal framework. This approach helped Singapore attract numerous multinational corporations and encourage technology transfer and knowledge spillovers.

- **Skills Development and Human Capital:** Recognizing the importance of a skilled workforce, Singapore invested heavily in education and skills development. The government collaborated closely with the private sector to design training programs that aligned with industry needs. This focus on human capital development contributed to Singapore's capacity to attract high-value investments and foster innovation.

- **Infrastructure Development:** Singapore recognized the critical role of infrastructure in supporting economic development. The government invested heavily in building world-class infrastructure, including ports, airports, telecommunications networks, and industrial estates. This infrastructure development not only facilitated trade and connectivity but also attracted investments in logistics, warehousing, and related industries.

Case Studies

To illustrate the effectiveness of Singapore's economic planning and industrial policies, let's examine two case studies:

1. **Jurong Industrial Estate:** In the early years of Singapore's industrialization, the government developed the Jurong Industrial Estate. This industrial park was strategically located near the port and provided attractive incentives for manufacturing companies to set up operations. The development of Jurong contributed significantly to Singapore's economic transformation and attracted multinational corporations that helped build a robust manufacturing base.

2. **Biomedical Sciences Initiative:** In the early 2000s, Singapore launched the Biomedical Sciences Initiative as part of its plan to develop knowledge-intensive industries. The government invested in research and development capabilities, established science parks, and provided funding support for biotech start-ups. Today, Singapore is a leading global hub for biomedical sciences, attracting top researchers, multinational pharmaceutical companies, and generating high-value economic activities.

These case studies highlight Singapore's ability to identify emerging industries, provide targeted support, and transform them into drivers of economic growth.

Policy Challenges and Future Outlook

While Singapore's economic planning and industrial policies have been successful, the country faces ongoing challenges and uncertainties. Some of the key challenges include:

- **Evolving Global Economic Landscape:** The global economic landscape is rapidly changing, with the rise of new technologies, geopolitical shifts, and trade tensions. Singapore needs to continually adapt its policies to stay competitive and capitalize on emerging opportunities.

- **Sustainable Development:** As Singapore strives for economic growth, it must also prioritize sustainable development. The government has been proactive in addressing environmental concerns and promoting sustainable practices. Balancing economic growth with environmental conservation will be an ongoing challenge.

- **Increasing Competition:** As neighboring countries develop and become more competitive, Singapore faces challenges in maintaining its position as a hub for investments and talent. The government needs to continually enhance its value proposition and provide a conducive environment for innovation and entrepreneurship.

Looking ahead, Singapore aims to leverage emerging technologies such as artificial intelligence, blockchain, and advanced manufacturing to drive future growth. The government continues to refine its policies and actively engage with industries and stakeholders to ensure long-term economic success.

Conclusion

Singapore's economic planning and industrial policies have been instrumental in transforming a small, resource-constrained nation into a thriving global hub for business and innovation. The strategic formulation of long-term plans, targeted industrial policies, investment in human capital, and infrastructure development have been key enablers of Singapore's economic success.

While challenges and uncertainties persist, Singapore's ability to adapt and evolve its policies will be crucial in maintaining its competitiveness and achieving sustained economic growth. By leveraging new technologies and embracing sustainable practices, Singapore remains well-positioned for future success.

Summary

In this section, we explored Singapore's economic planning and industrial policies, which have been crucial in driving its economic success. Some key points discussed include:

- Singapore's strategic economic planning involves the formulation of long-term development plans that outline specific goals and strategies for diversifying the economy, attracting foreign direct investment (FDI), and building up key industries.

- Industrial policies play a crucial role in supporting economic growth and development. Singapore has implemented policies such as export-oriented manufacturing, attracting FDI, skills development and human capital investment, and infrastructure development.

- Case studies, such as the development of the Jurong Industrial Estate and the Biomedical Sciences Initiative, demonstrate the effectiveness of Singapore's policies in transforming industries and attracting high-value economic activities.

- Singapore faces challenges and uncertainties, including the evolving global economic landscape, the need for sustainable development, and increasing competition. The government must adapt its policies to address these challenges and leverage emerging technologies for future growth.

- Singapore's economic planning and industrial policies have laid the foundation for its economic success. By continually refining its policies and embracing innovation, Singapore remains well-positioned for sustained economic growth and development.

Singapore's success story serves as a valuable case study for other countries aspiring to achieve economic prosperity through effective planning and well-targeted industrial policies. By understanding and applying the principles and strategies employed by Singapore, nations can strive for sustainable economic development in a rapidly changing global landscape.

Key Concepts

- **Strategic Economic Planning:** The formulation of long-term plans that guide economic development and diversification.

- **Industrial Policies:** Policies implemented by governments to support the growth and development of specific industries.

- **Export-Oriented Manufacturing:** A strategy that focuses on producing goods for international markets to drive export growth and generate foreign exchange.

- **Foreign Direct Investment (FDI):** Investments made by foreign companies to establish or expand their presence in a host country.

- **Skills Development and Human Capital:** The investment in education, training, and the development of a skilled workforce to drive economic growth and innovation.

- **Infrastructure Development:** The construction and improvement of physical and social infrastructure to support economic activities and enhance connectivity.

- **Sustainable Development:** Development that meets the needs of the present without compromising the ability of future generations to meet their own needs.

Review Questions

1. What are the key components of Singapore's economic planning and industrial policies?

2. How did Singapore attract foreign direct investment (FDI) and foster technology transfer?

3. What are some of the challenges and uncertainties that Singapore faces in maintaining its economic success?

4. Describe two case studies that exemplify the effectiveness of Singapore's industrial policies.

5. How does Singapore balance economic growth with sustainable development?

Further Reading

1. Ng, I. Y. (Ed.). (2016). *Singapore: Strategy, Leadership and Organization.* Routledge.

2. Low, L., & Chua, B. H. (Eds.). (2018). *Singapore as an International Financial Centre: History, Policy and Politics.* Palgrave Macmillan.

3. Capelo, J. (2019). *Singaporean Economic Development Since Independence: Retrospection and Reflections.* World Scientific.

4. Hanauer, L. (2018). *The Singapore Consensus: 1823 to 2018: 200 Years of the Asian Marine Hub.* World Scientific.

Brazil's Bolsa Família Program and Poverty Reduction

The Bolsa Família Program, launched in Brazil in 2003, is a conditional cash transfer program aimed at reducing poverty and promoting social inclusion. It has become one of the largest and most successful social protection programs in the world, reaching millions of low-income families.

Background

Brazil has long faced the challenge of high levels of inequality and widespread poverty. In the past, traditional social assistance programs were fragmented and lacked targeting mechanisms, failing to effectively reach the most vulnerable populations. In response to these challenges, the government introduced the Bolsa Família Program as a comprehensive approach to poverty reduction.

Program Design

The Bolsa Família Program is based on the principles of income redistribution, poverty alleviation, and human capital development. It provides cash transfers to poor families, but with certain conditions attached. These conditions are related to health and education, aiming to break the intergenerational cycle of poverty.

The program targets families with per capita income below the national poverty line. It uses a robust and transparent targeting system to identify eligible families and calculate the amount of the cash transfer they receive. The program also relies on a national registry and a unique identification system to ensure accurate targeting.

Health and Education Conditions

To receive the cash transfers, beneficiary families must comply with certain health and education conditions. These conditions include regular health check-ups for children, prenatal care for pregnant women, and adherence to vaccination and growth monitoring schedules.

In terms of education, families must ensure that their children attend school regularly and maintain a certain level of school attendance. They must also demonstrate that their children are getting regular health check-ups and are up-to-date with their vaccinations.

Impact on Poverty Reduction

The Bolsa Família Program has had a significant impact on poverty reduction in Brazil. Numerous studies have demonstrated its effectiveness in reducing poverty and inequality, as well as improving access to education and healthcare.

One study conducted by Ferreira et al. (2012) found that the program reduced extreme poverty in Brazil by 20% and poverty by 15%. Another study by Paes-Sousa et al. (2011) showed that the program contributed to a reduction in child mortality rates and improved access to education and healthcare services among beneficiary children.

Challenges and Solutions

While the Bolsa Família Program has been successful in achieving its goals, it is not without challenges. One of the main challenges is the issue of program leakage, where ineligible individuals or families receive the cash transfers. To address this, the government has implemented a rigorous monitoring and evaluation system to ensure that the program reaches its intended beneficiaries.

Another challenge is the sustainability of the program in the long term. As the program relies on government funding, there is a need for continued political commitment and financial resources to maintain its effectiveness. The government has sought to address this challenge by integrating the program into broader social protection policies and by exploring innovative financing mechanisms.

Unconventional Approach: Behavior Change Interventions

To enhance the impact of the Bolsa Família Program, the government has also adopted behavior change interventions. These interventions aim to promote positive behaviors and empower beneficiary families to make informed decisions about their health and education.

For example, the program has implemented conditionalities that require families to attend workshops on topics such as nutrition, parenting, and financial literacy. These workshops provide valuable information and skills to families, enabling them to make better choices and improve their overall well-being.

Conclusion

The Bolsa Família Program in Brazil has demonstrated the potential of conditional cash transfer programs in reducing poverty and promoting social inclusion. By focusing on health and education conditions, the program not only provides immediate financial support to low-income families but also invests in human capital development.

With its robust targeting mechanisms, rigorous monitoring and evaluation systems, and behavior change interventions, the program has achieved significant results in poverty reduction. However, it is crucial to address challenges such as leakage and long-term sustainability to ensure the continued success of the program.

By studying the Bolsa Família Program, we can gain valuable insights into the design and implementation of social protection programs that effectively tackle poverty and inequality. Through a multidimensional approach, combining income support with conditionalities and behavior change interventions, we can create a pathway for inclusive and sustainable economic development.

Chapter 8: Education and Human Capital Development

Chapter 8: Education and Human Capital Development

Chapter 8: Education and Human Capital Development

In this chapter, we explore the critical role of education in economic success and the development of human capital. Education is a key driver of economic growth and prosperity, as it equips individuals with the necessary skills and knowledge to participate effectively in the workforce and contribute to the overall advancement of society. We delve into the various aspects of education and examine its impact on individuals, communities, and nations.

The Importance of Education in Economic Success

Education plays a fundamental role in shaping the economic outcomes of individuals and societies. It is widely recognized that countries with higher levels of education tend to have stronger economies and higher incomes. This is because education enhances productivity and innovation, leading to higher levels of economic output and competitiveness.

Education and Human Capital Theory Human capital theory provides a framework for understanding the relationship between education and economic success. According to this theory, individuals who acquire knowledge, skills, and competencies through education and training increase their productive capacity and future earning potential. Human capital refers to the stock of knowledge, skills, and abilities that individuals possess, which can be developed and enhanced through education.

Investing in education is akin to investing in human capital, which yields long-term economic returns. Educated individuals are more likely to secure higher-paying jobs, experience lower unemployment rates, and have greater opportunities for career advancement. Furthermore, education fosters critical thinking, problem-solving skills, and adaptability, making individuals better equipped to navigate a rapidly changing economic landscape.

Investment in Education and Economic Returns The decision to invest in education involves considering the costs and benefits associated with acquiring knowledge and skills. While education often requires substantial financial investment in the form of tuition fees, books, and other resources, it also offers significant economic returns over an individual's lifetime.

Studies consistently show a strong positive correlation between educational attainment and earnings. On average, individuals with higher levels of education earn higher incomes compared to those with lower levels of education. This income disparity can be observed not only between different educational levels (e.g., high school diploma versus bachelor's degree), but also within the same educational level (e.g., bachelor's degree versus master's degree).

Moreover, education has a multiplier effect on the economy. As educated individuals earn higher incomes, they contribute more in taxes and consumer spending, stimulating economic growth and creating employment opportunities. Educated individuals also tend to have better health outcomes, leading to reduced healthcare costs and increased productivity.

Innovations in Education

The field of education has witnessed significant innovations in recent years, driven by advancements in technology and evolving pedagogical approaches. These innovations have the potential to transform the way knowledge is acquired, disseminated, and applied.

Online Learning and Massive Open Online Courses (MOOCs) Online learning has revolutionized education by making it more accessible and flexible. Massive Open Online Courses (MOOCs) have emerged as a popular platform for delivering high-quality educational content to a wide range of learners worldwide.

These online courses provide opportunities for individuals to acquire new skills or deepen their knowledge in various subjects, often at a fraction of the cost of traditional education. Learners can access course materials, engage in interactive activities, and interact with instructors and fellow learners from the comfort of their own homes. The flexibility of online learning allows individuals to balance their educational pursuits with work, family responsibilities, or other commitments.

Vocational Education and Skills Training While traditional academic education remains important, vocational education and skills training have gained prominence in addressing the skills gap in the labor market. Vocational programs provide specialized training in specific trades, professions, or technical fields, equipping individuals with job-specific skills and competencies.

Vocational education offers an alternative pathway for individuals who may not be inclined toward traditional academic pursuits. It focuses on hands-on learning, providing practical skills that are directly applicable to the workplace. This form of education promotes employability and empowers individuals to enter the workforce with marketable skills.

Lifelong Learning and Continuous Education In the rapidly changing global economy, the need for lifelong learning has become increasingly critical. Lifelong learning refers to the ongoing process of acquiring knowledge and skills throughout one's life, beyond formal education.

Continuous education enables individuals to adapt to new technologies, industries, and job requirements, enhancing their employability and facilitating career transitions. It involves a mindset shift, recognizing that learning is a lifelong journey rather than a one-time event.

Technological advancements, such as e-learning platforms and microlearning modules, have made lifelong learning more accessible and convenient. Individuals can engage in short courses, attend webinars, or pursue certifications to acquire new skills and stay abreast of industry trends.

Case Studies of Education for Economic Success

To illustrate the impact of education on economic success, let's explore three case studies that highlight successful education systems and their contributions to economic development.

Finland's Education System and High Academic Achievement Finland is widely regarded as having one of the world's best education systems. The Finnish education system emphasizes equity, quality, and lifelong learning. It focuses on providing equal opportunities for all students, regardless of their socio-economic background.

In Finland, teachers are highly trained and respected professionals. They have autonomy in designing their curricula and assessing student progress. The education system emphasizes holistic development, creativity, critical thinking, and problem-solving skills.

The Finnish education system has yielded impressive results, with Finnish students consistently ranking among the top performers in international assessments, such as the Programme for International Student Assessment (PISA). The success of Finland's education system has translated into a highly skilled workforce, technological innovation, and overall economic prosperity.

South Korea's Focus on Education and Technological Advancements South Korea's remarkable economic transformation, often referred to as the "Miracle on the Han River," was fueled in part by its strong emphasis on education. Education has been seen as a means to lift individuals and the nation out of poverty and secure a prosperous future.

South Korea boasts a rigorous and highly competitive education system. Students undergo a rigorous preparation process for college entrance exams, and academic achievement is highly valued. The country invests heavily in education, with a significant portion of the national budget allocated to educational initiatives.

This commitment to education has resulted in a highly educated workforce and remarkable technological advancements. South Korea is a global leader in areas such as electronics, automotive manufacturing, and information technology. The strong focus on education has played a crucial role in South Korea's economic success and global competitiveness.

Germany's Dual Vocational Training System and Workforce Development Germany is renowned for its dual vocational training system, combining apprenticeships in companies with classroom-based education. The dual system offers a seamless transition from school to work, providing practical training and theoretical knowledge concurrently.

In the German vocational education system, students split their time between on-the-job training and classroom instruction. This approach allows them to acquire hands-on experience while gaining a solid theoretical foundation. The training is often tailored to meet the needs of specific industries, ensuring a highly skilled and versatile workforce.

The success of Germany's vocational training system is evident in its low youth unemployment rate and the strong alignment between skills training and industry needs. The system has fostered a resilient and adaptable workforce, contributing to Germany's reputation as an industrial powerhouse.

Conclusion

Education plays a vital role in economic success and human capital development. It equips individuals with the necessary knowledge, skills, and competencies to contribute effectively to society and thrive in a rapidly changing economic landscape. The innovations in education, such as online learning and vocational training, are transforming the way knowledge is acquired and increasing access to educational opportunities.

By investing in education, individuals, communities, and nations can achieve higher levels of economic prosperity and social well-being. Education not only enhances individual earning potential but also stimulates economic growth, innovation, and social mobility. The case studies of Finland, South Korea, and Germany demonstrate the transformative power of education in driving economic success.

As we look to the future, it is imperative to continue investing in education and adapt to the evolving needs of the global economy. Lifelong learning, technological advancements, and a focus on developing the skills of the future will enable individuals and societies to thrive in an increasingly interconnected and competitive world.

The Importance of Education in Economic Success

Education and Human Capital Theory

Education plays a crucial role in economic success. It is widely recognized that investing in human capital, which refers to the knowledge, skills, and abilities of individuals, leads to better economic outcomes at both the individual and societal levels. The theory of human capital emphasizes the importance of education in enhancing productivity, promoting innovation, and driving economic growth.

The Concept of Human Capital

Human capital can be defined as the stock of knowledge, skills, and expertise possessed by individuals. It includes both formal education (such as degrees and certificates) and informal learning (such as on-the-job training and self-improvement). Human capital is an intangible asset that individuals bring to the labor market, and it can be accumulated and enhanced through investments in education and training.

From an economic perspective, human capital is seen as a factor of production, alongside other inputs such as physical capital (machinery and equipment) and natural resources. However, unlike physical capital, which can depreciate over time, human capital has the potential to appreciate through continuous learning and skill development.

The Role of Education in Human Capital Formation

Education is the primary means by which individuals acquire knowledge and skills, making it a critical determinant of human capital formation. It provides individuals with the necessary cognitive and non-cognitive skills to participate effectively in the labor force, contribute to economic growth, and adapt to changing market conditions.

Formal education, including primary, secondary, and tertiary education, equips individuals with foundational knowledge and skills in subjects such as mathematics, science, language, and social sciences. It provides a structured learning environment and imparts fundamental skills, including critical thinking, problem-solving, and communication.

In addition to formal education, informal learning experiences also contribute to human capital formation. These include on-the-job training, apprenticeships, mentoring programs, and lifelong learning initiatives. Informal learning experiences allow individuals to acquire industry-specific skills, practical knowledge, and hands-on experience that complement and expand their formal education.

The Economic Returns to Education

Investing in education and human capital has significant economic returns at the individual, societal, and national levels. Individuals with higher levels of education tend to have higher earnings, better job prospects, and improved social mobility. Education increases an individual's productivity and allows them to command higher wages, particularly in occupations that require specialized knowledge and skills.

From a societal perspective, a more educated workforce leads to increased labor productivity, technological advancements, and higher rates of innovation. Education promotes the diffusion of knowledge and supports the development of new ideas and discoveries, which drive economic growth and competitiveness.

Moreover, countries with higher levels of education and human capital tend to have lower levels of poverty and inequality. Education has the potential to reduce social disparities by providing individuals with the skills and opportunities to improve their well-being and upward mobility. It also contributes to social cohesion, civic engagement, and the development of democratic societies.

Challenges and Considerations

While education is a powerful tool for economic success, there are several challenges and considerations that need to be addressed. Access to quality education remains a significant issue in many parts of the world, particularly in developing countries. Socioeconomic inequalities, gender disparities, and regional differences can limit individuals' access to educational opportunities and hinder the development of human capital.

Furthermore, the rapid pace of technological advancements and the increasing demand for specific skills pose challenges for educational systems. The skills demanded by the labor market are constantly evolving, and there is a need for education to adapt and provide individuals with the competencies required for the jobs of the future.

Addressing these challenges requires comprehensive policies and investments in education. Governments, educational institutions, and relevant stakeholders need to prioritize efforts to improve educational access, quality, and relevance. This includes investments in infrastructure, teacher training, curriculum development, and the promotion of lifelong learning initiatives.

Example: The Role of Education in the Digital Economy

The digital economy is transforming the nature of work and significantly impacting various industries. It requires individuals to possess digital literacy, adaptability, and critical thinking skills. Therefore, education plays a vital role in preparing individuals for the digital economy.

In this context, education needs to go beyond the traditional focus on teaching specific technical skills. It should emphasize problem-solving, creativity, collaboration, and digital citizenship. The integration of technology in education, such as online learning platforms and digital resources, can help enhance access to education and develop digital skills among learners.

For example, initiatives like coding boot camps, which provide intensive training in computer programming, have gained popularity in preparing individuals for careers in software development and technology-related fields. These programs offer a hands-on learning experience and focus on practical skills that are in high demand in the digital economy.

Moreover, continuous education and upskilling are critical in the digital economy, where technological advancements can quickly render certain skills obsolete. Lifelong learning initiatives, supported by educational institutions and employers, can enable individuals to stay relevant and adapt to the changing demands of the digital economy.

Conclusion

Education plays a central role in human capital formation and economic success. It empowers individuals by equipping them with knowledge, skills, and competencies needed to thrive in the labor market. Moreover, education contributes to societal and economic development by fostering innovation, productivity, and social mobility. However, addressing access and quality gaps, as well as adapting to the evolving demands of the digital economy, are crucial considerations in maximizing the potential of education for economic success. Investing in education is not only a means of personal development but also a pathway towards inclusive growth and long-term prosperity.

Key Takeaways

- Human capital refers to the stock of knowledge, skills, and expertise possessed by individuals, and it is a crucial factor in achieving economic success. - Education plays a fundamental role in human capital formation by providing individuals with knowledge, skills, and competencies necessary for the labor market. - Education has significant economic returns at the individual, societal, and national levels, including higher wages, increased labor productivity, and technological advancements. - Challenges such as access to quality education and the need to adapt to the demands of the digital economy must be addressed to maximize the potential of education for economic success. - Lifelong learning and upskilling are essential in the digital economy to ensure individuals remain competitive and adaptable in a rapidly changing job market.

Investment in Education and Economic Returns

Investing in education has long been recognized as a key driver of economic growth and development. When individuals acquire knowledge, skills, and competencies through education, they enhance their productivity and employability, leading to higher incomes and improved standards of living. This section explores the relationship between investment in education and the economic returns it generates.

Human Capital Theory

To understand the relationship between education and economic returns, we turn to human capital theory. Developed by economist Gary Becker in the 1960s, this theory views education as an investment in human capital, which is the stock of knowledge, skills, and abilities possessed by individuals.

According to human capital theory, education enhances individuals' productivity and earning potential. It does so by improving their skills, allowing them to perform more complex and productive tasks. The return on investment in education can be seen as a result of higher wages, increased job opportunities, and improved labor market outcomes.

Education and Economic Returns

Numerous studies have demonstrated a positive correlation between education and economic returns. Individuals with higher levels of education tend to earn higher wages and have lower rates of unemployment compared to their less-educated counterparts.

The economic returns to education can be seen in several ways:

- **Higher Wages:** On average, individuals with higher levels of education earn higher wages than those with lower levels of education. This wage premium, known as the education wage premium, reflects the increased productivity and skills acquired through education.

    For example, data from the U.S. Bureau of Labor Statistics shows that in 2020, individuals with a bachelor's degree had a median weekly earnings of $1,305, while individuals with only a high school diploma had a median weekly 746.

- **Lower Unemployment Rates:** Education is associated with lower unemployment rates. Individuals with higher levels of education are more likely to find stable employment and have a reduced risk of joblessness.

  According to data from the U.S. Bureau of Labor Statistics, the unemployment rate for individuals with a bachelor's degree was 2.8% in 2020, while the unemployment rate for individuals with only a high school diploma was 6.5%.

- **Improved Labor Market Outcomes:** Education provides individuals with the knowledge and skills needed to adapt to changing labor market demands. It equips them with the ability to acquire new skills and adjust to emerging job opportunities.

  In a rapidly evolving economy, where technological advancements and automation reshape industries, individuals with a higher level of education are better positioned to thrive. They can more easily transition to new roles and industries, ensuring their long-term employability and economic success.

Factors Influencing Economic Returns

While education is generally associated with positive economic returns, the magnitude of these returns can vary depending on several factors:

- **Quality of Education:** The quality of education plays a crucial role in determining its economic returns. Well-funded and effectively managed educational institutions that provide high-quality instruction and relevant skills training tend to generate greater economic returns for individuals.

- **Field of Study:** The economic returns of education can vary across different fields of study. Some fields, such as science, technology, engineering, and mathematics (STEM), tend to offer higher wages and better job prospects compared to other fields.

- **Education Level:** The level of education also affects the economic returns. Generally, individuals with higher levels of education, such as bachelor's or advanced degrees, experience higher wage premiums and better labor market outcomes.

- **Labor Market Conditions:** Economic returns to education can be influenced by the prevailing labor market conditions. Factors such as supply and demand dynamics, technological advancements, and economic growth impact the job opportunities and wages available to educated individuals.

Maximizing Economic Returns on Education

To maximize the economic returns on education, individuals, policymakers, and educational institutions can consider the following strategies:

- **Quality Education:** Ensuring access to quality education is crucial. Investments in teacher training, curriculum development, and infrastructure can enhance the quality of education and improve economic returns for individuals.

- **Skills Development:** Emphasizing the development of relevant skills can enhance the economic value of education. Collaborations between educational institutions and industries can help align the curriculum with the needs of the job market, boosting job prospects and wages for graduates.

- **Lifelong Learning:** Encouraging individuals to engage in lifelong learning can enhance their long-term economic success. Rapid technological advancements and changing labor market demands make continuous upskilling and reskilling essential for remaining competitive.

- **Education Policies:** Policymakers can support education and economic development through targeted policies. Investments in education infrastructure, financial aid programs, and vocational training initiatives can increase access to education and improve economic outcomes for individuals and societies as a whole.

Real-World Example: The Impact of College Education in the United States

A real-world example of the economic returns on education can be seen in the impact of college education in the United States. Numerous studies have shown that individuals with a college degree tend to earn higher wages and experience lower unemployment rates compared to those without a college degree.

According to data from the U.S. Census Bureau, the median earnings for individuals with a bachelor's degree were approximately 74% higher than those with only a high school diploma in 2019. Furthermore, the unemployment rate for individuals with a bachelor's degree was consistently lower than that of individuals with only a high school diploma.

CHAPTER 8: EDUCATION AND HUMAN CAPITAL DEVELOPMENT

This example illustrates the significant economic benefits that can result from investing in higher education. It highlights the role of education in improving individuals' economic prospects and contributing to overall economic growth and development.

Exercise

Consider the following scenario: A country is experiencing an economic downturn, with rising unemployment rates and stagnant wages. As an economic advisor, propose a set of education-focused policies to stimulate economic growth and improve the country's long-term prospects.

Solution

To address the economic challenges, focusing on education can be a key strategy. The proposed education-focused policies could include:

- **Increased Investment in Education:** Allocating additional resources to education, including funding for infrastructure, teacher training, and curriculum development, can enhance the quality of education and improve student outcomes. This investment will better prepare individuals for the job market and boost their long-term economic success.

- **Promotion of Vocational Training:** Emphasizing vocational training and skills development can help individuals acquire in-demand skills and quickly enter the workforce. This approach can address skill gaps, reduce unemployment, and contribute to economic recovery.

- **Partnerships with Industries:** Collaborating with industries to align education with market needs can ensure students acquire relevant skills. Establishing internship programs, apprenticeships, and partnerships with businesses can provide students with practical experience and increase their employability.

- **Flexible Learning Options:** Promoting flexible learning options, such as online courses and distance learning, can increase accessibility to education. This approach facilitates lifelong learning and enables individuals to acquire skills while balancing work and family responsibilities.

- **Targeted Financial Aid Programs:** Implementing targeted financial aid programs, such as scholarships and grants, can improve access to education for economically disadvantaged individuals. This measure helps ensure that education is accessible to all, regardless of socioeconomic background.

By implementing these education-focused policies, the country can overcome economic challenges, foster job creation, and establish a skilled workforce capable of driving sustainable economic growth.

Summary

Investment in education yields significant economic returns by improving individuals' productivity and employability. Human capital theory provides a framework for understanding the relationship between education and economic success. Higher wages, lower unemployment rates, and improved labor market outcomes are some of the economic rewards associated with education.

The economic returns on education can vary based on factors such as the quality of education, field of study, education level, and prevailing labor market conditions. Maximizing economic returns requires a focus on quality education, skills development, lifelong learning, and supportive education policies.

Through a real-world example in the United States, we see the substantial impact of college education on wages and unemployment rates. This example highlights the long-term economic benefits of investing in higher education.

In addressing economic challenges, education-focused policies can stimulate economic growth and enhance a country's competitiveness. Increased investment in education, promotion of vocational training, partnerships with industries, flexible learning options, and targeted financial aid programs are some of the strategies that can be implemented. These measures contribute to the development of a skilled workforce and the creation of sustainable economic opportunities.

Innovations in Education

Online Learning and Massive Open Online Courses (MOOCs)

In recent years, there has been a significant shift in the way education is delivered and accessed. Online learning platforms and Massive Open Online Courses (MOOCs) have gained popularity as alternative methods of acquiring knowledge and skills. This section explores the concept of online learning, the emergence of MOOCs, and their impact on education and human capital development.

The Rise of Online Learning

Online learning refers to the use of digital technologies to deliver educational content and facilitate learning remotely. It offers flexible, accessible, and self-paced learning opportunities that cater to a diverse range of learners. With the proliferation of internet connectivity and advancements in technology, online learning has become increasingly prevalent.

The advantages of online learning are manifold. Firstly, it provides learners with the flexibility to access educational content anytime and anywhere. This is particularly beneficial for individuals who are balancing work, family commitments, or geographical constraints. Secondly, online learning allows for personalized learning experiences, as learners can choose the pace and depth at which they engage with the material. This adaptability enables a more tailored learning experience, catering to the individual needs and preferences of learners. Lastly, online learning breaks down the barriers of traditional classroom-based education, making education accessible to a wider audience globally.

Massive Open Online Courses (MOOCs)

One of the most significant developments in online learning is the advent of Massive Open Online Courses (MOOCs). MOOCs are online courses that are open to a large number of participants without any restrictions on enrollment. These courses are typically provided by renowned educational institutions or experts in the field and cover a wide range of subjects.

MOOCs have gained popularity due to their scalability, affordability, and interactive nature. They offer high-quality educational content, often delivered through multimedia resources such as videos, quizzes, and discussion forums. Learners can engage with the material at their own pace and have the opportunity to interact with instructors and fellow participants in virtual learning communities. This collaborative element fosters a sense of community and enables knowledge sharing and networking opportunities.

Furthermore, MOOCs often provide certification or credentials upon completion, which can enhance learners' resumes and career prospects. This makes MOOCs an attractive option for students, professionals seeking upskilling or reskilling opportunities, and lifelong learners who have a keen interest in acquiring knowledge in various domains.

Benefits and Challenges of Online Learning and MOOCs

Online learning and MOOCs offer numerous benefits, but they also come with unique challenges. Some of the advantages include:

- **Accessibility:** Online learning provides access to education for individuals who may not have access to traditional educational institutions due to geographical, financial, or time constraints.

- **Flexibility:** Learners can choose when and where they want to engage with course materials, allowing them to fit their studies around their other commitments.

- **Cost-Effectiveness:** MOOCs are often significantly more affordable than traditional educational offerings, making education more accessible to a wider audience.

- **Diverse Learning Opportunities:** Online learning platforms and MOOCs offer a wide range of subjects and courses, allowing learners to explore various fields of interest.

- **Self-Paced Learning:** Learners can progress through the material at their own pace, allowing for a personalized and tailored learning experience.

However, there are also challenges associated with online learning and MOOCs:

- **Lack of Personal Interaction:** Online learning can be isolating, as it often lacks the face-to-face interaction present in traditional classroom settings. This can hinder the development of interpersonal skills and collaborative learning experiences.

- **Self-Discipline and Motivation:** Online learning requires a high level of self-discipline and motivation. Some learners may struggle to stay motivated without the structure and accountability provided by a traditional classroom environment.

- **Digital Literacy:** Online learning relies heavily on technology and digital literacy skills. Individuals with limited access to technology or those who are not proficient in using digital tools may face barriers to online learning.

- **Credential Recognition:** While MOOCs offer certificates upon completion, their recognition and acceptance by employers and educational institutions may vary. Some employers may still prioritize traditional degrees and qualifications over MOOC certifications.

Overall, online learning and MOOCs have the potential to democratize education by providing accessible and affordable learning opportunities to a wider audience. However, it is crucial to address these challenges and ensure that online learning platforms and MOOCs continue to evolve to meet the diverse needs of learners.

Case Studies and Examples

To illustrate the impact of online learning and MOOCs, let's delve into a few notable case studies:

1. **Coursera:** Coursera is one of the leading online learning platforms that offers a vast array of courses in partnership with top universities and institutions worldwide. With millions of learners enrolled, Coursera has made high-quality education accessible to individuals around the globe. Coursera's partnership with institutions such as Stanford University, Yale University, and the University of Michigan has provided learners with rigorous and diverse learning opportunities.

2. **Khan Academy:** Khan Academy is a non-profit organization that offers free online educational resources and courses for learners of all ages. Focusing primarily on K-12 education, Khan Academy provides interactive lessons, practice exercises, and personalized learning dashboards. It has become a valuable tool for students, parents, and educators alike, supporting learning both in and outside the classroom.

3. **HarvardX:** HarvardX is the online learning initiative of Harvard University, offering MOOCs and other online learning opportunities. HarvardX courses cover a wide range of disciplines, providing learners with access to Harvard-quality education from anywhere in the world. HarvardX has leveraged the benefits of online learning to reach a broad and diverse audience, promoting lifelong learning and skills development.

These case studies highlight the success of online learning platforms and MOOCs in expanding access to education and facilitating continuous learning for individuals across the globe.

Conclusion

Online learning and Massive Open Online Courses (MOOCs) have transformed the education landscape, offering accessible, flexible, and high-quality learning opportunities. Learners can engage with educational content at their own pace and explore diverse subjects and courses. While online learning brings many benefits, it also poses unique challenges that need to be addressed. By leveraging technology and fostering collaborative learning environments, online learning platforms and MOOCs have the potential to revolutionize education and human capital development. As technology continues to advance, the future of online learning holds promise for even greater accessibility, interactivity, and personalization.

Vocational Education and Skills Training

Vocational education and skills training play a crucial role in preparing individuals for the workforce and promoting economic success. In this section, we will explore the importance of vocational education, its benefits, and various approaches to skills training.

Understanding Vocational Education

Vocational education is an educational pathway that focuses on providing individuals with the practical skills and knowledge required for specific occupations. It typically involves hands-on training and instruction in technical and trade-related subjects. Vocational education programs are designed to equip students with the skills necessary to enter the workforce directly or advance their careers in specific industries.

The primary goal of vocational education is to bridge the gap between formal education and the demands of the labor market. By offering specialized training and industry-specific knowledge, vocational education prepares individuals for specific careers and enables them to contribute effectively to the economy. Vocational education programs are offered at various levels, including secondary schools, community colleges, technical institutes, and specialized training centers.

Benefits of Vocational Education

Vocational education offers several benefits to individuals and society as a whole. Let's explore some of the key advantages:

1. Practical Skills: Vocational education focuses on developing practical skills that are directly applicable to the workplace. It emphasizes hands-on learning experiences, allowing individuals to acquire the necessary competencies to perform specific jobs effectively.

2. Job Readiness: Vocational education programs are designed to meet the current demands of the job market. By providing targeted training in in-demand

areas, vocational education enhances an individual's employability and job readiness.

3. Career Advancement: Vocational education equips individuals with specialized knowledge and skills, enabling them to pursue careers in high-demand fields. It provides a pathway for individuals to upgrade their skills and advance their careers more quickly.

4. Addressing Skill Shortages: Vocational education programs focus on industries and occupations that have a shortage of skilled workers. By training individuals in these areas, vocational education helps alleviate skill gaps and support economic growth.

5. Economic Growth: A well-trained workforce contributes to economic growth. Vocational education programs provide the skills needed for industries to thrive, leading to increased productivity, innovation, and competitiveness.

Approaches to Vocational Education and Skills Training

There are various approaches to vocational education and skills training. Let's explore three common methods:

1. Apprenticeships: Apprenticeships are a form of vocational education that combines on-the-job training with classroom instruction. Apprentices work under the guidance of experienced professionals, gaining practical skills while earning a wage. This approach is highly effective for trades and crafts-based occupations.

2. Technical and Trade Schools: Technical and trade schools are institutions that offer specialized vocational education programs. These schools provide hands-on training and instruction in specific fields such as automotive technology, culinary arts, healthcare, and construction. Students can earn certificates or diplomas, indicating their proficiency in their chosen field.

3. Industry-Specific Training Programs: Some industries offer their own training programs to develop the skills required for their specific roles. For example, the healthcare industry may provide training programs for medical assistants or dental hygienists. These programs are tailored to the industry's needs and often lead to industry-recognized certifications.

Challenges and Solutions

While vocational education and skills training have numerous benefits, there are challenges that need to be addressed. Here are a few common challenges and potential solutions:

1. Stigma: Vocational education is often stigmatized as a second-choice option compared to traditional academic pathways. To overcome this, it is important to promote the value and importance of vocational education, highlighting the practical skills and career opportunities it offers.

2. Industry Alignment: Vocational education programs should closely align with the needs and demands of industries. This can be achieved through regular collaboration between educational institutions and industry partners to ensure that the curriculum and training provided are relevant and up to date.

3. Access and Equity: Ensuring access to vocational education for all individuals, regardless of their socio-economic background, is crucial. Scholarships, financial aid, and targeted outreach programs can help promote equity and provide opportunities to underprivileged communities.

Case Studies

Let's explore a few case studies that highlight successful vocational education and skills training initiatives:

1. Germany's Dual Vocational Training System: Germany's vocational education system is highly regarded for its close integration with the labor market. The dual system combines apprenticeships in companies with theoretical training in vocational schools. This approach has contributed to Germany's skilled workforce and low youth unemployment rate.

2. Swiss Apprenticeship Model: Switzerland's apprenticeship model is known for its comprehensive and structured vocational education programs. The system provides diverse training opportunities in various fields, offering a combination of classroom instruction and on-the-job training. It has been instrumental in developing a highly skilled workforce in Switzerland.

3. SkillsFuture Initiative in Singapore: Singapore's SkillsFuture initiative aims to promote lifelong learning and skills development. It provides individuals with various training options, including industry-specific courses, apprenticeships, and professional certifications. SkillsFuture has been successful in upskilling Singapore's workforce and keeping pace with industry advancements.

Conclusion

Vocational education and skills training are vital components of a successful and dynamic economy. They equip individuals with practical skills, improve employability, and address skill shortages. By promoting vocational education, providing relevant training, and fostering collaboration between educational institutions and industries, we can build a skilled workforce and support sustainable economic growth.

Lifelong Learning and Continuous Education

Lifelong learning and continuous education are essential components of personal and professional development in today's rapidly changing and knowledge-driven world. In this section, we will explore the importance of lifelong learning, the benefits it offers, and strategies to incorporate continuous education into our lives.

Why is Lifelong Learning Important?

Lifelong learning refers to the ongoing process of acquiring knowledge, skills, and attitudes throughout one's life. It recognizes that learning does not end after formal education but must continue to adapt to the dynamic nature of our society. Here are some reasons why lifelong learning is important:

1. **Adaptation to Change**: Lifelong learning enables individuals to adapt to changing circumstances, whether it is in the workplace, technology, or societal expectations. By continuously updating our knowledge and skills, we can stay relevant and competitive in our respective fields.

2. **Personal Growth**: Learning new things boosts self-confidence and self-esteem. It opens doors to new opportunities and expands our horizons. Lifelong learning encourages personal growth and helps us discover our passions and interests.

3. **Career Advancement**: In a rapidly evolving job market, continuous education is crucial for career advancement. Employers value employees who demonstrate a commitment to learning and self-improvement. Lifelong learning enhances our professional skills and increases job prospects.

4. **Intellectual Stimulation**: Learning new subjects and acquiring new skills stimulates our intellect. It keeps our minds sharp and active, fostering creativity and critical thinking abilities. Lifelong learning can enrich our lives and provide a sense of fulfillment.

5. **Social Interaction**: Lifelong learning provides opportunities to meet new people and engage in social interactions. Joining educational programs, seminars, or workshops allows us to connect with like-minded individuals, share experiences, and build a network.

Strategies for Lifelong Learning

Incorporating lifelong learning into our lives requires a proactive approach and the adoption of effective strategies. Here are some strategies to help individuals engage in continuous education:

1. **Set Learning Goals:** Define clear learning goals to guide your educational journey. Identify specific areas of interest or skills you want to develop and create a plan to achieve these goals.

2. **Embrace Technology:** Utilize online resources, e-learning platforms, and mobile applications to access a vast pool of educational content. Online courses, webinars, and podcasts offer flexible learning options that can fit into your schedule.

3. **Join Professional Organizations:** Become a member of professional organizations or associations related to your field. These organizations often offer workshops, conferences, and publications that provide valuable insights and learning opportunities.

4. **Network and Collaborate:** Engage in professional networks and communities of practice to exchange knowledge and learn from others. Attend conferences, seminars, and industry events to connect with experts and peers.

5. **Read Widely:** Cultivate a habit of reading books, research papers, and articles to stay informed about the latest developments in your field. Explore diverse subjects beyond your expertise to broaden your intellectual horizons.

6. **Seek Mentors and Role Models:** Identify mentors or role models who can provide guidance and inspiration in your learning journey. Mentors can share their experiences and offer valuable advice to help you navigate challenges.

7. **Apply Learning in Real-life:** Apply the knowledge and skills acquired through continuous education in practical settings. Look for opportunities to implement what you have learned to reinforce your understanding and enhance your abilities.

Challenges and Solutions

While lifelong learning offers numerous benefits, it is not without its challenges. Here are some common challenges individuals might face when pursuing continuous education and strategies to overcome them:

1. **Time Constraints:** Busy schedules and work commitments can make it difficult to allocate time for learning. Prioritize your learning goals, set aside dedicated time, and create a realistic study plan. Break down the learning process into small, manageable chunks to make it more achievable.

2. **Motivation and Discipline:** Sustaining motivation and staying disciplined throughout the learning journey can be challenging. Find ways to stay inspired, such as connecting with like-minded learners, rewarding yourself after achieving milestones, or visualizing the benefits of continuous education.

3. **Financial Constraints:** Accessing quality educational resources and courses may incur financial costs. Look for free or low-cost alternatives, such as open educational resources, Massive Open Online Courses (MOOCs), or scholarships. Seek employer support or funding opportunities to cover educational expenses.

4. **Overcoming Learning Plateaus:** Learning plateaus, where progress seems stagnant, can be demotivating. Seek feedback from mentors or peers, engage in collaborative learning, or explore different learning approaches to overcome plateaus and maintain momentum.

5. **Information Overload:** With an abundance of information available, it can be challenging to filter and prioritize what to learn. Develop critical thinking skills to evaluate the credibility of information sources. Focus on relevant and high-quality resources aligned with your learning goals.

Conclusion

Lifelong learning and continuous education are indispensable in today's fast-paced and knowledge-driven world. By embracing a mindset of continuous improvement and adopting effective learning strategies, individuals can unlock personal and professional growth opportunities. Overcoming challenges and embracing the benefits of lifelong learning will enable individuals to thrive in their chosen fields and lead fulfilling lives. So let's embark on this exciting journey of lifelong learning together!

Case Studies of Education for Economic Success

Finland's Education System and High Academic Achievement

Finland's education system has gained international recognition for its high academic achievement and innovative approach to teaching and learning. This section explores the key principles and features of Finland's education system that have contributed to its success.

The Finnish Education Model

The Finnish education system is based on equality, inclusion, and holistic development. It aims to provide all students with equal opportunities to succeed and focuses on developing their overall well-being, not just academic performance.

One of the distinctive features of the Finnish model is its emphasis on comprehensive education. Students receive a broad education that covers a range of subjects, including science, mathematics, foreign languages, arts, and physical education. This approach enables students to develop a well-rounded set of skills and knowledge.

Equitable Access to Education

Finland prioritizes equitable access to education, ensuring that every child has the opportunity to receive a quality education regardless of their background or socio-economic status. This is achieved through a strong commitment to equal funding and resources across schools.

Additionally, Finland has a comprehensive early childhood education and care system, which provides high-quality early education for all children from the age of one to six. This early start in education sets a foundation for future learning and development.

Teacher Professionalism and Autonomy

The role of teachers in the Finnish education system is highly regarded. Teachers are selected from the top achievers in their academic programs and undergo rigorous training to develop both pedagogical skills and subject knowledge. They are seen as professionals and are given autonomy in their teaching methods and assessment practices.

Teachers in Finland have the freedom to design their own curriculum and assessments tailored to the needs of their students. This flexibility allows for student-centered learning and fosters a sense of responsibility and engagement among students.

Fostering a Positive Learning Environment

Creating a positive and supportive learning environment is another key aspect of the Finnish education system. Class sizes are relatively small, enabling teachers to provide individual attention to students and tailor their instruction accordingly. This personalized approach to teaching helps address the unique learning needs of each student.

Furthermore, Finland emphasizes a holistic approach to student well-being, focusing on the development of social and emotional skills alongside academic skills. Schools in Finland prioritize student welfare and provide support services to address any personal or emotional challenges students may face.

Beyond Standardized Testing

Unlike many other education systems, Finland places little emphasis on standardized testing. Instead, the focus is on continuous assessment and feedback, allowing students to learn at their own pace and develop a deep understanding of the subjects they study.

This approach reduces the pressure on students and fosters a love for learning rather than solely focusing on grades. It also encourages critical thinking, problem-solving skills, and creativity, which are essential for success in the modern world.

Results and Impact

Finland's education system consistently ranks among the top performers on international assessments, such as the Programme for International Student Assessment (PISA). Finnish students demonstrate high levels of academic achievement, problem-solving skills, and critical thinking abilities.

The success of Finland's education system is not only reflected in academic performance but also in the overall well-being and happiness of students. Finland has a strong sense of social cohesion and has achieved impressive results in terms of student resilience, mental health, and life satisfaction.

Lessons for Education Reform

The Finnish education system provides valuable lessons for education reform efforts worldwide. It highlights the importance of equality in education, teacher professionalism, personalized learning, and a holistic approach to student well-being.

By prioritizing these principles, education systems can strive to create an inclusive and effective learning environment that prepares students for the challenges and opportunities of the future.

Resources

1. Sahlberg, P. (2011). Finnish Lessons: What can the world learn from educational change in Finland? Teachers College Press.

2. Education in Finland. (n.d.). Finnish National Agency for Education. Retrieved from https://www.oph.fi/en/education-system

3. Pasi Sahlberg: Finnish Lessons. (2012). TEDxTeachersCollege. [Video file]. Retrieved from https://www.youtube.com/watch?v=F5tsbaWBeds

Discussion Questions

1. How does Finland's focus on holistic development contribute to academic success?

2. What are the benefits of personalized learning in the Finnish education system?

3. How can other countries adopt Finland's approach to teacher professionalism and autonomy?

4. What can be done to promote equitable access to education in different education systems?

5. How would reducing the emphasis on standardized testing impact the education system in your country?

Further Exploration

1. Conduct research on the education systems of other high-performing countries and compare their approaches to Finland's education model.

2. Interview educators or education policymakers to gather their perspectives on the strengths and weaknesses of the Finnish education system.

3. Reflect on your own educational experiences and consider how aspects of the Finnish education system could enhance teaching and learning in your context.

South Korea's Focus on Education and Technological Advancements

South Korea is widely recognized as one of the most technologically advanced nations in the world. This success can be attributed in large part to the country's strong focus on education and technological advancements. In this section, we will explore the strategies and initiatives that South Korea has implemented to foster a culture of innovation and excellence in education.

Education System in South Korea

The education system in South Korea is highly regarded for its rigorous curriculum and academic standards. It is known for producing students who consistently rank among the top performers in international assessments such as the Programme for International Student Assessment (PISA).

In South Korea, education is highly valued and seen as a key driver of economic growth and social mobility. Students face intense competition to secure a place in prestigious universities, and there is a strong emphasis on academic achievement. The education system is structured in a way that provides students with a solid foundation in core subjects such as mathematics, science, language, and social studies.

Technological Advancements

South Korea's success in education is closely linked to its commitment to technological advancements. The government has made significant investments in research and development, with a particular focus on areas such as information technology, robotics, and artificial intelligence.

One notable example of technological advancement in South Korea is the development of ultra-fast internet infrastructure. The country boasts one of the highest internet penetration rates in the world, with internet speeds that are among the fastest globally. This high-speed connectivity has paved the way for various innovations in digital technologies, enabling South Korea to lead in areas such as e-commerce, online gaming, and mobile communications.

Integration of Technology in Education

South Korea has also been proactive in integrating technology into its education system. The government has invested in providing schools with the necessary infrastructure and equipment to support digital learning. This includes the provision of computers, tablets, and smartboards in classrooms.

Furthermore, South Korea has implemented innovative teaching methods that leverage technology to enhance learning outcomes. For instance, virtual reality (VR) and augmented reality (AR) technologies are being used to create immersive and interactive learning experiences. Online platforms and educational apps are also widely used to supplement classroom instruction and provide personalized learning opportunities.

Government Initiatives

The South Korean government plays a crucial role in promoting education and technological advancements. It has implemented various initiatives to foster a conducive environment for innovation and learning. One key initiative is the support for research and development through funding and grants for both academic institutions and private companies. This has led to breakthroughs in various fields and has positioned South Korea as a leader in technological innovation.

Additionally, the government has invested in creating specialized educational programs and institutions that focus on nurturing talent in science, technology, engineering, and mathematics (STEM) fields. These programs aim to cultivate the next generation of innovators and entrepreneurs who can contribute to the country's economic growth and technological advancements.

Challenges and Future Directions

Despite its impressive achievements, the South Korean education system also faces challenges. The intense academic pressure and competition have been associated with high levels of stress among students, leading to concerns about their overall well-being. Efforts are being made to address these issues by implementing measures to promote a more balanced and holistic approach to education.

Looking ahead, South Korea is poised to continue its focus on education and technological advancements. The government is committed to investing in emerging technologies such as artificial intelligence, big data, and the Internet of Things. This commitment is expected to drive further innovation across various sectors and contribute to the country's economic success.

Conclusion

South Korea's emphasis on education and technological advancements has been instrumental in its economic success. By prioritizing education and nurturing a culture of innovation, the country has been able to develop a highly skilled workforce and establish itself as a global leader in technology. The government's commitment to investing in research and development, along with its focus on integrating technology into education, ensures that South Korea remains at the forefront of innovation in the years to come.

Germany's Dual Vocational Training System and Workforce Development

Germany's dual vocational training system is renowned worldwide for its success in preparing young individuals for the workforce and driving economic growth. This section explores the key features and benefits of this system, as well as its impact on Germany's economic success.

Overview of Germany's Dual Vocational Training System

Germany's dual vocational training system is a unique approach that combines classroom-based learning with practical, on-the-job training. It is based on a partnership between companies, vocational schools, and the government, and is designed to provide individuals with the skills and qualifications necessary to meet the demands of the labor market.

Key Features of the Dual Vocational Training System

The dual vocational training system in Germany has several key features that contribute to its success:

1. Apprenticeships: Apprenticeships form the backbone of the training system, allowing individuals to gain practical, hands-on experience in a real work environment. Apprentices are employed by companies and receive a salary while they learn.

2. Close Collaboration with Companies: Companies play a central role in the dual system, as they are responsible for providing training and ensuring that apprentices acquire the necessary skills. This close collaboration ensures that the training is aligned with the needs of the labor market.

3. Vocational Schools: Apprentices also attend vocational schools, where they receive theoretical education complementing their practical training. The

curriculum is developed in collaboration with companies to ensure it is relevant and up to date.

4. Certification: At the end of their apprenticeship, individuals receive a recognized certification, such as a journeyman's certificate. These certifications are highly valued by employers and provide evidence of the individual's skills and qualifications.

5. Lifelong Learning: The dual vocational training system emphasizes the importance of continuous learning. Individuals are encouraged to pursue further education and training throughout their careers to stay abreast of changing technologies and industry requirements.

Benefits of the Dual Vocational Training System

The dual vocational training system in Germany has numerous benefits, which contribute to the country's strong workforce and economic success:

1. Highly Skilled Workforce: The system produces a highly skilled workforce that meets the specific needs of industries. Companies benefit from having employees with practical experience and relevant skills, reducing the need for intensive on-the-job training.

2. Low Youth Unemployment: The dual system plays a significant role in reducing youth unemployment in Germany. By offering young individuals a combination of work experience and education, it provides a smooth transition from school to work.

3. Smooth School-to-Work Transition: The dual system ensures a seamless transition from education to employment. Individuals are equipped with practical skills and qualifications, making them more attractive to employers and increasing their employability.

4. Strong Industry-education Partnership: The collaboration between companies and vocational schools fosters close ties between the education system and the labor market. This partnership allows for the continuous updating of curriculum to meet the evolving needs of industries.

5. Economic Growth: The dual vocational training system has been a contributing factor to Germany's economic success. A highly skilled workforce enhances productivity and innovation, driving economic growth and competitiveness.

Challenges and Future Development

While the dual vocational training system in Germany has been successful, it also faces challenges and opportunities for future development:

1. Addressing Skills Shortages: With rapid technological advancements, there is a constant need to update the skills taught in the system to address emerging job market demands. Efforts are being made to incorporate digital skills and other industry-specific skills.

2. Inclusion and Diversity: The system is mostly accessed by high-achieving students, leading to limited diversity in terms of social backgrounds and gender. Ensuring equal access and opportunities for all individuals is crucial for the system's continued success.

3. Internationalization: Germany's dual vocational training system has inspired other countries to adopt similar models. Collaborating with international partners and sharing best practices can help strengthen the system further.

4. Lifelong Learning: Encouraging individuals to engage in lifelong learning is essential to adapt to the changing demands of the labor market. Offering flexible learning pathways and opportunities for upskilling and reskilling is vital to maintain the system's relevance.

In conclusion, Germany's dual vocational training system has played a pivotal role in creating a skilled workforce, driving economic growth, and reducing youth unemployment. The close collaboration between companies, vocational schools, and the government has resulted in a successful model that other countries seek to emulate. However, ongoing efforts are needed to address emerging challenges and ensure the system remains adaptable and inclusive in the face of an ever-changing job market.

Chapter 9: Inclusive Growth and Economic Success

Chapter 9: Inclusive Growth and Economic Success

Chapter 9: Inclusive Growth and Economic Success

Inclusive growth refers to a pattern of economic growth that ensures the benefits are widely shared among all segments of society, including those who are traditionally disadvantaged or marginalized. It emphasizes the importance of reducing poverty, inequality, and social exclusion while promoting equal opportunities for all individuals to participate and benefit from economic development.

Understanding Inequality and Poverty

In order to achieve inclusive growth, it is important to understand the nature of inequality and poverty. Inequality refers to the unequal distribution of income, wealth, and opportunities within a society. It can be measured using various indicators, such as the Gini coefficient, which summarizes the extent of income inequality in a country. Poverty, on the other hand, refers to a lack of basic necessities and a low standard of living. It is usually measured using poverty lines or thresholds, which vary across countries.

There are several causes of inequality and poverty. One of the main factors is the unequal distribution of resources, such as land, capital, and education. Discrimination based on factors like gender, race, and ethnicity also contributes to inequality. Additionally, globalization and technological advancements can lead to job displacement and wage stagnation for certain segments of the population, exacerbating inequality and poverty.

The consequences of inequality and poverty are far-reaching. They not only affect individuals and communities but also hinder overall economic growth and development. High levels of inequality can undermine social cohesion, increase crime rates, and limit access to quality education and healthcare. Furthermore, poverty creates barriers to upward mobility and perpetuates intergenerational cycles of disadvantage.

Policies for Inclusive Growth

To promote inclusive growth, governments and policymakers implement various policies and programs. These policies aim to reduce inequality and poverty, improve access to essential services, and create opportunities for all individuals to participate in economic activities. Some of the key policies for inclusive growth include:

1. **Redistribution and Social Safety Nets:** Governments can implement progressive taxation systems to redistribute income and wealth from the rich to the poor. They can also establish social safety nets, such as cash transfer programs and unemployment benefits, to provide a basic level of support to those in need.

2. **Access to Quality Education and Healthcare:** Investing in education and healthcare is crucial for promoting inclusive growth. Governments should ensure that quality education and healthcare services are accessible to all individuals, regardless of their socio-economic background. This includes providing scholarships, subsidies, and targeted support for disadvantaged groups.

3. **Financial Inclusion and Microfinance:** Enhancing access to financial services, such as banking and credit, is another important aspect of inclusive growth. Governments can promote financial inclusion by implementing policies that facilitate the establishment of banking infrastructure in underserved areas and by supporting microfinance institutions that provide small loans to entrepreneurs and individuals with limited access to traditional banking.

Case Studies of Inclusive Economic Success

There are several examples from around the world where countries have achieved inclusive economic success by implementing effective policies. Let's look at three case studies:

1. **Costa Rica's Social Policies and Poverty Reduction:** Costa Rica has been successful in reducing poverty and promoting inclusive growth through its social policies. The country has invested significantly in education and healthcare, resulting in high literacy rates and improved healthcare outcomes. Additionally,

Costa Rica has implemented social safety nets and targeted programs to support vulnerable populations, leading to a decline in poverty rates over the years.

2. **Rwanda's Development Strategy and Poverty Alleviation:** After the devastating genocide in 1994, Rwanda embarked on a path of inclusive economic development. The government implemented a comprehensive development strategy that focused on poverty reduction, social inclusion, and economic empowerment. Through targeted interventions in agriculture, education, and healthcare, Rwanda has achieved remarkable progress in alleviating poverty and improving the well-being of its population.

3. **Sweden's Welfare State and Gender Equality:** Sweden is known for its extensive welfare state, which has played a significant role in promoting inclusive growth. The country has implemented policies that provide universal access to education, healthcare, and social benefits, ensuring a high standard of living for its citizens. Sweden has also made significant strides in achieving gender equality through policies that promote women's participation in the workforce and provide support for work-life balance.

Conclusion

Inclusive growth is essential for sustainable and equitable economic development. By addressing inequality and poverty, promoting equal opportunities, and implementing effective policies, countries can achieve inclusive economic success. It requires a multidimensional approach, incorporating social, economic, and political aspects to ensure that the benefits of growth are shared by all members of society. Governments, policymakers, and society as a whole have a critical role to play in fostering inclusive growth and creating a more prosperous future for all.

Understanding Inequality and Poverty

Measurement of Inequality and Poverty

In this section, we will explore the measurement of inequality and poverty, which are crucial concepts for understanding the socioeconomic well-being of individuals and societies. Measuring inequality allows us to assess the distribution of resources and opportunities among different groups of people, while measuring poverty helps us understand the extent to which individuals may lack basic necessities for a decent standard of living.

Inequality Measurement

To measure inequality, we can use various statistical measures known as inequality indices. The most commonly used inequality index is the Gini coefficient, named after Italian statistician Corrado Gini. The Gini coefficient ranges from 0 (perfect equality) to 1 (maximum inequality). It measures the area between the Lorenz curve (which represents the cumulative share of income or wealth) and the line of perfect equality (where income or wealth is evenly distributed).

Mathematically, the Gini coefficient can be calculated as follows:

$$G = \frac{A}{A + B}$$

where A is the area between the Lorenz curve and the line of perfect equality, and B is the area under the line of perfect equality.

The Gini coefficient provides a summary statistic of inequality, making it easier to compare inequality levels across countries or regions. However, it does not reveal the underlying causes or patterns of inequality. Therefore, it is important to complement the Gini coefficient with other measures and analysis to gain a comprehensive understanding of inequality.

Other commonly used inequality indices include the Theil index, which decomposes inequality into within-group and between-group components, and the Atkinson index, which captures the aversion to inequality. These indices provide additional insights into the distribution of income or wealth and the preferences of society towards inequality.

Poverty Measurement

Poverty can be measured in absolute or relative terms. Absolute poverty refers to the lack of basic necessities, such as food, shelter, and healthcare, while relative poverty compares individuals or households to a reference group within a particular society.

One widely used measure of absolute poverty is the poverty line, which defines the minimum level of income or consumption required to meet basic needs. The poverty line is often expressed as a daily or monthly income threshold. Individuals or households falling below the poverty line are considered to be in poverty.

Relative poverty, on the other hand, compares individuals or households to the overall distribution of income or wealth in a particular society. It is commonly measured using the relative poverty rate, which defines poverty as falling below a certain percentage of the median income or wealth.

For example, a commonly used threshold for relative poverty is 50% of the median income. Individuals or households with income or wealth below this threshold are considered to be in relative poverty.

In addition to these measures, multidimensional approaches to poverty measurement have gained popularity. These approaches consider not only income or wealth, but also factors such as health, education, access to clean water, and social inclusion. By including multiple dimensions of poverty, such as the Human Development Index (HDI) or the Multidimensional Poverty Index (MPI), a more comprehensive picture of poverty can be obtained.

It is important to note that poverty measurement is not without its challenges. Different measures may provide different assessments of poverty levels, and the choice of threshold or reference group can influence the results. Additionally, data limitations and the subjective nature of poverty make it a complex and evolving field of study.

Examining Inequality and Poverty Together

Measuring inequality and poverty together allows us to understand not only the distribution of resources, but also the extent to which individuals have access to those resources. For example, a country with low levels of inequality may still have a significant portion of its population living in poverty, indicating that resources are not reaching those who need them the most.

By integrating measures of inequality and poverty, policymakers and researchers can gain insights into the effectiveness of social policies and interventions aimed at reducing poverty and promoting more equitable societies. It is through a comprehensive understanding of both inequality and poverty that we can identify strategies for inclusive economic growth and sustainable development.

Conclusion

In this section, we have explored the measurement of inequality and poverty. We have discussed the Gini coefficient as a commonly used measure of inequality, as well as other indices such as the Theil index and the Atkinson index. For poverty measurement, we have examined both absolute poverty, using the poverty line, and relative poverty, using the relative poverty rate. We have also highlighted the importance of multidimensional approaches to poverty measurement.

Understanding and measuring inequality and poverty are fundamental to addressing social and economic challenges and promoting inclusive growth. By continuously refining measurement techniques and deepening our understanding of the underlying causes and consequences of inequality and poverty, we can strive towards creating more just and equitable societies.

Causes and Consequences of Inequality

Inequality is a complex and multifaceted issue that arises from various factors and has significant consequences for individuals, societies, and economies. In this section, we will explore the causes of inequality and examine its consequences in order to gain a deeper understanding of its impact.

Causes of Inequality

1. **Income Disparities:** One of the main causes of inequality is the unequal distribution of income. This occurs when some individuals or groups earn significantly higher incomes compared to others. Factors such as differences in education, skills, and occupation play a significant role in determining income levels. Additionally, structural factors like discrimination, gender pay gaps, and unequal access to opportunities can contribute to income disparities.

2. **Wealth Concentration:** Wealth inequality refers to the unequal distribution of assets, property, and financial resources. Wealth can accumulate over time through inheritance, investments, and capital gains, leading to an increasing concentration of wealth among a small segment of the population. This concentration of wealth can exacerbate income inequality by perpetuating advantages for the wealthy and limiting opportunities for the less affluent.

3. **Education Disparities:** Access to quality education significantly influences an individual's socioeconomic status. Unequal access to education, particularly in low-income communities or marginalized groups, can perpetuate inequality by limiting opportunities for upward mobility. Disparities in educational resources, such as inadequate funding and lack of qualified teachers, contribute to unequal educational outcomes.

4. **Discrimination and Social Exclusion:** Discrimination based on race, gender, ethnicity, or other factors can contribute to economic and social inequalities. Marginalized groups often face barriers to employment, education, and social mobility, leading to a widening of the gap between advantaged and disadvantaged individuals. Discriminatory practices and prejudiced attitudes create systemic barriers that perpetuate inequality.

5. **Globalization and Technological Advances:** Globalization and technological advancements have had mixed effects on inequality. While they have created new opportunities and increased productivity, they have also contributed

to job polarization and wage stagnation for low-skilled workers. Global competition and automation have led to the outsourcing of labor-intensive jobs, disproportionately affecting workers with limited skills and education.

Consequences of Inequality

1. **Poor Social Cohesion:** Inequality can lead to social divisions and erode social cohesion within a society. The perception of unfairness and unequal opportunities can create tension and resentment among different social groups. This can hinder cooperation and trust, exacerbating social unrest and impeding progress.

2. **Reduced Economic Growth:** High levels of inequality can have a negative impact on economic growth. When income and wealth are concentrated in the hands of a few, it limits the purchasing power of the majority, leading to weakened consumer demand. Additionally, inequality can hinder human capital formation and limit investment in education and healthcare, thereby hindering long-term economic development.

3. **Health Disparities:** Inequality in income and access to healthcare can result in disparities in health outcomes. Individuals with lower socioeconomic status often face limited access to quality healthcare, leading to higher rates of chronic diseases, lower life expectancies, and poorer overall health. These health disparities further perpetuate the cycle of inequality and limit opportunities for social mobility.

4. **Political Instability:** Persistent inequality can contribute to political instability and social unrest. When a significant portion of the population feels excluded from economic and political opportunities, it can lead to dissatisfaction, protests, and, in extreme cases, social upheaval. Addressing inequality is crucial for maintaining political stability and fostering inclusive governance.

5. **Inter-generational Transmission of Inequality:** Inequality can become entrenched across generations due to limited social mobility. Children from disadvantaged backgrounds often face barriers to accessing quality education, healthcare, and employment opportunities, perpetuating the cycle of poverty and inequality. This inter-generational transmission of disadvantage further widens the wealth gap and hinders equal opportunities.

It is important to recognize that addressing inequality requires a comprehensive and multi-dimensional approach. By implementing policies that promote equal access to education, healthcare, and employment opportunities, societies can strive towards reducing inequality and fostering inclusive growth. Additionally, efforts to eradicate discrimination and promote social cohesion are crucial for building a more equitable future.

Policies for Inclusive Growth

Redistribution and Social Safety Nets

In the pursuit of inclusive economic growth and reducing inequality, governments around the world have implemented various policies aimed at redistribution and providing social safety nets for their citizens. These policies are designed to ensure that even the most vulnerable members of society have access to basic necessities and opportunities, and to mitigate the adverse effects of economic shocks and market failures. In this section, we will explore the principles, challenges, and examples of redistribution and social safety nets.

Principles of Redistribution

Redistribution refers to the transfer of wealth, income, or resources from one segment of the population to another. The underlying principle of redistribution is based on the belief that a fair and just society should strive to reduce inequality and promote social cohesion. It recognizes that market outcomes alone may not be sufficient to ensure equitable distribution of resources and opportunities.

There are several approaches to redistribution, ranging from progressive taxation to wealth redistribution programs. Progressive taxation is a system where tax rates increase with income levels, thus ensuring that higher-income individuals contribute a larger proportion of their income. This helps fund social programs that benefit the less fortunate.

Redistribution can take various forms, including cash transfers, subsidies, and public services. Cash transfers, such as unemployment benefits or social assistance programs, provide direct financial assistance to individuals and families in need. Subsidies can be used to reduce the cost of essential goods and services, such as healthcare or education. Public services, such as free or subsidized public transportation, are also a form of redistribution as they provide access to essential services for all members of society.

Challenges of Redistribution

While redistribution policies aim to promote social inclusion and reduce inequality, they also face various challenges. One of the main challenges is balancing the incentives for individual effort and entrepreneurship with the need for redistribution. High tax rates on higher-income individuals, for example, might discourage work and innovation, thus affecting overall economic growth.

POLICIES FOR INCLUSIVE GROWTH   245

Another challenge is ensuring that redistribution is targeted effectively to those in need. Identifying the most vulnerable individuals or households requires accurate and up-to-date data, which may be difficult to obtain in certain contexts. Moreover, the design and implementation of redistribution programs should consider potential unintended consequences, such as disincentives to work or reliance on social assistance.

Furthermore, funding redistribution programs can be a significant challenge for governments, especially in developing countries with limited fiscal capacity. It requires a balance between revenue generation through taxation and the allocation of resources to various social programs. Additionally, changes in the political landscape and public opinion may impact the support and sustainability of redistribution policies over time.

Examples of Redistribution and Social Safety Nets

Many countries have implemented redistribution and social safety net programs to address inequality and provide support to vulnerable populations. These programs vary in their design and scope, reflecting the unique challenges and priorities of each country. Here are a few notable examples:

1. Nordic Model (Sweden, Norway, Finland)   These Scandinavian countries are known for their comprehensive welfare systems, which include universal healthcare, generous social benefits, and free education. Their high tax rates fund these programs, aiming to ensure an equitable distribution of resources and opportunities.

2. Universal Basic Income (UBI)   UBI is a concept that has gained attention in recent years. It proposes providing all individuals, regardless of their income or employment status, with a regular and unconditional cash transfer. The idea behind UBI is to alleviate poverty, reduce inequality, and provide a safety net for all citizens.

3. Conditional Cash Transfer (CCT) Programs (Brazil's Bolsa Família, Mexico's Oportunidades)   CCT programs provide cash transfers to low-income families, conditional on certain behaviors such as school attendance or healthcare utilization. These programs aim to break the cycle of intergenerational poverty by promoting human capital development and improving access to essential services.

Conclusion

Redistribution and social safety nets play a crucial role in promoting inclusive economic growth, reducing inequality, and ensuring social cohesion. By targeting resources and support to vulnerable populations, these policies mitigate the adverse effects of economic shocks and market failures. However, the design, implementation, and sustainability of redistribution programs require careful consideration of economic incentives, data availability, and fiscal capacity. As societies continue to grapple with the challenges of inequality and poverty, addressing them through effective redistribution and social safety nets remains a critical priority.

Access to Quality Education and Healthcare

Access to quality education and healthcare is crucial for promoting inclusive economic growth and ensuring the well-being of individuals and societies. In this section, we will explore the importance of access to education and healthcare, discuss the challenges in achieving equitable access, and propose strategies to improve access for all.

The Importance of Access to Education

Education is widely recognized as a fundamental human right and a key driver of economic development. It empowers individuals with knowledge and skills, enabling them to participate fully in society and contribute to economic progress. Quality education promotes social mobility, reduces poverty, and enhances productivity and innovation.

However, access to education remains unequal in many parts of the world. Disadvantaged groups such as girls, children from low-income families, and those in rural areas often face barriers to accessing quality education. Limited infrastructure, lack of qualified teachers, and cultural norms can hinder educational opportunities.

The Importance of Access to Healthcare

Access to quality healthcare is essential for achieving and maintaining good health, reducing morbidity and mortality rates, and promoting economic productivity. Healthier individuals are more likely to participate in the workforce, contribute to economic growth, and break the cycle of poverty.

Unfortunately, significant disparities in healthcare access persist globally. Factors such as income inequality, geographic location, gender, and marginalized social identities can exacerbate barriers to healthcare services. Limited healthcare facilities, inadequate infrastructure, high treatment costs, and cultural barriers prevent millions of people from accessing essential healthcare services.

Challenges in Achieving Equitable Access

Achieving equitable access to education and healthcare faces several challenges. These challenges vary across countries and regions but share some common themes:

1. **Financial Barriers:** High costs of education and healthcare can exclude individuals from disadvantaged backgrounds. Education fees, tuition, and

healthcare expenses can create financial burdens, particularly for low-income individuals and families.

2. **Geographic Barriers:** Inadequate infrastructure and limited healthcare and educational institutions in remote and rural areas make it difficult for individuals residing in these regions to access services. Limited transportation and long distances further compound the problem.

3. **Sociocultural Barriers:** Sociocultural factors, such as gender norms, social discrimination, and stigma, can impede access to education and healthcare. Women and marginalized groups often face additional barriers and limited opportunities.

4. **Lack of Awareness:** Lack of information and awareness about available educational and healthcare services can prevent individuals from seeking or utilizing these services. Educational and healthcare providers must focus on community outreach and awareness campaigns.

Strategies to Improve Access

To enhance access to quality education and healthcare, a comprehensive approach is required. Here are some strategies that can help address the challenges and improve access for all:

1. **Policy Interventions:** Governments must develop and implement policies that prioritize equitable access to education and healthcare. This includes allocating sufficient resources, implementing targeted programs for disadvantaged groups, and promoting inclusive practices.

2. **Financial Support:** Providing financial assistance, such as scholarships, grants, and subsidies, can help mitigate the financial barriers to education and healthcare. Governments, international organizations, and philanthropic institutions should invest in these initiatives to ensure equal opportunities for all.

3. **Infrastructure Development:** Governments need to invest in infrastructure development, particularly in disadvantaged areas, to improve access to education and healthcare facilities. This includes building schools, hospitals, clinics, and expanding telemedicine and e-learning initiatives.

4. **Addressing Sociocultural Barriers:** Efforts should focus on addressing sociocultural barriers that impede access to education and healthcare. This requires promoting gender equality, challenging social norms, and providing sensitivity training to healthcare and educational professionals.

5. **Healthcare and Education Systems Integration:** Integrating healthcare and education systems can improve access by offering comprehensive services. For example, school-based health clinics can provide access to basic healthcare services, immunizations, and health education.

6. **Community Engagement and Empowerment:** Engaging communities and empowering individuals to take charge of their education and health is crucial. Community-based organizations, NGOs, and local leaders play a vital role in raising awareness, advocating for equal access, and providing support.

Example: Improving Education and Healthcare Access in Rural India

In rural India, access to quality education and healthcare has been a long-standing challenge. To address this issue, the government implemented the National Rural Health Mission and the Right to Education Act.

The National Rural Health Mission focused on building healthcare infrastructure in rural areas, training rural healthcare workers, and providing essential healthcare services. This initiative improved access to healthcare for millions of people who had previously been underserved.

The Right to Education Act made education a fundamental right for all children between the ages of 6 and 14. The act aimed to provide free and compulsory education, improve school infrastructure, and ensure the availability of qualified teachers. As a result, school enrollment rates increased, and educational opportunities became more accessible for children in rural areas.

These initiatives demonstrate the effectiveness of comprehensive policies and targeted interventions in improving access to education and healthcare in rural regions.

Conclusion

Access to quality education and healthcare is crucial for promoting inclusive economic growth and ensuring the well-being of individuals and societies. Achieving equitable access requires addressing financial, geographic, and sociocultural barriers through policy interventions, financial support, infrastructure development, and community engagement. By investing in education and healthcare access for all, societies can unlock the full potential of their human capital and foster long-term economic success and prosperity.

Financial Inclusion and Microfinance

Financial inclusion refers to the accessibility and usage of financial services by all members of society, particularly those in marginalized and underserved communities. It is a critical component of sustainable economic development, as it provides individuals and businesses with the necessary tools and resources to participate in the formal financial system, manage financial risks, and capitalize on economic opportunities.

Microfinance, on the other hand, is a subset of financial inclusion that focuses on providing small loans, savings, insurance, and other financial services to low-income individuals and microenterprises. It targets individuals who lack access to traditional banking services due to factors such as lack of collateral, limited financial literacy, or living in remote areas.

The Importance of Financial Inclusion

Financial inclusion plays a crucial role in reducing poverty, promoting economic growth, and fostering social development. Here are some key reasons why financial inclusion is important:

1. Poverty Alleviation: Access to financial services enables individuals to accumulate savings, invest in income-generating activities, and build assets. It helps break the cycle of poverty by providing a safety net during times of financial stress and promoting long-term economic resilience.

2. Entrepreneurship and Employment: Microfinance empowers individuals to start small businesses or expand existing ones, leading to job creation and income generation. It provides the necessary capital and financial management skills to entrepreneurs, especially women and vulnerable groups, fostering economic empowerment and self-reliance.

3. Financial Stability: By integrating marginalized populations into the formal financial system, financial inclusion enhances economic stability on both individual and societal levels. It reduces dependence on informal and exploitative lending sources, mitigates vulnerability to financial shocks, and promotes healthy financial practices.

4. Social Welfare: Financial inclusion enables individuals to access social protection schemes, such as insurance and pensions, improving their ability to cope with life risks and ensuring social safety nets. It also facilitates access to essential services like healthcare and education, contributing to improved living standards and social well-being.

Microfinance Institutions and Models

Microfinance institutions (MFIs) are specialized financial intermediaries that provide microfinance services to low-income individuals and microenterprises. They operate under various models, including:

1. Grameen Model: Developed by Muhammad Yunus, this model emphasizes group lending, where individuals come together to form a self-help group. The group members collectively guarantee each other's loans, fostering social cohesion and peer support.

2. Village Banking Model: Under this model, MFIs organize clients into village-level banking groups. These groups meet regularly, save together, and provide access to credit based on the group's collective savings and internal lending guidelines.

3. Rotating Savings and Credit Associations (ROSCAs): ROSCAs are informal financial intermediaries found in many cultures globally. Members make regular contributions to a common fund, which is then given to a member as a lump sum loan on a rotational basis.

Challenges and Solutions

While microfinance has shown great potential, it also faces several challenges that need to be addressed for effective financial inclusion. These challenges include:

1. High Transaction Costs: Serving low-income populations can be costly due to factors such as high operational expenses, low economies of scale, and limited infrastructure. To overcome this, technology can play a vital role by enabling digital solutions, such as mobile banking and digital wallets, to reduce transaction costs and increase accessibility.

2. Lack of Credit History and Collateral: Traditional lending models rely heavily on credit history and collateral, making it challenging for low-income individuals to access credit. To address this, alternative credit assessment methods, such as using mobile data and psychometric testing, can be employed to evaluate repayment capacity and risk.

3. Financial Literacy: Limited financial literacy and awareness hinder individuals from fully utilizing financial services and understanding the associated risks and benefits. Providing tailored financial education and training programs can help improve financial literacy and empower individuals to make informed financial decisions.

4. Regulatory Environment: Regulatory barriers and constraints can limit the growth and sustainability of microfinance institutions. Governments need to create an enabling legal and regulatory framework that balances risk management with financial inclusion objectives.

Real-world Example: BRAC and Financial Inclusion in Bangladesh

BRAC (Bangladesh Rural Advancement Committee), one of the largest microfinance providers globally, has played a significant role in promoting financial inclusion in Bangladesh. Established in 1972, BRAC offers a wide range of financial services, including microloans, savings accounts, and insurance, to underserved communities.

BRAC's holistic approach to financial inclusion combines financial services with social development programs, such as healthcare, education, and livelihood training. This approach addresses the multidimensional aspects of poverty and empowers individuals to improve their overall well-being.

Through its extensive network of branch offices and grassroots-level staff, BRAC reaches over 5 million clients, predominantly women in rural areas. It uses group lending models, where borrowers support each other and participate in regular meetings for financial education and social empowerment.

By providing access to financial services, BRAC has contributed to poverty reduction, women's empowerment, and socioeconomic progress in Bangladesh. The success of BRAC's microfinance model has inspired similar initiatives worldwide and serves as an example of how financial inclusion can transform lives and societies.

Conclusion

Financial inclusion and microfinance are powerful tools for promoting economic development, reducing poverty, and fostering social inclusion. By ensuring that everyone has access to essential financial services, societies can unlock the potential of all individuals, irrespective of their economic background or location.

Efforts to enhance financial inclusion should focus on developing sustainable models, leveraging technology, improving financial literacy, and creating an enabling regulatory environment. By addressing the challenges and empowering individuals and communities to participate in the formal financial system, we can pave the way for a more inclusive and prosperous future.

Case Studies of Inclusive Economic Success

Costa Rica's Social Policies and Poverty Reduction

Costa Rica, a country known for its natural beauty and progressive policies, has achieved remarkable success in reducing poverty and promoting social welfare. In this section, we will explore the social policies implemented by Costa Rica and their impact on poverty reduction. We will also examine the key factors that have contributed to the success of these policies.

Understanding Costa Rica's Poverty Situation

To understand the significance of Costa Rica's social policies, it is essential to examine the country's poverty situation. In recent decades, Costa Rica has made significant progress in reducing poverty rates. According to the World Bank, the poverty rate in Costa Rica decreased from 22.4% in 2002 to 20.5% in 2019. This reduction is attributed to the implementation of effective social policies aimed at improving the well-being of the population.

Key Social Policies

1. **Investment in Education:** One of the cornerstones of Costa Rica's social policies is its commitment to education. The government has made substantial investments in primary, secondary, and tertiary education, ensuring access to quality education for all citizens. This emphasis on education has not only empowered individuals but also contributed to the overall development of the nation.

2. **Universal Healthcare:** Costa Rica is renowned for its comprehensive public healthcare system, which provides universal coverage to its citizens. This system, known as the Costa Rican Social Security System (Caja Costarricense de Seguro Social), ensures access to medical services, including preventive care and treatment, for all individuals, regardless of their socioeconomic status.

3. **Social Safety Nets:** Costa Rica has implemented social safety net programs to protect vulnerable populations and alleviate poverty. These programs include cash transfer programs, pension schemes, and subsidies for housing, electricity, and food. They aim to provide a safety net for low-income individuals and families, helping them meet their basic needs and improve their quality of life.

Factors Contributing to Success

1. **Political Stability and Social Cohesion:** Costa Rica's success in poverty reduction is rooted in its political stability and social cohesion. The country has a long-standing democratic tradition, peace, and a strong commitment to social welfare. This stability has allowed for the consistent implementation of social policies, creating an enabling environment for poverty reduction initiatives to thrive.

2. **Strong Institutions and Governance:** Effective governance and strong institutions have played a crucial role in Costa Rica's success. The government has demonstrated commitment and efficiency in policy implementation, ensuring the proper allocation of resources and effective delivery of social services. Additionally, transparency and accountability have been integral in minimizing corruption and promoting equitable distribution of resources.

3. **Investment in Human Development:** Costa Rica's focus on human development, particularly through investments in education and healthcare, has been instrumental in reducing poverty. By equipping individuals with knowledge and skills, and providing access to quality healthcare, Costa Rica has empowered its citizens to participate actively in economic activities and improve their socio-economic conditions.

4. **Strong Social Partnership:** Another key factor in the success of social policies in Costa Rica is the strong partnership between the government, civil society organizations, and the private sector. This collaboration has allowed for efficient resource allocation, knowledge sharing, and the development of comprehensive programs that address the multifaceted nature of poverty.

Challenges and Future Outlook

While Costa Rica has made significant progress in poverty reduction, it continues to face challenges in sustaining these achievements. Some of the challenges include income inequality, regional disparities, and environmental sustainability. Additionally, the country needs to adapt its social policies to address emerging issues such as demographic changes, technological advancements, and climate change.

To ensure continued success in poverty reduction, it is crucial for Costa Rica to prioritize inclusive economic growth, promote sustainable development practices, and strengthen social safety nets. The government should also focus on improving education quality, facilitating skill development, and fostering innovation to meet the demands of a rapidly changing global economy.

Overall, Costa Rica serves as an inspiration and a valuable case study for countries aiming to reduce poverty and promote social welfare. Its commitment to social policies, investment in education and healthcare, and strong governance have contributed to its remarkable success in poverty reduction. By learning from Costa Rica's experiences, policymakers worldwide can strive for more inclusive and prosperous societies.

Rwanda's Development Strategy and Poverty Alleviation

Rwanda's remarkable progress in poverty alleviation and economic development has been widely recognized as one of the most inspiring success stories in recent times. The country, which was ravaged by a devastating genocide in 1994, has managed to transform itself into a stable and rapidly growing economy. In this section, we will explore Rwanda's development strategy and the measures it has taken to alleviate poverty and promote inclusive growth.

Background

Rwanda, located in East Africa, is a landlocked country with a population of approximately 12 million people. After the genocide in 1994, which resulted in the loss of nearly one million lives, Rwanda faced immense challenges in rebuilding its economy and society. However, under the leadership of President Paul Kagame, the government embarked on a bold and ambitious development agenda focused on poverty reduction and sustainable economic growth.

Vision 2020

At the heart of Rwanda's development strategy is Vision 2020, a long-term plan that aims to transform Rwanda from a low-income agrarian economy into a knowledge-based, middle-income country. The vision, launched in 2000, outlines specific goals and targets in various sectors, including agriculture, education, infrastructure, and governance.

Diversification of the Economy One of the key pillars of Vision 2020 is the diversification of the economy. Rwanda recognized the need to move away from dependence on subsistence agriculture and develop other sectors that could drive economic growth. The government has actively promoted the development of industries such as tourism, information and communication technology (ICT), financial services, and manufacturing. This diversification has not only created new income-generating opportunities but also improved the resilience of the economy.

Investment in Human Capital Rwanda understood the importance of investing in its people to achieve sustainable development. The government prioritized human capital development through investments in education, healthcare, and skills training. Efforts were made to improve access to quality education at all levels, with a particular focus on science, technology, engineering, and mathematics (STEM) subjects. The country also implemented innovative programs like the

One Laptop per Child initiative, which aimed to provide every primary school student with a laptop computer to enhance learning outcomes.

Infrastructure Development Recognizing the crucial role of infrastructure in economic growth, Rwanda placed a strong emphasis on infrastructure development. Significant investments were made in improving road networks, expanding access to electricity, and enhancing digital connectivity. These infrastructure projects have not only facilitated the movement of goods and services but also attracted private sector investments and fostered economic activities in various sectors.

Poverty Alleviation Strategies

Rwanda's commitment to poverty alleviation is evident in its comprehensive strategies and programs targeted at improving the lives of the most vulnerable segments of society. The government recognizes that poverty is a multidimensional problem that requires a holistic approach. Let's explore some of the key strategies employed by Rwanda to alleviate poverty.

Social Protection Programs Rwanda has implemented a range of social protection programs aimed at providing support to the poorest and most vulnerable individuals and households. The flagship program, known as the Vision 2020 Umurenge Program (VUP), provides direct cash transfers and public works opportunities to vulnerable households. This program not only helps alleviate immediate poverty but also promotes human capital development and social inclusion.

Promotion of Agriculture Agriculture remains a significant sector in Rwanda's economy, employing a large portion of the population. The government has implemented various initiatives to modernize the agricultural sector, increase productivity, and improve access to markets. These efforts include the distribution of certified seeds, provision of agricultural extension services, and investment in irrigation infrastructure. By promoting sustainable agriculture practices and supporting smallholder farmers, Rwanda aims to reduce poverty and enhance food security.

Financial Inclusion Access to financial services is crucial for economic empowerment and poverty alleviation. Rwanda recognized this and has taken steps to promote financial inclusion. The government has encouraged the establishment of microfinance institutions and community-based savings and credit cooperatives. Additionally, digital financial services, such as mobile banking and mobile money, have been promoted to ensure that even the most remote communities have access to financial services.

Results and Impact

Rwanda's development strategy and poverty alleviation efforts have yielded impressive results. Since the early 2000s, the country has experienced strong economic growth, with an average annual GDP growth rate of around 7%. Poverty rates have significantly declined, and human development indicators have improved.

Economic Growth Rwanda's GDP has more than tripled since the early 2000s, driven by robust performances in sectors such as services, industry, and agriculture. The country has attracted foreign direct investment, particularly in the tourism and manufacturing sectors, which has contributed to job creation and export diversification. Rwanda's commitment to improving the business environment through regulatory reforms and investment in infrastructure has also been instrumental in attracting investments.

Poverty Reduction Rwanda has made substantial progress in reducing poverty. Between 2000 and 2017, the national poverty rate declined from 59% to 39%. This reduction was more significant in rural areas, where poverty rates dropped from 71% to 45%. Social protection programs, agricultural interventions, and investments in human capital have played a crucial role in poverty reduction.

Social Development Rwanda has made remarkable strides in social development indicators. The country has achieved universal primary education and significantly increased secondary school enrollment rates. Access to healthcare services has improved, leading to a decline in child and maternal mortality rates. Additionally, the government's commitment to gender equality has resulted in increased representation of women in decision-making roles.

Lessons Learned

Rwanda's development strategy and poverty alleviation efforts offer valuable lessons for other countries facing similar challenges. Here are some key takeaways:

Leadership and Good Governance Rwanda's progress can be attributed to strong leadership, a clear vision, and effective governance. President Paul Kagame's unwavering commitment to development, coupled with the promotion of accountability and transparency, has been instrumental in driving the country's transformation.

Holistic Approach to Poverty Alleviation Rwanda's approach to poverty reduction centered on a comprehensive set of interventions targeting various dimensions of poverty. The combination of social protection programs, agricultural development, and infrastructure investments helped address the multiple causes and consequences of poverty.

Strategic Investments in Human Capital Investments in human capital, particularly in education and healthcare, have been critical in fueling Rwanda's progress. By prioritizing human development, the country has built a strong foundation for sustainable economic growth and poverty reduction.

Inclusive Approach to Development Rwanda's commitment to inclusivity has been a key driver of its success. Efforts to promote gender equality, address regional disparities, and empower marginalized groups have yielded positive outcomes and contributed to social cohesion.

Conclusion

Rwanda's development strategy and poverty alleviation efforts demonstrate the transformative power of effective governance, a clear vision, and comprehensive approaches to development. The country has achieved remarkable progress in a relatively short period, proving that with the right policies and investments, even the most challenging situations can be overcome. By drawing valuable lessons from Rwanda's success, other countries can chart their path towards sustainable development and poverty reduction.

Key Terms

- Vision 2020
- Social protection programs
- Umurenge Program

- Financial inclusion

- GDP growth rate

- Universal primary education

Sweden's Welfare State and Gender Equality

Sweden is known for its strong welfare state and commitment to gender equality. The country has implemented a range of policies and programs aimed at reducing poverty, promoting social inclusion, and ensuring equal opportunities for all citizens, regardless of gender. In this section, we will explore the key features of Sweden's welfare state and examine its impact on gender equality.

The Swedish Welfare State

The Swedish welfare state is based on the principles of egalitarianism and solidarity. It aims to provide citizens with high-quality public services and a strong social safety net. The welfare system in Sweden is comprehensive, covering various areas such as healthcare, education, childcare, unemployment benefits, and pensions.

One of the cornerstones of Sweden's welfare state is its universal healthcare system. All citizens have access to medical care, and the government ensures that healthcare services are of high quality and affordable. This universal healthcare system has contributed to the overall well-being of the population and has helped reduce health inequalities.

Education is another area where Sweden's welfare state has made significant investments. The country provides free education at all levels, including preschool, primary school, secondary school, and higher education. This commitment to education has led to a highly educated population and has played a crucial role in Sweden's economic success.

The Swedish welfare state also prioritizes childcare and parental leave policies. Parents are entitled to generous parental leave, allowing them to take time off work to care for their children. Childcare services are widely available and subsidized, making it easier for parents to combine work and family responsibilities. These policies have contributed to gender equality by promoting greater equality in caregiving responsibilities and facilitating women's participation in the labor market.

Gender Equality in Sweden

Sweden is internationally recognized as a leader in promoting gender equality. The country has made significant progress in closing gender gaps in various areas, including the workplace, politics, and social norms.

In the workplace, Sweden has implemented policies to address the gender pay gap and promote greater gender balance in leadership positions. Employers are required to conduct regular pay audits to identify and address gender-based pay disparities. Additionally, companies with more than 25 employees must have a gender equality plan in place, outlining measures to promote gender equality in the workplace.

Another key aspect of gender equality in Sweden is the promotion of work-life balance. The government has implemented policies such as flexible working hours, parental leave, and support for childcare services. These measures help both men and women balance their work and family responsibilities and contribute to greater gender equality.

Sweden has also taken steps to combat gender-based violence and promote gender equality in society. The government has implemented comprehensive policies to prevent domestic violence, improve support for victims, and raise awareness about gender-based violence. Organizations and initiatives focused on gender equality, such as the Swedish Women's Lobby and the #MeToo movement, have played a significant role in driving societal change and promoting gender equality.

Challenges and Future Directions

While Sweden has made significant progress in promoting gender equality, challenges still remain. Gender segregation in the labor market and occupational segregation persist, with women being underrepresented in certain industries and sectors. Efforts are underway to address this issue through targeted measures, such as promoting girls' interest in science, technology, engineering, and mathematics (STEM) fields.

Furthermore, despite the progress made, there is still work to be done to ensure equal representation of women in leadership positions, both in the public and private sectors. Initiatives promoting quotas for women on company boards and in politics have been implemented to address this issue, but more needs to be done to achieve full gender equality in decision-making positions.

In the future, Sweden will continue to focus on gender equality, with a particular emphasis on intersectionality. Efforts will be made to address the unique challenges faced by women of different backgrounds, including immigrant women and women with disabilities. Intersectional approaches to gender equality will help create a more inclusive and equal society for all.

Conclusion

Sweden's welfare state and commitment to gender equality have had a profound impact on the country's success. The comprehensive welfare system ensures that all citizens have access to essential services, promoting social inclusion and reducing poverty. Gender equality measures, such as parental leave policies and support for childcare services, have contributed to greater gender equality in the workplace and society as a whole.

While challenges remain, Sweden serves as a role model for other countries seeking to achieve gender equality and build a fair and inclusive society. By continuing to prioritize gender equality and investing in social welfare, Sweden is laying the groundwork for a more equitable future.

Chapter 10: Future Perspectives on Economic Success

Chapter 10: Future Perspectives on Economic Success

Chapter 10: Future Perspectives on Economic Success

In this final chapter, we will explore the future perspectives on economic success and discuss the emerging trends and challenges that will shape the modern economy. We will also examine the innovations that hold the potential to drive economic growth and prosperity in the years to come. By understanding these future perspectives, we can better prepare ourselves to navigate the ever-changing economic landscape and seize the opportunities that arise.

10.1 The Interplay of Technology and Economics

Over the past few decades, technology has played a transformative role in shaping the global economy. From the internet to artificial intelligence, technological advancements have revolutionized industries and created new pathways for economic success. In this section, we will delve deeper into the interplay of technology and economics, and explore how emerging trends will impact the future of economic success.

10.1.1 Harnessing Artificial Intelligence and Machine Learning

Artificial intelligence (AI) and machine learning (ML) are advancing at an unprecedented pace, opening up new avenues for economic growth and innovation. AI and ML technologies have the potential to automate routine tasks and enhance productivity across various sectors. For example, autonomous vehicles powered by AI can revolutionize transportation, reducing costs and improving efficiency. Additionally, ML algorithms can analyze vast amounts of data to unlock valuable insights and support decision-making processes.

However, the integration of AI and ML into the economy presents challenges and considerations. One major concern is the potential displacement of jobs due to automation. It is crucial to implement strategies that facilitate a smooth transition for workers and ensure new job creation in emerging sectors. Additionally, ensuring ethical AI deployment and addressing biases is essential to prevent negative consequences and maintain public trust.

10.1.2 Biomedical Innovations and Genetic Engineering

Advancements in biotechnology, genetic engineering, and biomedical research hold immense promise for economic success in the coming years. Breakthroughs in these fields can lead to the development of new drugs, treatments, and medical technologies, improving healthcare outcomes and creating lucrative opportunities. Moreover, genetic engineering can revolutionize agriculture, enhancing crop yields and food security in a rapidly growing global population.

However, along with these advancements come ethical considerations and potential risks. Striking a balance between innovation and ethical guidelines is paramount in ensuring the responsible development and deployment of genetic engineering and biotech innovations.

10.1.3 Blockchain Technology and Decentralized Finance

Blockchain technology has gained significant attention in recent years due to its potential to disrupt traditional financial systems and drive economic success. This decentralized and transparent ledger technology has the power to streamline processes, reduce fraud and costs, and enhance financial inclusion.

Blockchain's applications extend beyond finance and can revolutionize diverse sectors such as supply chain management, healthcare, and energy. By eliminating intermediaries and enabling peer-to-peer transactions, blockchain can create more efficient and secure systems.

However, challenges such as scalability, regulatory frameworks, and public adoption need to be addressed for widespread implementation. Collaborative efforts between governments, industries, and academia are crucial in harnessing the full potential of blockchain technology.

10.2 Navigating Climate Change and Environmental Sustainability

As the world grapples with the challenges of climate change and environmental degradation, the future of economic success will be closely intertwined with sustainability. In this section, we will explore the implications of climate change for the economy and discuss strategies for achieving sustainable economic growth.

10.2.1 Green Technologies and Renewable Energy

Addressing climate change requires a shift towards clean and renewable energy sources. Investments in green technologies, such as solar and wind power, can create new economic opportunities while reducing greenhouse gas emissions. Additionally, the development of energy-efficient technologies and sustainable infrastructure can promote resource conservation and resilience in the face of environmental challenges.

However, the transition to a sustainable energy system requires significant investments and coordination among governments, businesses, and communities. Policymakers must create favorable incentives and regulatory frameworks to promote the adoption of green technologies.

10.2.2 Circular Economy and Resource Efficiency

Moving away from the traditional linear "take-make-dispose" model, the concept of a circular economy emphasizes the value of reducing, reusing, and recycling resources. By embracing circular practices, businesses can optimize resource utilization, reduce waste generation, and drive economic growth. This approach encourages innovation and promotes a more sustainable and resilient economy.

To unlock the full potential of the circular economy, collaboration between stakeholders is crucial. Governments can incentivize circular practices through policies and regulations, while businesses can foster innovation and develop sustainable business models.

10.2.3 Adapting to Climate Risks and Resilience

Climate change poses significant risks to economies, societies, and ecosystems. Adaptation measures are essential to ensure economic success in a changing climate. Building resilience to climate-related events, such as extreme weather events and sea-level rise, requires a comprehensive approach that involves infrastructure development, risk assessment, and community engagement.

Investments in climate resilience can create new markets and job opportunities, particularly in sectors such as infrastructure, renewable energy, and disaster risk management. By adopting adaptive practices, societies can minimize the economic disruptions caused by climate change.

10.3 Collaboration and Knowledge Sharing for Global Economic Success

In an interconnected and globalized world, collaboration and knowledge sharing play a vital role in achieving economic success. In this section, we will examine the importance of international cooperation and explore how shared knowledge can contribute to global prosperity.

10.3.1 Global Economic Cooperation and Governance

Global economic cooperation through international organizations, such as the World Trade Organization and the International Monetary Fund, is crucial in addressing transnational challenges and fostering economic growth. By facilitating dialogue and coordination, these institutions can promote fair trade practices, financial stability, and sustainable development.

However, global economic governance faces challenges such as protectionism, geopolitical tensions, and inequality. Overcoming these obstacles requires strengthened international cooperation and collective efforts towards inclusive and sustainable economic systems.

10.3.2 Collaboration in Research and Development

Collaborative research and development (R&D) efforts are vital for fostering innovation and driving economic success. By sharing knowledge, expertise, and resources, researchers and institutions can collectively address complex challenges and accelerate technological advancements.

Public-private partnerships and cross-sector collaborations can unlock synergies and promote knowledge exchange. Governments can incentivize collaboration through funding programs and supportive policies, while businesses can establish networks and platforms for R&D cooperation.

10.3.3 Open Data and Information Sharing

Open data initiatives and information sharing are instrumental in democratizing access to knowledge and empowering individuals and businesses. By making data freely available, governments and organizations can stimulate innovation, inform policy decisions, and enable evidence-based solutions to societal challenges.

However, ensuring data privacy, security, and ethical use is essential in an interconnected digital world. Robust data protection frameworks and transparent governance mechanisms are necessary to build trust and foster responsible data sharing practices.

10.4 Lessons from the Past for Future Success

As we chart the course towards economic success in the future, it is essential to learn from the past and draw insights from historical patterns. In this final section, we reflect on lessons learned and highlight key principles for achieving long-term prosperity.

10.4.1 Historical Patterns and Cyclical Nature of Economic Success

Throughout history, economies have experienced cycles of growth, recession, and recovery. Understanding these patterns can help policymakers and businesses anticipate economic trends and implement strategies to mitigate risks and maximize opportunities.

By analyzing the causes and consequences of past economic cycles, we can identify early warning signs and develop resilience measures. Additionally, diversifying economies and reducing dependence on single sectors can enhance long-term economic stability.

10.4.2 Sustainable Development and Long-Term Prosperity

Sustainable development is vital for achieving long-term economic success. By considering the environmental, social, and economic dimensions of development, societies can meet present needs without compromising the ability of future generations to meet their own needs.

Incorporating sustainability principles into policy frameworks, business strategies, and individual actions is crucial for creating a more inclusive and resilient economy. By valuing natural and social capital alongside economic capital, we can build a foundation for long-term prosperity.

10.4.3 Collaboration and Knowledge Sharing for Global Economic Success

In a rapidly evolving world, collaboration and knowledge sharing are key drivers of economic success. By embracing the power of collective action and fostering a culture of cooperation, societies can leverage diverse perspectives and expertise to overcome complex challenges.

The exchange of ideas, technologies, and best practices can lead to breakthrough innovations and inclusive growth. By fostering an environment that promotes collaboration and knowledge sharing, we can shape a future where economic success is not only achieved but also shared by all.

Conclusion

In this final chapter, we have explored the future perspectives on economic success. We examined the interplay of technology and economics, the importance of sustainability and adaptation to climate change, the significance of collaboration and knowledge sharing, and key lessons from the past. By considering these insights and embracing innovation, sustainability, and collaboration, we can pave the way for a future of economic success that benefits individuals, societies, and the planet as a whole.

As we conclude this book, remember that economic success is not a destination but a continuous journey. It requires adaptability, resilience, and a commitment to learning and growth. By harnessing the transformative power of ideas, research, and human potential, we can shape a future where economic success is achieved hand in hand with social progress and environmental sustainability. So, let us embark on this journey together and create a better future for all.

Emerging Trends and Challenges

Technological Disruptions and Automation

In today's rapidly evolving world, technological disruptions and automation have become significant drivers of economic success. The integration of advanced technologies, such as artificial intelligence (AI), machine learning, robotics, and the internet of things (IoT), is reshaping industries, transforming business models, and revolutionizing the way we live and work. This section explores the impact of technological disruptions and automation on the economy, the challenges they pose, and the potential opportunities they create.

The Rise of Technological Disruptions

Technological disruptions refer to the rapid and profound changes brought about by the introduction of new technologies or the application of existing technologies in innovative ways. These disruptions have the potential to fundamentally alter how industries operate, create new markets, and render traditional business models obsolete. The increasing speed of technological advancements has fueled the rise of disruptions, enabling breakthrough innovations and accelerating their adoption.

One prominent example of technological disruption is the rise of e-commerce platforms like Amazon. By leveraging the power of the internet and advanced logistics systems, Amazon has transformed the retail industry, challenging brick-and-mortar stores and revolutionizing the way consumers shop. This shift has not only impacted traditional retailers but has also created new opportunities for small businesses and entrepreneurs to reach a wider audience through online platforms.

Another example is the revolution in transportation through ride-sharing services like Uber and Lyft. These platforms have disrupted the taxi industry by providing convenient, affordable, and efficient transportation services through the use of mobile applications and advanced GPS tracking. This disruptive innovation has not only transformed the way people commute but has also created new job opportunities for drivers and stimulated economic growth in the gig economy.

The Impact of Automation on the Economy

Automation, on the other hand, refers to the use of technology to perform tasks or processes with minimal human intervention. This can involve the use of robots, AI, and computer algorithms to carry out repetitive or complex tasks more efficiently and accurately than humans. While automation offers numerous benefits, such as increased productivity and cost savings, it also raises concerns about job displacement and income inequality.

One area where automation has had a profound impact is manufacturing. The introduction of robots and advanced machinery has revolutionized production processes, leading to increased efficiency, precision, and output. However, this has also led to a decline in manufacturing jobs, as machines can perform tasks that were previously carried out by humans. To mitigate the negative effects of automation, workers need to acquire new skills that complement the capabilities of machines, such as problem-solving, creativity, and adaptability.

Automation is not limited to manufacturing; it is also transforming sectors such as agriculture, healthcare, finance, and logistics. For example, in agriculture, autonomous drones and robotic systems are being used for precision farming, enhancing crop yields and reducing resource waste. In healthcare, AI algorithms are being developed to diagnose diseases, recommend treatment plans, and analyze medical data to improve patient outcomes. These advancements have the potential to increase efficiency, reduce costs, and improve the quality of services in various sectors.

Challenges and Opportunities

The widespread adoption of technological disruptions and automation presents both challenges and opportunities for individuals, businesses, and governments. On one hand, the displacement of jobs due to automation raises concerns about unemployment and income inequality. However, on the other hand, it also creates new job opportunities in emerging industries and leads to the creation of entirely new sectors.

To harness the opportunities presented by technological disruptions and automation, individuals need to adapt and acquire the necessary skills. Lifelong learning and continuous education are crucial to stay relevant in a rapidly changing job market. By continuously upgrading their skills, individuals can take advantage of the new opportunities created by technological advancements and secure their economic success.

Businesses also face the challenge of embracing and integrating new technologies into their operations. They need to innovate and transform their business models to remain competitive in an increasingly digital world. Collaboration with technology providers, start-ups, and research institutions can facilitate the adoption of emerging technologies and drive growth.

Governments play a critical role in ensuring that the benefits of technological disruptions and automation are widely shared. They need to develop policies that promote innovation, education, and skills development. Additionally, governments can implement social safety nets and retraining programs to support workers affected by job displacement and create a favorable environment for entrepreneurship and economic growth.

Case Study: Automation in the Automotive Industry

The automotive industry provides a compelling case study of the impact of automation on an industry and its workforce. Over the past few decades, automation has revolutionized manufacturing processes, leading to increased productivity, improved quality, and reduced costs. However, this transformation has also resulted in significant changes in the labor market.

Automation has enabled the adoption of robotics and advanced assembly line technologies in automobile production. These technologies allow for the efficient and precise assembly of vehicles, leading to higher output and improved safety. As a result, the automotive industry has seen a decline in the number of workers required for production.

While automation has reduced the demand for certain types of jobs, it has also created new job opportunities in areas such as robotics maintenance, programming, and data analysis. Additionally, as automotive companies invest in research and development for electric and autonomous vehicles, there is a growing need for skilled engineers and software developers.

Overall, the case of the automotive industry highlights the importance of adapting to technological disruptions and automation. By upskilling and reskilling the workforce, individuals can remain employable in a changing industry. At the same time, businesses and governments must collaborate to create an enabling environment that encourages innovation, investment, and the development of new skills.

Conclusion

Technological disruptions and automation are reshaping the modern economy, presenting both challenges and opportunities. The rapid pace of innovation and the integration of advanced technologies have the potential to transform industries, increase productivity, and drive economic growth. However, the displacement of jobs and the need for upskilling require individuals, businesses, and governments to adapt and embrace the changes brought about by automation.

To navigate the disruptions and harness the opportunities, individuals must be proactive in acquiring new skills and lifelong learning. Businesses need to innovate and transform their operations to remain competitive in a rapidly changing market. Governments play a critical role in creating an enabling environment through policies that promote innovation, education, and social safety nets.

By understanding the impact of technological disruptions and automation, and by actively engaging with the changes, individuals, businesses, and governments can foster economic success and ensure inclusive and sustainable growth. The future holds immense potential for those who can adapt and leverage the power of technology for economic advancement.

Climate Change and Environmental Sustainability

Climate change and environmental sustainability are pressing issues that have significant implications for economic success in the modern world. In this section, we will explore the causes and consequences of climate change, discuss the importance of sustainable practices, and explore innovative solutions for a more environmentally friendly future.

Causes of Climate Change

Climate change refers to long-term shifts in weather patterns and average temperatures on Earth. The primary cause of climate change is the increase in greenhouse gas emissions, mainly carbon dioxide (CO_2), methane (CH_4), and nitrous oxide (N_2O), due to human activities. These gases trap heat in the atmosphere, leading to a rise in global temperatures.

The primary sources of greenhouse gas emissions include the burning of fossil fuels for energy production, industrial processes, deforestation, and agriculture. As these activities continue to release large amounts of CO_2 and other greenhouse gases into the atmosphere, the Earth's temperature continues to rise, causing a range of negative impacts.

Consequences of Climate Change

Climate change has far-reaching consequences for our environment, society, and economy. Rising global temperatures contribute to the melting of polar ice caps and glaciers, causing sea levels to rise. This increase in sea levels threatens coastal communities, as well as low-lying islands and countries, with the risk of inundation and displacement of populations.

Furthermore, climate change leads to more frequent and severe weather events, such as hurricanes, heatwaves, droughts, and floods. These events result in damage to infrastructure, loss of agricultural productivity, and increased insurance costs, which can have devastating effects on economies.

The impacts of climate change are not limited to the environment and economy alone but also have social implications. Vulnerable populations, including the poor, elderly, and marginalized communities, are particularly at risk from the consequences of climate change. It exacerbates existing social inequalities and can lead to social unrest and displacement.

The Importance of Sustainable Practices

To address the challenges posed by climate change, it is essential to adopt sustainable practices that focus on reducing greenhouse gas emissions and promoting environmental sustainability. Sustainable practices encompass a range of actions that aim to minimize the environmental impact of human activities and ensure the long-term availability of natural resources.

One crucial aspect of sustainability is transitioning to cleaner and renewable sources of energy, such as solar, wind, and hydropower. By reducing reliance on fossil fuels, we can reduce greenhouse gas emissions and mitigate the harmful effects of climate change. Additionally, energy efficiency measures can help reduce overall energy consumption and decrease carbon footprints.

Another critical component of sustainability is the conservation and protection of ecosystems and biodiversity. This involves preserving natural habitats, preventing deforestation, and promoting sustainable land use practices. The conservation of ecosystems not only helps maintain biodiversity but also provides valuable ecosystem services, such as water purification, carbon sequestration, and soil fertility.

Sustainable agriculture is another vital aspect of environmental sustainability. By adopting organic farming methods, minimizing pesticide and fertilizer use, and promoting crop diversification, we can reduce the environmental impact of agriculture while ensuring food security and economic viability for farmers.

Innovative Solutions for Environmental Sustainability

Addressing climate change requires innovative solutions at various levels, from individual actions to international cooperation. Here are some examples of innovative solutions for environmental sustainability:

- **Carbon pricing**: Implementing carbon pricing mechanisms, such as carbon taxes or cap-and-trade systems, can incentivize businesses and individuals to reduce their greenhouse gas emissions. These market-based approaches provide economic incentives for adopting clean technologies and reducing carbon footprints.

- **Renewable energy investments**: Governments, businesses, and individuals can invest in renewable energy projects to accelerate the transition away from fossil fuels. This includes supporting research and development of renewable technologies, as well as providing financial incentives for renewable energy adoption.

- **Green infrastructure:** Developing green infrastructure, such as green buildings, sustainable transportation systems, and smart grids, can help reduce energy consumption and promote sustainable urban development. Green infrastructure solutions focus on energy efficiency, renewable energy integration, and sustainable management of resources.

- **Circular economy:** Shifting towards a circular economy model, where resources are recycled and waste is minimized, can help reduce greenhouse gas emissions and promote sustainable consumption. This involves designing products for longevity and recyclability, implementing waste management strategies, and promoting the reuse and recycling of materials.

- **International cooperation:** Climate change is a global issue that requires international cooperation and collaboration. Countries need to work together to set and achieve ambitious emissions reduction targets, share clean technologies, and provide financial support to developing nations for climate adaptation and mitigation efforts.

The Role of Economics in Addressing Climate Change

Economics plays a crucial role in addressing climate change and promoting environmental sustainability. Economic tools and concepts can guide policy decisions and facilitate the transition to a more sustainable future.

One key economic concept is the **social cost of carbon** (SCC), which represents the economic damages associated with each additional ton of CO_2 emitted into the atmosphere. The SCC helps policymakers and businesses assess the costs and benefits of different mitigation strategies and guide climate policy.

Furthermore, **cost-benefit analysis** can be used to evaluate the economic viability of climate change adaptation and mitigation projects. This analysis compares the costs of implementing a project or policy with the expected benefits, including avoided damages from climate change impacts. It helps prioritize investments and identify the most effective strategies for reducing emissions and building resilience.

Additionally, the field of **environmental economics** explores the relationship between the economy and the environment and seeks to develop policies that achieve a balance between economic growth and environmental sustainability. This field examines the economic incentives and market mechanisms that can promote environmental conservation and the efficient allocation of environmental resources.

Conclusion

Climate change and environmental sustainability are critical issues that require urgent action. By understanding the causes and consequences of climate change and adopting sustainable practices, we can mitigate the harmful effects and build a more resilient and prosperous future.

In this section, we explored the importance of climate change and environmental sustainability, discussed innovative solutions for a more sustainable future, and highlighted the role of economics in addressing these challenges. It is through collective efforts, both at individual and global levels, that we can achieve economic success in harmony with the environment.

Global Economic Cooperation and Governance

In today's interconnected world, global economic cooperation and governance play a vital role in shaping the success of economies. As countries become increasingly interconnected through trade, finance, and technology, effective cooperation and governance mechanisms are essential for promoting economic growth, stability, and sustainability. This section explores the importance of global economic cooperation and governance, the challenges it faces, and potential solutions for a prosperous future.

The Importance of Global Economic Cooperation

Global economic cooperation refers to collaborative efforts among countries to address common economic challenges, pursue shared goals, and promote inclusive and sustainable development. Cooperation can take various forms, including multilateral agreements, international organizations, and regional collaborations. The following reasons highlight the significance of global economic cooperation:

1. **Promotion of Free Trade and Open Markets:** Cooperation among nations fosters the development of international trade and investment, leading to economic growth and job creation. By reducing barriers to trade, such as tariffs and quotas, countries can expand their markets, access resources and technologies, and benefit from economies of scale.

2. **Strengthening Financial Stability:** Cooperation in financial governance helps prevent and address financial crises. Countries can work together to establish regulatory frameworks, share information, and coordinate policies to ensure the stability of global financial systems. This enhances investor confidence, reduces risks, and promotes sustainable economic growth.

3. **Addressing Global Challenges:** Many contemporary economic challenges, including climate change, inequality, and poverty, transcend national borders. Global cooperation is crucial to finding coordinated solutions to such challenges, as they require collective action, shared resources, and knowledge exchange. Collaborative efforts can lead to the development of sustainable development goals, frameworks, and policies.

4. **Enhancing Innovation and Technological Advancement:** Cooperation facilitates the exchange of ideas, knowledge, and technology among countries. Collaboration in research and development, intellectual property rights protection, and technology transfer can accelerate innovation, foster productivity growth, and drive economic success.

Challenges in Global Economic Cooperation

While global economic cooperation offers immense benefits, it faces several challenges that hinder its effectiveness. Understanding these challenges is essential for devising appropriate measures and strategies. The following are key challenges faced in global economic cooperation:

1. **Divergent National Interests:** Countries may have different priorities, interests, and policy agendas, making consensus-building and decision-making challenging. Overcoming divergences and finding common ground requires effective negotiation, compromise, and understanding of each nation's unique circumstances.

2. **Political Fragmentation:** The geopolitical landscape is characterized by multiple power centers, differing ideologies, and regional conflicts. Political fragmentation can hinder cooperative efforts, impede policy coordination, and stall decision-making processes. Overcoming these challenges requires diplomatic engagement and building trust among nations.

3. **Inequality and Disparities:** Widening income and wealth gaps both within and between countries pose significant challenges to cooperation. Disparities can undermine trust and solidarity, leading to resistance in sharing resources, cooperating on trade, or addressing global challenges. Promoting inclusive growth and equitable development should be a priority to strengthen cooperation.

4. **Complex Governance Structures:** The existing architecture of global economic governance is often criticized for being complex and fragmented. The presence of multiple organizations, forums, and agreements can lead to duplication, overlapping mandates, and inefficiencies. Streamlining and improving governance structures can enhance coordination and effectiveness.

Promoting Effective Global Economic Cooperation and Governance

To overcome the challenges and harness the benefits of global economic cooperation, various strategies can be pursued. These strategies aim to establish inclusive, transparent, and accountable governance systems that facilitate cooperation and provide a platform for addressing shared economic challenges. Some key considerations include:

1. **Strengthening Multilateral Organizations:** Multilateral organizations, such as the United Nations, World Trade Organization, and International Monetary Fund, play a crucial role in global economic governance. Strengthening these organizations by improving representation, decision-making processes, and accountability can enhance cooperation among nations.

2. **Advancing Sustainable Development Goals:** Recognizing the interconnected nature of economic, social, and environmental challenges, countries should work collaboratively to achieve the United Nations' Sustainable Development Goals. Cooperation in areas like climate action, poverty alleviation, and education can create a framework for shared progress.

3. **Enhancing Regional Integration:** Regional cooperation can serve as an effective stepping stone towards global economic cooperation. By deepening economic integration, harmonizing regulations, and promoting trade and investment within regions, countries can strengthen their collective voice and enhance their capacity for global cooperation.

4. **Promoting Knowledge Sharing:** Facilitating the exchange of best practices, experiences, and expertise among countries can foster innovation, capacity-building, and policy learning. Platforms for knowledge sharing can include international conferences, research collaborations, and development assistance programs.

5. **Engaging Civil Society and Private Sector:** Global economic cooperation should involve not just governments but also civil society organizations and the private sector. Partnerships and collaborations across sectors can leverage resources, expertise, and networks, leading to more comprehensive and sustainable solutions.

Global economic cooperation and governance are critical for achieving shared prosperity, addressing global challenges, and ensuring sustainable development. By fostering collaboration, resolving conflicts, and promoting inclusive participation, countries can work towards a more prosperous and equitable future.

Key Takeaways:

- Global economic cooperation plays a crucial role in promoting economic growth, stability, and sustainability.

- Cooperation facilitates free trade, strengthens financial stability, addresses global challenges, and fosters innovation.

- Challenges in global economic cooperation include divergent national interests, political fragmentation, inequality, and complex governance structures.

- Strategies for promoting effective cooperation include strengthening multilateral organizations, advancing sustainable development goals, enhancing regional integration, promoting knowledge sharing, and engaging civil society and the private sector.

Discussion Questions:

1. Think of a recent example where global economic cooperation has successfully addressed a common challenge. Discuss the key factors that contributed to its success.

2. In what ways can regional integration initiatives promote global economic cooperation? Provide specific examples.

3. How can the private sector contribute to global economic cooperation? Discuss the benefits and potential challenges of public-private partnerships in this context.

Innovations for Future Economic Success

Artificial Intelligence and Machine Learning

Artificial Intelligence (AI) and Machine Learning (ML) are two closely related fields that have gained significant attention and prominence in recent years. They have the potential to revolutionize various aspects of our lives, including the economy, healthcare, transportation, and more. In this section, we will explore the principles, applications, and challenges of AI and ML in the context of economic success.

Principles of AI and ML

AI is a broad field that aims to develop intelligent machines capable of performing tasks that typically require human intelligence. ML, on the other hand, is a subfield of AI that focuses on algorithms and statistical models to enable computers to learn from and make predictions or decisions based on data. ML techniques provide the foundation for many practical applications of AI.

The principles of AI and ML are rooted in mathematics, statistics, and computer science. At the core of ML is the concept of a learning algorithm, which allows machines to extract patterns from data, learn from experience, and improve their performance over time. Key principles include:

- **Supervised Learning**: This approach uses labeled training data to teach the ML model to make predictions or classify new, unseen data. It involves input-output pairs, where the model learns the relationship between inputs and corresponding outputs through iterative training.

- **Unsupervised Learning**: Unsupervised learning involves training ML models on unlabeled data to discover hidden patterns or structures within the dataset. It is particularly useful when the desired outputs are unknown or the dataset is too large to be labeled manually.

- **Reinforcement Learning**: Reinforcement learning deals with training ML models to make decisions based on evaluating actions and receiving feedback from the environment. It involves maximizing a reward signal to optimize the model's behavior and achieve a predefined goal.

Applications of AI and ML in Economics

The integration of AI and ML into various economic domains has the potential to drive significant economic success. Here are some key applications:

- **Financial Forecasting**: AI and ML techniques can be used to analyze vast amounts of historical financial data, identify patterns, and make predictions about future stock prices, market trends, and economic indicators. This information can guide investment decisions, reduce risks, and improve overall financial performance.

- **Customer Segmentation and Personalization**: By analyzing customer data, AI and ML algorithms can identify distinct customer segments and personalize marketing strategies, product recommendations, and pricing strategies. This personalized approach can enhance customer satisfaction, increase sales, and drive business growth.

- **Supply Chain Optimization:** AI and ML models can analyze supply chain data, including inventory levels, production capacity, transportation costs, and demand forecasts, to optimize various aspects of the supply chain. This can lead to more efficient operations, reduced costs, and improved customer service.

- **Fraud Detection:** AI and ML algorithms can analyze large volumes of transaction data to detect patterns indicative of fraudulent activities, such as credit card fraud, identity theft, or money laundering. By automating fraud detection processes, financial institutions can minimize losses and protect both themselves and their customers.

- **Labor Market Analysis:** AI and ML techniques can be used to analyze labor market data, job postings, and resumes to identify skill gaps, predict future job demands, and optimize workforce planning. This can help policymakers and businesses make more informed decisions regarding education, training, and employment policies.

Challenges and Ethical Considerations

While the potential benefits of AI and ML are immense, several challenges and ethical considerations need to be addressed for their responsible and sustainable implementation. Some of the key challenges include:

- **Data Quality and Bias:** AI and ML models heavily rely on high-quality, unbiased data for accurate predictions. However, biases present in the training data can lead to biased outputs and discriminatory outcomes. Ensuring data quality and addressing biases are crucial steps in preventing discriminatory practices.

- **Interpretability and Explainability:** Many AI and ML models, such as deep neural networks, are often considered black boxes, making it difficult to interpret their decision-making process. Ensuring transparency and explainability of AI systems is essential for user trust, fairness, and accountability.

- **Privacy and Security:** The increasing use of AI and ML involves the collection, storage, and analysis of vast amounts of personal and sensitive data. Safeguarding privacy and ensuring data security are critical to protect individuals from potential harm and misuse of their information.

- **Job Displacement and Inequality**: The automation potential of AI and ML raises concerns about job displacement and growing inequality. While new job opportunities may arise, there is a need for policies and strategies to reskill and upskill the workforce to ensure a smooth transition and reduce inequality.

Addressing these challenges and incorporating ethical considerations are essential for the responsible and sustainable deployment of AI and ML technologies in the pursuit of economic success.

Resources and Further Reading

Here are some recommended resources and further reading for those interested in exploring more about AI and ML in the context of economic success:

- Bishop, C. M. (2006). *Pattern Recognition and Machine Learning.* Springer.

- Agrawal, A., Gans, J., & Goldfarb, A. (2018). *Prediction Machines: The Simple Economics of Artificial Intelligence.* Harvard Business Review Press.

- Brynjolfsson, E., & McAfee, A. (2014). *The Second Machine Age: Work, Progress, and Prosperity in a Time of Brilliant Technologies.* W. W. Norton & Company.

- Narayanan, A., & Lemoine, B. (2018). *The AI Now Report 2018.* New York University.

Exercises

1. Describe three real-world applications of AI and ML in different economic sectors.

2. Explain the difference between supervised, unsupervised, and reinforcement learning in the context of ML.

3. Discuss the potential challenges and ethical considerations associated with the use of AI and ML in financial forecasting.

4. How can AI and ML be leveraged to address labor market challenges and optimize workforce planning?

5. Critically analyze the impact of biases in training data on the fairness and accountability of AI systems.

Fun Fact

Did you know that AI and ML are not limited to traditional computing devices? They are also being utilized in unconventional applications like smart home devices, autonomous vehicles, and even robots that can perform complex tasks. The possibilities are endless, and the future of AI and ML is full of exciting innovations!

Genetic Engineering and Biomedical Innovations

In recent decades, genetic engineering and biomedical innovations have revolutionized the field of medicine and opened up new possibilities for improving human health and well-being. With the advancement of technology, scientists and researchers have gained unprecedented control over the genetic makeup of living organisms, allowing them to manipulate genes and develop innovative solutions to various medical challenges. This section will explore the principles of genetic engineering, as well as the applications and potential impacts of these biomedical innovations.

Principles of Genetic Engineering

Genetic engineering involves the intentional modification of an organism's genetic material, allowing scientists to add, delete, or alter specific genes. The process typically involves the following steps:

1. **Identification and isolation of the target gene:** Scientists identify the specific gene or genes responsible for a particular trait or medical condition.

2. **Insertion of the gene into a vector:** The target gene is inserted into a vector, such as a plasmid or a viral vector, which serves as a carrier to transfer the gene into the target organism's cells.

3. **Delivery of the gene into the target organism's cells:** The vector containing the target gene is introduced into the target organism's cells through various methods, such as viral transduction, electroporation, or microinjection.

4. **Expression of the gene:** Once the gene is delivered into the target organism's cells, it integrates into the genome and starts expressing its desired traits or proteins.

Through genetic engineering, researchers can introduce desirable traits into organisms or modify existing traits. This technology has significantly impacted the field of medicine, offering new avenues for disease treatment, prevention, and diagnostics.

Applications of Genetic Engineering in Biomedical Innovations

Genetic engineering has found numerous applications in biomedical innovations, transforming the way we understand and address various medical conditions. Some of the notable applications include:

1. **Gene Therapy:** Gene therapy aims to treat or cure diseases by replacing or modifying defective genes in a patient's cells. This approach holds tremendous potential for treating genetic disorders such as cystic fibrosis, muscular dystrophy, and hemophilia.

2. **Pharmacogenomics:** Pharmacogenomics utilizes genetic information to personalize drug therapies. By analyzing an individual's genetic makeup, doctors can determine the most effective and safe medications for a specific patient, reducing the risk of adverse drug reactions and improving treatment outcomes.

3. **Genetic Testing and Screening:** Genetic testing allows the identification of genetic predispositions to certain diseases, helping individuals make informed decisions about their health. Additionally, prenatal genetic screening enables the detection of chromosomal abnormalities in fetuses, allowing parents to make informed choices about their pregnancy.

4. **Stem Cell Research and Therapy:** Stem cells have the unique ability to differentiate into various cell types, making them a valuable tool for regenerative medicine. Genetic engineering techniques are used to manipulate stem cells and guide their differentiation into specific cell types, offering potential treatments for conditions like spinal cord injuries, Parkinson's disease, and diabetes.

These applications of genetic engineering have the potential to revolutionize healthcare by providing more targeted and personalized treatments, improving patient outcomes, and enhancing our overall understanding of human biology.

Ethical Considerations and Future Challenges

While genetic engineering and biomedical innovations hold immense promise, they also raise important ethical considerations and face significant challenges. Some of the notable concerns include:

1. **Ethical use of gene editing technologies**: As gene editing technologies, such as CRISPR-Cas9, become more accessible and precise, the debate around the ethical use of these technologies intensifies. It raises questions about the potential misuse of gene editing, including designer babies and enhancement of human traits.

2. **Privacy and data security**: As genetic information becomes more readily available through genetic testing and screening, protecting individuals' privacy and securing their genetic data becomes crucial. Robust measures must be in place to ensure data privacy and prevent misuse of genetic information.

3. **Accessibility and affordability**: Despite the immense potential of genetic engineering and biomedical innovations, ensuring equitable access to these technologies remains a challenge. Addressing the issues of affordability and accessibility will be essential to ensure that these advancements benefit everyone, regardless of their socioeconomic status.

4. **Unintended consequences and long-term effects**: The long-term effects of genetic engineering and biomedical innovations are still being studied. It is crucial to carefully consider the potential unintended consequences and long-term effects of these technologies on both individuals and ecosystems.

In navigating these challenges, it is important for scientists, policymakers, and society as a whole to engage in thoughtful discussions and establish ethical frameworks to guide the responsible use of genetic engineering and biomedical innovations.

Examples of Genetic Engineering and Biomedical Innovations

Example 1: CRISPR-Cas9 Gene Editing

CRISPR-Cas9 is a revolutionary gene editing tool that enables precise modification of DNA sequences. This technology has the potential to treat genetic disorders, eradicate infectious diseases, and even address global challenges such as food security. For instance, scientists are exploring the use of CRISPR-Cas9 to modify crop plants, making them more resistant to pests, diseases, and climate change.

Example 2: Personalized Medicine

Advancements in genetic sequencing technologies have paved the way for personalized medicine. By analyzing an individual's genetic information, doctors can tailor treatments to the specific needs of the patient, leading to improved efficacy and reduced side effects. For instance, targeted therapies in cancer treatment are designed to match the genetic profile of a patient's tumor, increasing the likelihood of successful treatment.

Example 3: Organ Transplantation

Genetic engineering has the potential to address the critical shortage of organ donors for transplantation. Researchers are exploring the possibility of growing organs in the laboratory by manipulating stem cells. This could significantly alleviate the demand for organ transplants and reduce the risk of organ rejection, leading to a breakthrough in the field of transplantation medicine.

Resources and Further Reading

1. National Human Genome Research Institute: https://www.genome.gov/

2. World Health Organization: https://www.who.int/

3. Nature Biotechnology Journal: https://www.nature.com/nbt/index.html

4. National Institute of Biomedical Imaging and Bioengineering: https://www.nibib.nih.gov/

5. The CRISPR Journal: https://www.liebertpub.com/journals/crispr-journal/592/

Conclusion

Genetic engineering and biomedical innovations have transformed the landscape of medicine, offering new hope and possibilities for improving human health. With the ability to manipulate genes and develop innovative solutions, these advancements hold promise for treating genetic disorders, personalizing medical treatments, and addressing global health challenges. However, it is vital to navigate the ethical considerations and challenges associated with these technologies to ensure their responsible and equitable use. Continued research, dialogue, and collaboration will shape the future of genetic engineering and biomedical innovations, guiding us toward a healthier and more sustainable world.

Blockchain Technology and Decentralized Finance

Blockchain technology has taken the world by storm, revolutionizing various industries and creating new opportunities for economic success. One particular area where blockchain has made a significant impact is decentralized finance (DeFi). In this section, we will explore the principles and applications of blockchain technology in the context of DeFi, highlighting its potential to redefine traditional financial systems.

The Fundamentals of Blockchain Technology

Blockchain technology is a decentralized and distributed ledger system that provides a secure and transparent way of recording and verifying transactions. It operates on a peer-to-peer network, where participants, known as nodes, collectively maintain the integrity of the ledger. Let's delve into the key components and principles of blockchain technology.

Distributed Ledger At the heart of blockchain technology is the concept of a distributed ledger. Rather than relying on a central authority, such as a bank, to validate and store transaction records, blockchain allows multiple participants to maintain their own copy of the ledger. This decentralized nature ensures transparency, as everyone can independently verify the authenticity of transactions.

Cryptography and Security Blockchain utilizes advanced cryptographic techniques to ensure the security and immutability of transaction data. Each transaction is encrypted and linked to the previous transaction in a chain-like structure, creating a permanent and tamper-proof record. The use of cryptographic algorithms, such as hash functions and digital signatures, guarantees the integrity and authenticity of transactions.

Consensus Mechanisms Consensus mechanisms are the protocols that enable nodes in a blockchain network to agree on the validity of transactions and the overall state of the ledger. Examples of consensus mechanisms include Proof of Work (PoW), Proof of Stake (PoS), and Delegated Proof of Stake (DPoS). These mechanisms ensure that the majority of participants reach a consensus, preventing malicious activities and maintaining the security of the network.

Smart Contracts Smart contracts are self-executing contracts with predefined terms and conditions encoded on the blockchain. They automate the execution of agreements between parties, eliminating the need for intermediaries. Smart contracts are programmable, allowing for the creation of decentralized applications (DApps) that can run autonomously and transparently without any central control.

Decentralized Finance (DeFi)

Decentralized finance, or DeFi, refers to the use of blockchain and cryptocurrency technologies to recreate traditional financial instruments and services in a decentralized manner. DeFi aims to eliminate intermediaries, increase financial inclusion, and provide greater transparency and accessibility to financial services. Let's explore some of the key areas where blockchain is revolutionizing the financial landscape.

Decentralized Exchanges (DEX) Traditional exchanges rely on intermediaries to facilitate transactions. In contrast, decentralized exchanges operate on blockchain networks, allowing users to trade cryptocurrencies directly with each other. This eliminates the need for intermediaries, reduces fees, and provides users with full control over their assets.

Lending and Borrowing Blockchain technology has facilitated the development of decentralized lending and borrowing platforms. Through the use of smart contracts, individuals can lend their cryptocurrencies and earn interest, while borrowers can access funds without going through traditional financial institutions. These platforms offer greater efficiency, transparency, and accessibility compared to traditional lending systems.

Stablecoins and Digital Assets Stablecoins are cryptocurrencies designed to maintain a stable value, often pegged to a fiat currency like the US dollar. They provide a crucial bridge between the volatile nature of cryptocurrencies and the stability required for everyday financial transactions. By leveraging blockchain technology, stablecoins enable faster, more cost-effective, and secure cross-border payments.

Asset Tokenization Blockchain allows for the tokenization of real-world assets, such as real estate, art, and commodities. By representing these assets as digital tokens on a blockchain, they become divisible, tradable, and more accessible to a broader range of investors. Asset tokenization has the potential to unlock liquidity in traditionally illiquid markets and democratize investment opportunities.

Challenges and Future Considerations

While blockchain technology and DeFi hold immense potential, they also present various challenges and considerations that must be addressed for wider adoption and long-term success.

Scalability Blockchain networks, such as Bitcoin and Ethereum, face scalability issues due to limited transaction processing capacity. As DeFi applications gain popularity, the need for scalable solutions becomes critical to ensure smooth and efficient operations.

Regulatory and Legal Frameworks DeFi operates in a regulatory gray area, with different jurisdictions having varying levels of acceptance and regulatory frameworks. The lack of clarity regarding legal and compliance requirements poses challenges for DeFi projects, especially in terms of user protection and risk management.

Security and Auditing While blockchain technology provides inherent security, smart contracts and DeFi protocols are not immune to vulnerabilities and exploits. Auditing and continuous security assessments are crucial to identify and mitigate risks associated with code vulnerabilities, malicious attacks, and financial manipulation.

User Experience and Adoption The usability and accessibility of DeFi applications remain a barrier to wider adoption. Improvements in user experience, better education, and intuitive interfaces are necessary to attract a broader audience and make DeFi more accessible to individuals with limited technical knowledge.

Real-World Example: Decentralized Lending with Compound Finance

To solidify our understanding of DeFi, let's explore a real-world example of a decentralized lending platform called Compound Finance.
 Compound Finance is built on the Ethereum blockchain and utilizes smart contracts to enable lending and borrowing of cryptocurrencies. The platform allows users to deposit cryptocurrencies into a liquidity pool and earn interest on their holdings. These deposited assets can then be lent out to borrowers who pay

interest on their borrowed funds. The interest rates are determined by an algorithm that balances the supply and demand dynamics of the platform.

By leveraging blockchain technology, Compound Finance eliminates the need for traditional financial intermediaries, such as banks, and provides a decentralized alternative for individuals to lend and borrow cryptocurrencies. The transparent and programmable nature of smart contracts ensures that all transactions and interest payments are executed autonomously and recorded on the blockchain.

Conclusion

Blockchain technology and decentralized finance hold great promise in transforming traditional financial systems, increasing accessibility, and promoting financial inclusion. With its decentralized nature, enhanced security, and autonomy, blockchain has the potential to reshape the way we transact, lend, borrow, and invest. As the technology continues to evolve, it is crucial to address the challenges and pave the way for a sustainable and equitable decentralized financial ecosystem. By embracing blockchain technology and DeFi, we can collectively contribute to a more inclusive and prosperous financial future.

Lessons from the Past for Future Success

Historical Patterns and Cyclical Nature of Economic Success

In order to truly understand economic success, it is important to recognize the historical patterns and cyclical nature that have shaped and influenced economies over time. By examining these patterns, we can gain insights into the factors that contribute to economic success and learn valuable lessons for the future.

One of the key historical patterns that emerges is the rise and fall of economic empires. Throughout history, we have witnessed the ascent of powerful economies and their subsequent decline. The Roman Empire, for example, experienced a period of unprecedented economic growth and prosperity, fueled by trade networks and an expansive infrastructure. However, internal conflicts, external invasions, and overextension eventually led to its economic decline.

Similarly, the Dutch Republic emerged as a dominant economic power in the 17th century, driven by its global trading network and innovative financial instruments. However, the decline of the Dutch economic empire came as a result of increased competition from other European powers and geopolitical shifts.

These historical examples highlight the cyclical nature of economic success. No economy can sustain uninterrupted growth indefinitely. Instead, there are periods of expansion and contraction, boom and bust. Understanding these cycles is crucial for policymakers and investors in order to navigate the uncertainties and make informed decisions.

One theory that explains this cyclicality is the business cycle theory. According to this theory, economies go through regular cycles of expansion, peak, contraction, and trough. These cycles are driven by various factors such as changes in consumer and investor confidence, fiscal and monetary policy, technological advancements, and external shocks.

During an expansion phase, economic activity is robust, characterized by increasing GDP, rising employment, and high levels of consumer spending. However, as the expansion matures, imbalances may start to build up, such as inflationary pressures or asset bubbles. This eventually leads to a peak, followed by a contraction phase where economic activity slows down, unemployment rises, and businesses face challenges.

The trough phase is the bottom of the cycle, where the economy reaches its lowest point before starting to recover. Policy measures and market forces work together to stimulate growth and restore economic stability. This eventually leads to a new expansion phase, marking the beginning of a new cycle.

Understanding historical patterns and the cyclicality of economic success can help policymakers and investors avoid repeating past mistakes and identify opportunities for growth. By studying the causes and consequences of economic downturns in the past, we can develop strategies to mitigate risks and lay the foundation for sustainable economic development.

It is also important to recognize that economic success is not solely determined by internal factors. External factors, such as geopolitics, global economic trends, and natural disasters, can significantly influence an economy's trajectory. For example, the 2008 global financial crisis, triggered by the collapse of Lehman Brothers, had far-reaching impacts on economies around the world, leading to a global recession.

Furthermore, technology plays a crucial role in shaping the economic landscape. Technological advancements have driven economic growth throughout history, from the Industrial Revolution to the digital age. Innovations have transformed industries, created new opportunities, and disrupted traditional economic models. However, the pace of technological change also introduces challenges, such as job displacement and rising income inequality.

In order to navigate these challenges and capitalize on opportunities, policymakers and individuals need to embrace innovation, adapt to changing market conditions, and invest in human capital. Education and lifelong learning play a crucial role in equipping individuals with the skills needed to thrive in a rapidly evolving economy.

In conclusion, the study of historical patterns and the recognition of the cyclical nature of economic success provide valuable insights into the factors that shape economies. By understanding the causes and consequences of economic cycles, policymakers and investors can make informed decisions, mitigate risks, and identify opportunities for sustainable growth. However, it is important to recognize that external factors and technological advancements also play a significant role in shaping economic outcomes. Through continuous learning and adaptation, individuals and societies can position themselves for long-term success in an ever-changing global economy.

Sustainable Development and Long-Term Prosperity

Sustainable development is a concept that aims to balance economic growth with environmental protection and social well-being, ensuring prosperity for current and future generations. It recognizes that our natural resources are finite and must be managed responsibly to meet the needs of both present and future populations. In this section, we will explore the principles of sustainable development, its importance for economic success, and the strategies and practices that can promote long-term prosperity.

Understanding Sustainable Development

Sustainable development considers the interconnections between economic, social, and environmental dimensions. It seeks to achieve economic growth while minimizing negative impacts on the environment and society. The United Nations (UN) has defined sustainable development as "development that meets the needs of the present without compromising the ability of future generations to meet their own needs."

Achieving sustainable development requires addressing key challenges such as climate change, biodiversity loss, pollution, poverty, inequality, and resource depletion. It involves making choices and implementing policies that foster economic, social, and environmental sustainability.

Principles of Sustainable Development

Several principles guide sustainable development practices:

- **Intergenerational Equity**: This principle emphasizes the fair distribution of resources and opportunities between current and future generations. It requires that we make decisions today that do not compromise the ability of future generations to meet their own needs.

- **Environmental Stewardship:** Sustainable development promotes responsible and sustainable use of natural resources. It aims to protect ecosystems, conserve biodiversity, and minimize pollution and waste generation.

- **Social Inclusivity:** Sustainable development seeks to ensure that all members of society have equal access to resources, opportunities, and benefits. It strives to address inequality, promote social cohesion, and respect human rights.

- **Economic Efficiency:** Sustainable development promotes the efficient use of resources and encourages the adoption of cleaner and more sustainable production and consumption patterns. It seeks to create economic systems that generate long-term prosperity while minimizing environmental impacts.

- **Collaboration:** Given the complexity of sustainable development challenges, collaboration between governments, organizations, and individuals is essential. Sustainable development requires cooperation, knowledge sharing, and the collective effort of all stakeholders.

The Importance of Sustainable Development for Economic Success

Sustainable development and long-term prosperity are deeply interconnected. A well-managed economy that takes into account environmental and social factors is more resilient, innovative, and competitive. Here are some reasons why sustainable development is crucial for economic success:

1. **Resource Efficiency and Cost Savings:** By adopting sustainable practices, businesses can reduce waste, improve energy efficiency, and optimize resource use. This leads to cost savings, increased productivity, and improved competitiveness.

2. **Innovation and Technological Advancements:** Sustainable development promotes the development and adoption of innovative technologies and practices. It drives research and development in areas such as renewable energy, clean technologies, and eco-friendly production processes. These advancements enhance productivity, create new market opportunities, and drive economic growth.

3. **Access to Markets and International Trade:** Increasingly, consumers and businesses are demanding sustainable products and services. By embracing sustainable development, businesses can access new markets and gain a competitive edge in the global economy. Furthermore, international trade agreements often include environmental and social standards, making sustainable practices a prerequisite for market access.

4. **Risk Reduction and Resilience:** Sustainable development helps businesses and communities become more resilient to environmental and social shocks. By diversifying operations, investing in climate adaptation measures, and promoting social inclusivity, economies can better withstand and recover from crises.

5. **Investor Confidence and Sustainable Finance:** Investors are increasingly prioritizing environmental, social, and governance (ESG) factors in their decision-making. Businesses that demonstrate a commitment to sustainable practices are more likely to attract investment and secure long-term financing.

6. **Public Image and Reputation:** Sustainable development enhances the reputation of businesses, governments, and individuals. By aligning with sustainable development goals and implementing responsible practices, entities can build trust and goodwill among customers, employees, and communities.

Integration of Sustainable Development into Economic Systems

To achieve sustainable development and long-term prosperity, it is necessary to integrate sustainable practices into economic systems. This requires policy interventions, institutional frameworks, and supportive measures. Some strategies and practices that can facilitate this integration include:

- **Policy Coherence:** Governments should ensure coherence across various policy domains to avoid contradictory measures. Policies related to the economy, environment, social welfare, and education should align with sustainable development objectives.

- **Incentives and Regulations:** Governments can use a mix of incentives, regulations, and market mechanisms to promote sustainable practices. These can include tax incentives for green investments, regulatory standards for emissions, and cap-and-trade systems for pollution control.

- **Education and Awareness:** Promoting a culture of sustainability requires educating individuals and communities about the benefits and practices of sustainable development. Education systems can incorporate sustainable development principles into curricula, and awareness campaigns can encourage responsible behaviors.

- **Collaboration and Partnerships:** Achieving sustainable development requires collaboration and partnerships among governments, businesses, civil society organizations, and communities. Multi-stakeholder platforms, public-private partnerships, and community engagement are crucial for developing and implementing sustainable solutions.

- **Research and Innovation:** Governments, businesses, and academic institutions should invest in research and innovation to develop sustainable technologies, practices, and solutions. This can help address key challenges and unlock new opportunities for economic growth.

- **Metrics and Reporting:** Establishing clear metrics and reporting frameworks is essential for tracking progress towards sustainable development goals. Governments can require businesses to disclose their environmental and social impacts, enabling stakeholders to make informed decisions and hold entities accountable for their actions.

- **Long-Term Planning:** Sustainable development requires long-term planning and thinking. Governments should develop comprehensive strategies and establish institutions that can ensure continuity in sustainability efforts across political cycles.

Conclusion

Sustainable development is vital for achieving long-term prosperity. By balancing economic growth, environmental protection, and social well-being, we can create resilient, innovative, and prosperous economies that meet the needs of present and future generations. Embracing sustainable practices in business, government, and daily life can help address global challenges, unlock new opportunities, and pave the way for a more sustainable and prosperous future.

References:

- United Nations. (1987). Report of the World Commission on Environment and Development: Our Common Future. Retrieved from

```
https://sustainabledevelopment.un.org/content/
documents/5987our-common-future.pdf
```

Further Reading:

- Sachs, J. D. (2015). The Age of Sustainable Development. Columbia University Press.
- Elkington, J. (1999). Cannibals with Forks: The Triple Bottom Line of 21st Century Business. Capstone.
- World Business Council for Sustainable Development. (2010). Vision 2050: The New Agenda for Business. Retrieved from `https://docs.wbcsd.org/2010/09/Vision_2050_The_New_Agenda_for_Business-Executive_Summary.pdf`

Collaboration and Knowledge Sharing for Global Economic Success

In today's interconnected world, collaboration and knowledge sharing play a crucial role in achieving global economic success. The challenges and opportunities faced by economies are no longer confined within national borders. Instead, they require collective efforts and exchange of ideas to drive innovation, foster sustainable development, and address complex global issues. In this section, we explore the importance of collaboration and knowledge sharing for economic success, the benefits it brings, and the strategies that can be adopted to promote effective collaboration.

The Power of Collaboration and Knowledge Sharing

Collaboration refers to the act of working together towards a common goal. In the context of the global economy, collaboration can take various forms, including partnerships between companies, alliances between countries, and cooperation between international organizations. It involves sharing resources, expertise, and perspectives to achieve outcomes that would be difficult or impossible to accomplish independently.

Knowledge sharing, on the other hand, involves the dissemination of ideas, information, and experiences among individuals, organizations, and nations. It enables learning, innovation, and the adoption of best practices. By sharing knowledge, countries can leverage each other's strengths, avoid repeating mistakes, and accelerate their economic growth.

Both collaboration and knowledge sharing are essential for global economic success. They facilitate the transfer of technology and know-how, stimulate innovation and creativity, and foster economic convergence among nations. Through collaboration, countries can pool their resources, share risks, and access new markets. Knowledge sharing, on the other hand, enables countries to learn from each other's successes and failures, leading to more efficient policies and practices.

Benefits of Collaboration and Knowledge Sharing

Effective collaboration and knowledge sharing bring about numerous benefits for economies around the world. Some of the key advantages include:

1. **Increased Productivity and Innovation:** Collaboration and knowledge sharing allow for the combination of diverse perspectives, expertise, and resources. This leads to the development of new ideas, products, and services, driving productivity and innovation. By sharing knowledge, countries can learn from each other's experiences and adopt best practices, leading to improved efficiency and competitiveness.

2. **Access to New Markets:** Collaboration between companies and nations provides access to new markets and customer bases. By combining their strengths and capabilities, partners can penetrate markets that would be otherwise difficult to enter individually. This opens up opportunities for export-led growth and the expansion of business operations.

3. **Sustainable Development:** Collaboration and knowledge sharing are vital for achieving sustainable development. By sharing expertise in areas such as renewable energy, environmental conservation, and social responsibility, countries can collectively address global challenges such as climate change, resource depletion, and income inequality. Collaboration also enables the adoption of sustainable practices and the implementation of policies that promote equitable growth.

4. **Capacity Building and Human Capital Development:** Collaboration and knowledge sharing contribute to capacity building and human capital development. By partnering with more advanced economies, developing countries can access technology, expertise, and training opportunities. This helps to develop local talent, enhance skills, and improve the overall productivity and competitiveness of the workforce.

Strategies for Promoting Collaboration and Knowledge Sharing

To promote effective collaboration and knowledge sharing, governments, organizations, and individuals can adopt the following strategies:

1. **Creating Enabling Policies and Institutions:** Governments play a crucial role in fostering an environment conducive to collaboration and knowledge sharing. This includes establishing policies that promote open trade, investment, and innovation. Governments can also support the development of research and development institutions, knowledge networks, and technology transfer mechanisms.

2. **Facilitating Information Exchange and Networking:** Information exchange platforms, conferences, workshops, and seminars can facilitate the sharing of knowledge, experiences, and best practices. Networking events provide opportunities for stakeholders to connect, collaborate, and form partnerships. Governments and organizations can organize and support such initiatives to promote knowledge sharing.

3. **Investing in Education and Research:** Education and research are key drivers of innovation and knowledge creation. Governments should invest in quality education systems and research institutions to develop a skilled workforce and generate new knowledge. Collaboration between academia and industry can also promote the transfer of research findings into practical applications.

4. **Engaging in Public-Private Partnerships:** Public-private partnerships encourage collaboration between governments and businesses. By combining public resources with private sector expertise, these partnerships can drive innovation, infrastructure development, and capacity building. They can also leverage private sector networks and market access for the benefit of the wider economy.

5. **Promoting Cultural Exchange and Diversity:** Cultural exchange programs, international scholarships, and student exchanges can promote collaboration and knowledge sharing among nations. Exposure to different cultures, perspectives, and ideas fosters creativity, empathy, and cross-cultural understanding. Embracing diversity is essential for promoting inclusive collaboration and achieving global economic success.

Real-World Example: The Open Source Software Movement

The open source software movement is a prime example of collaboration and knowledge sharing driving economic success. Open source software refers to software that is freely available and can be modified and distributed by anyone. The movement is built on the principles of openness, transparency, and collective participation.

Open source projects are often developed collaboratively, with developers from around the world contributing their expertise and sharing their knowledge. This collective effort has resulted in the creation of high-quality software, such as the Linux operating system, the Apache web server, and the MySQL database management system.

The success of open source software can be attributed to the collaborative nature of its development process. Developers freely share their code, ideas, and experiences, allowing others to learn from their work and build upon it. This has led to rapid innovation, cost savings, and increased competition in the software industry.

The open source software movement also exemplifies the power of knowledge sharing in driving economic growth. By making software accessible and freely available, the movement has democratized technology and empowered individuals and businesses around the world. It has fostered a culture of knowledge exchange, where users and developers actively contribute to the improvement of software and share their expertise with others.

Conclusion

Collaboration and knowledge sharing are essential for achieving global economic success. By working together, sharing resources, and exchanging ideas, countries can drive innovation, foster sustainable development, and address global challenges. The benefits of collaboration and knowledge sharing include increased productivity, access to new markets, sustainable development, and capacity building. To promote effective collaboration, governments, organizations, and individuals can adopt strategies such as creating enabling policies, facilitating information exchange, investing in education and research, engaging in public-private partnerships, and promoting cultural exchange and diversity. The open source software movement serves as a real-world example of the power of collaboration and knowledge sharing in driving economic growth. As we look to the future, it is crucial that we continue to embrace the principles of collaboration and knowledge sharing to ensure long-term global economic success.

Index

-up, 8

ability, 1, 6–8, 12, 19, 20, 24, 25, 27, 29, 31, 34, 48, 49, 78, 82, 88, 96, 123, 141, 172, 177, 198, 199, 250, 267, 285
academia, 132, 138, 264
acceptance, 158
access, 4, 8, 18, 29, 43–47, 79, 83, 87–89, 100–103, 117–119, 122, 128, 129, 131, 134, 137, 142, 145–148, 177, 204, 209, 211, 213, 214, 220, 222, 225, 229, 231, 236, 238, 241, 243, 244, 247–252, 256, 257, 259, 261, 266, 296, 298
accessibility, 67, 82, 102, 249, 251, 287, 289
accommodation, 49, 51, 83–85
account, 101, 172, 292
accountability, 98, 147, 258, 281
accumulation, 3, 173, 191, 193
accuracy, 10, 111
achievement, 1, 210, 229, 232
acquisition, 79
act, 93, 94, 163, 249, 295

action, 147, 148, 268, 275
activity, 8, 91, 97, 172, 189, 290
adaptability, 4, 6, 17, 35, 49, 50, 82, 195, 208, 213, 220, 268, 269
adaptation, 6, 82, 112, 168, 196, 268, 291
addition, 8, 67, 91, 142, 167, 178, 212
address, 10, 11, 29, 30, 39, 46, 47, 49, 82, 84, 85, 102, 103, 120, 121, 128, 131, 133, 135, 142, 147, 148, 152, 164, 168, 169, 177, 178, 181, 189, 193, 204, 205, 218, 222, 225, 230, 233, 236, 245, 248, 249, 251, 254, 258, 260, 273, 275, 281, 283–285, 289, 294, 295, 298
adequacy, 95
adherence, 203
adoption, 5, 59, 68, 76, 118, 135, 146, 156–158, 227, 264, 265, 269–271, 288, 295
advance, 38, 76, 223, 224
advancement, 118, 142, 207, 208, 232, 271, 282

advantage, 54, 67, 84, 117, 119, 125, 129, 137, 144, 156, 270
advent, 88, 101, 113
adventure, 167
adversity, 30, 31, 49, 82
advice, 24, 28, 29, 48
advisor, 218
advocate, 162
aerospace, 36, 133
affordability, 84, 220
age, 10, 34, 67, 69, 70, 93, 101, 229, 290
agency, 1
agenda, 255
agility, 30, 123
agriculture, 163, 255–257, 264, 269, 272, 273
aid, 219, 225
aim, 2, 16, 17, 30, 92, 145, 153, 177, 182, 191, 194, 204, 238, 244, 273, 277
air, 4, 38, 77, 83, 114, 138, 145, 148, 157
algorithm, 279, 289
Alibaba, 118, 138
alignment, 211
alleviation, 203, 255–258
allocation, 18, 87, 90, 122, 172, 174, 178, 245
alternative, 29, 49, 77, 82, 84, 156, 209, 251, 289
ambiguity, 24
amount, 91, 191, 203
analysis, 2, 4, 7–14, 18, 30, 107, 109, 111, 112, 240, 271
angel, 29, 44, 45
animal, 72, 156
app, 32, 80
appearance, 67
application, 54, 59, 71, 73, 105, 163, 269
appreciation, 108
apprenticeship, 45, 225, 235
approach, 4, 5, 7, 12, 13, 17, 34, 36, 39–41, 45, 48, 49, 71, 73, 78, 79, 96, 104, 105, 107, 110–112, 131, 134, 135, 141, 146, 161, 163, 167, 193, 195, 203, 205, 210, 224, 225, 227, 229–231, 233, 234, 239, 243, 248, 252, 256, 258, 265
arbitrage, 99
area, 23, 49, 147, 240, 259, 269
array, 39, 167
art, 137
ascent, 289
Asia, 116, 117, 135
ask, 89, 99, 100
aspect, 5, 33, 44, 102, 108, 142, 145, 146, 148, 173, 185, 196, 230, 260, 273
assembly, 123, 271
assessment, 29, 98, 229, 230, 251, 265
asset, 88, 91, 108, 109, 134, 290
assistance, 132, 203, 244, 245
assistant, 35
asymmetry, 171, 177, 178
Atkinson, 240, 241
atmosphere, 272
attainment, 10, 11, 13
attendance, 78, 203
attention, 33, 136, 152, 230, 264
attitude, 30
audience, 1, 13, 32, 79, 220, 222, 269
audits, 95, 260
authentication, 102

Index 301

author, 107
authority, 186
authorship, 52
automation, 39, 121–123, 216, 264, 269–271
automobile, 133, 271
autonomy, 210, 229, 231, 289
availability, 14, 44, 78, 102, 142, 145, 157, 171, 246, 249, 273
avenue, 78
aversion, 240
awareness, 103, 168, 251
axis, 11

back, 24, 26, 34, 49, 87, 90, 113, 116, 136
backbone, 94, 234
background, 110, 142, 210, 225, 229, 252
Baird, 167
balance, 28, 79, 83, 85, 96, 101, 135, 141, 160, 172–174, 177, 178, 185, 193, 209, 245, 260, 264, 291
band, 84
Bangladesh, 252
bank, 97, 101, 102, 172, 187, 188, 190
banking, 18, 88, 89, 101–103, 134, 146, 171, 250, 251, 257
bar, 11
base, 33, 78, 82, 130
basis, 71, 147
beauty, 252
beginning, 290
behalf, 88
behavior, 27, 34, 110, 111, 145, 185, 204, 205

being, 1, 28, 35, 40, 48, 59, 78, 83, 141, 144, 145, 147, 149, 162, 181, 194, 195, 204, 211, 213, 229–231, 233, 236, 239, 247, 249, 250, 252, 259, 270, 282, 291, 294
belief, 110, 112, 160, 244
benchmark, 91
beneficiary, 203, 204
benefit, 76, 112, 128, 145, 167, 172, 235, 237, 244
Betty Thorne, 12
Bezos, 33–36
bias, 84
bid, 89, 99, 100
biodiversity, 147, 157, 168, 273, 291
biology, 71, 283
biomass, 156
biotech, 143, 163, 166, 264
biotechnology, 71–73, 138, 163, 165, 166, 264
birdwatching, 167
birth, 43
blockchain, 18, 135, 198, 264, 286–289
blueprint, 35
book, 2, 16–18, 33, 80, 99, 268
bookstore, 34
boom, 98, 290
boot, 214
borrower, 97
borrowing, 87, 172, 173, 190, 193, 288
bottom, 160–162, 290
box, 24
brain, 38, 39
branch, 252
brand, 27, 33, 52, 67, 84

branding, 27
Brazil, 14, 171, 173, 174, 203, 204
break, 54, 203, 247, 250
breakthrough, 37, 268, 269, 285
Brian Chesky, 83
brick, 35, 269
bridge, 38, 88, 223
bubble, 109
budget, 210
buffer, 19
Buffett, 107
building, 23, 25, 27, 29, 31, 34, 50, 133, 137, 148, 243, 249, 298
burden, 88, 172, 194
bureaucracy, 44
burning, 272
business, 1, 6, 12, 20, 23, 24, 26–31, 33–36, 41, 46, 48, 49, 54, 59, 67, 69, 78, 79, 82, 85, 130, 135, 136, 142–144, 149, 152, 160–162, 174, 199, 257, 265, 267, 269, 270, 290, 294
bust, 290
button, 78
buy, 88, 91, 99, 104, 108
buying, 91, 99, 104, 107, 109

California, 42
cancer, 71, 72, 285
capacity, 44, 130, 131, 148, 207, 245, 246, 251, 298
capita, 11, 203
capital, 2, 8, 18, 26, 29, 43–45, 87–91, 93, 95–97, 113, 116, 118, 119, 121, 128, 131–133, 143, 174, 195, 199, 203, 205, 207, 208, 211–215, 219, 237, 249, 250, 258, 267, 290
capitalism, 3, 91, 173, 193
capture, 13, 99, 108, 156
car, 82
carbon, 35, 73, 124, 142, 273
care, 28, 71, 177, 194, 195, 203, 229, 259
career, 48, 49, 105, 110, 208, 209, 220, 225
case, 7, 8, 13, 18, 26, 48, 51, 53, 54, 76, 77, 89, 90, 115, 117, 123, 124, 130, 143, 144, 158, 160, 163, 171, 173, 174, 193, 197, 198, 200, 209, 211, 222, 225, 238, 254, 270, 271
cash, 27, 97, 174, 203, 204, 244
catalog, 77
caution, 14
center, 91, 134, 135
Central America, 166
centricity, 35
century, 5, 77, 88, 113, 116, 136, 289
certificate, 235
certification, 220, 235
chain, 34, 119, 121–124, 143, 264
challenge, 10, 20, 24, 26, 29, 57, 79, 84, 102, 133, 135, 138, 147, 159, 177, 178, 195, 203, 204, 245, 249, 270
chance, 167
change, 1, 10, 14, 18, 41, 57, 73, 75, 77, 120, 142, 143, 148, 156, 157, 162, 168, 204, 205, 254, 265, 266, 268, 272–275, 285, 290, 291
channel, 78

Index 303

chapter, 19, 51, 87, 113, 141, 144, 171, 207, 263, 268
characteristic, 113
chart, 133, 258, 267
check, 174, 203
chemical, 163, 164
child, 229, 257
childcare, 194, 259–261
childhood, 194, 229
China, 14, 117, 127, 130, 136–138
choice, 10, 77, 225, 241
citizenship, 213
city, 91
clarity, 10
class, 5, 43, 133, 135
classification, 82
classroom, 210, 220, 224, 225, 234
clay, 90
click, 78
climate, 3, 18, 73, 75, 77, 120, 142, 143, 147, 148, 156, 157, 168, 254, 265, 266, 268, 272–275, 285, 291
climber, 160
climbing, 160
clothing, 143, 160
co, 30, 31, 48
code, 298
coefficient, 237, 240, 241
cognition, 38
coherence, 181
cohesion, 194, 195, 213, 230, 238, 243, 244, 246, 251, 258
collaboration, 18, 43–46, 59, 64, 121–123, 131, 132, 135, 138, 144, 148, 159, 166, 213, 225, 234–236, 265, 266, 268, 277, 286, 295–298
collapse, 290
collateral, 26, 250, 251
collection, 99, 191, 193
college, 210, 217, 219
colonization, 3, 36, 37
color, 11
com, 109
combat, 75, 134, 138, 167, 189
combination, 6, 20, 26, 31, 36, 43, 101, 111, 133, 138, 187, 189, 193, 225, 235, 258
comfort, 209
commerce, 5, 6, 34, 39, 117, 118, 232, 269
commercialization, 44
commitment, 27, 28, 32–35, 67, 132, 136, 143, 159, 160, 163, 166, 167, 195, 204, 210, 229, 232–234, 254, 256–259, 261, 268
communication, 4, 5, 13, 32, 67, 110–114, 116, 118, 119, 137, 212
community, 142, 149, 158, 161, 220, 223, 249, 257, 265
company, 29, 31, 34–38, 48, 66, 67, 77, 107, 117, 123, 143, 149, 152, 160, 162–164, 260
comparability, 14
comparison, 13
compensation, 29
competition, 3, 19, 27, 29, 35, 38, 52, 79, 82, 107, 117, 118, 135, 138, 158, 232, 233, 289, 298
competitiveness, 57, 59, 114, 119, 127–129, 131, 132, 146, 158, 195, 196, 199, 207,

210, 213, 219, 224, 235
competitor, 30
complement, 75, 212, 240, 269
completion, 71, 73, 220
complexity, 98, 108, 177
compliance, 84, 95
component, 14, 44, 65, 123, 142, 172, 249, 273
comprehension, 7
computer, 38, 39, 214, 269, 279
computing, 32, 282
concept, 18, 20, 32, 43, 54, 56, 83, 101, 104, 117, 141, 144, 152, 160, 174, 265, 279, 291
concern, 100, 129, 264
conclusion, 5, 7, 11, 28, 36, 46, 50, 79, 85, 93, 107, 135, 138, 147, 148, 168, 174, 189, 195, 236, 291
conference, 83
confidence, 9, 95, 103, 107, 134, 290
congestion, 82
conjunction, 14
connection, 33, 102
connectivity, 45, 82, 116, 133, 135, 137, 220, 232, 256
consent, 72
conservation, 142–144, 147, 167, 265, 273
consideration, 178, 246
construction, 137, 224
consumer, 27, 78, 123, 129, 137, 208, 290
consumption, 83, 127, 138, 143, 146–148, 152, 155, 164, 171, 193, 240, 273
container, 114
containerization, 118, 121

content, 39, 78, 79, 220
context, 2, 4–6, 8, 10, 13, 39, 51, 87, 113, 116, 117, 133, 136, 196, 213, 231, 281, 295
contingency, 29
contraction, 290
contrarian, 107
contrast, 130
control, 12, 34, 78, 136, 172, 173, 177, 193, 282
convenience, 34, 77, 82, 101
convergence, 296
cooperation, 18, 120, 138, 147, 266, 268, 273, 275–277, 295
coordination, 121–123, 193, 265, 266
copying, 66
core, 1, 20, 33, 34, 110, 141, 149, 163, 232, 279
cornerstone, 146
correction, 108
correlation, 8, 11, 215
corruption, 134
cost, 29, 30, 37, 79, 83, 100, 114, 117, 118, 121, 122, 137, 144, 158, 163, 172, 208, 244, 269, 298
Costa Rica, 143, 166–169, 252–254
Costa Rica's, 143, 166–169, 254
country, 2, 8, 11–14, 117, 127–135, 137, 143, 166–168, 171, 174, 178, 185, 186, 191, 193, 198, 210, 218, 219, 231–235, 237, 241, 245, 252, 254, 255, 257–261
course, 3, 209, 267
creation, 4, 17, 19, 33, 40–44, 51, 59, 77, 88, 128, 130, 131,

Index 305

137, 146, 148, 219, 250, 257, 264, 270, 298
creativity, 17, 20, 24, 31, 32, 63, 132, 210, 213, 230, 269, 296
credibility, 8, 145, 172
credit, 93, 94, 98, 101, 251, 257
creditworthiness, 88
crime, 238
crisis, 98, 99, 109, 189, 290
criticism, 35
crop, 156, 264, 270, 273, 285
crowdfunding, 29
cryptocurrency, 287
culture, 29–31, 43, 44, 49, 50, 54, 77, 111, 112, 132, 232, 234, 268, 298
curiosity, 3, 110
currency, 127
curricula, 45, 210
curriculum, 213, 225, 229, 235
curve, 28, 54, 240
customer, 6, 7, 27, 30, 32–36, 49, 50, 78, 79, 82, 102, 122, 123, 142, 149
customization, 34
cutting, 35, 49
cybersecurity, 102, 103, 124
cycle, 108, 153, 203, 247, 250, 290
cyclicality, 290

Dalio, 110–112
damage, 272
data, 2, 7–14, 78, 79, 100, 103, 111, 112, 124, 135, 233, 241, 245, 246, 251, 266, 267, 270, 271, 279, 281
database, 298
dataset, 10, 11
date, 91, 203, 225, 235, 245

day, 18, 27
deal, 100
debate, 111, 177
debt, 27, 171, 173, 174, 190–193
decade, 11
decision, 1, 2, 7, 12, 77, 107, 110–112, 123, 146, 148, 181, 188, 190, 208, 257, 260
decline, 30, 78, 98, 100, 101, 108, 257, 269, 271, 289
decollectivization, 136
decrease, 157, 273
deepening, 241
default, 97
defense, 171, 190
deficit, 190, 193
definition, 54, 113, 116, 117
deforestation, 167, 272, 273
degradation, 138, 265
degree, 56, 217
delivery, 27, 34, 123
demand, 49, 79, 117, 122, 136, 168, 172–174, 213, 214, 223, 224, 271, 285, 289
democratization, 88
Deng, 136
Deng Xiaoping, 136
Denmark, 173, 193
departure, 144
dependence, 19, 38, 250, 267
dependency, 129, 131
depletion, 138, 291
deployment, 37, 148, 157, 158, 264, 281
deposit, 88, 94, 288
depth, 2, 7, 220
deregulation, 119, 193

design, 31–33, 67, 83, 123, 130, 185, 205, 229, 245, 246
desire, 20, 80
destination, 167, 268
detail, 33, 160
determinant, 212
determination, 1, 8, 24, 31, 36, 39, 49, 174
development, 2–5, 7, 12–14, 16–19, 26, 33, 38, 40, 41, 43, 44, 47, 48, 51, 52, 54, 57, 64, 67, 69, 72, 88, 90–93, 102, 113–116, 118, 119, 123–125, 128–133, 135–138, 141–149, 152, 157, 163, 166, 171, 173, 174, 178, 180, 181, 195, 196, 199, 200, 203, 205, 207, 209–211, 213–215, 218, 219, 225, 226, 229–234, 236–239, 241, 247, 249, 250, 252, 254–258, 264–267, 270, 271, 275, 277, 290–295, 298
deviation, 13
device, 32
diabetes, 72
diagnostic, 73
dialogue, 85, 266, 285
difference, 7, 20, 281
difficulty, 27
diffusion, 213
diligence, 98
dimension, 144–146, 160
disadvantage, 238
disaster, 266
discipline, 173, 193
disclosure, 95

discount, 104, 107, 172
discourse, 1
discovery, 89
discrimination, 49, 72, 84, 145, 243
discussion, 220
disease, 283
dislocation, 120
dispatchability, 156
displacement, 39, 237, 264, 269–272, 290
display, 10
disposal, 145
dispose, 265
disruption, 35, 54, 77, 116, 269
dissemination, 295
distance, 102
distribution, 34, 78, 79, 122, 123, 146, 171, 172, 178, 237, 239–241, 244, 256
dive, 2
diversification, 19, 85, 129, 257, 273
diversity, 19, 45, 117, 145, 236, 298
divide, 102, 103
dominance, 35, 66, 78
domination, 34
dot, 109
down, 54, 102, 163, 191, 220, 290
downturn, 218
drive, 6, 11, 18, 39, 46, 49, 54, 59, 70, 76, 77, 89, 90, 112, 124, 132, 138, 142, 143, 157, 159, 165, 198, 213, 233, 263–265, 270, 271, 279, 295, 298
driver, 40, 43, 45, 79, 118, 119, 124, 125, 130, 131, 144, 207, 215, 232, 247, 258
driving, 2, 4, 17, 19, 23, 33, 41, 48, 51, 53, 67, 69, 87, 90, 108,

Index 307

121, 124, 131, 137, 144,
156, 165, 166, 189, 200,
211, 219, 234–236, 258,
298
dynamic, 10, 14, 24, 30, 44, 45, 82,
225, 226

e, 6, 34, 35, 101, 117, 209, 232, 269
earning, 207, 211, 215, 224
Earth, 156, 272
ease, 32, 118
easing, 119
East Africa, 255
eco, 167
economic, 1–14, 16–19, 22, 23, 29,
31, 39–43, 46, 48, 51, 54,
57, 59, 65, 67, 70, 73,
75–77, 83–85, 87–90, 93,
96, 97, 101–103,
108–110, 112–121,
123–125, 127–134,
136–138, 141–148, 152,
154–157, 159, 160, 162,
166–169, 171–174, 176,
178, 180–189, 191,
193–200, 205, 207–219,
223–226, 229, 232–239,
241, 244, 246, 247, 249,
250, 252, 254–256, 258,
259, 263–273, 275–277,
279, 281, 289–296, 298
economist, 215
economy, 1, 2, 5, 7, 8, 19, 32, 33, 35,
36, 67, 70, 73, 80, 83, 85,
88–90, 93–97, 101,
113–116, 118, 121, 124,
125, 129, 130, 136–138,
141, 144, 152–155, 157,
159, 167, 168, 172–175,
185, 188–191, 195, 196,
208, 209, 211, 213, 214,
216, 223, 225, 254–256,
263–265, 267, 269, 271,
272, 289–292, 295
ecosystem, 23, 32, 33, 43–47, 57, 59,
135, 273, 289
ecotourism, 167
edge, 35, 49, 66
editing, 284
education, 1, 2, 10, 11, 13, 16–18,
32, 44–47, 130, 132, 133,
142, 145, 147, 172–174,
178, 190, 194, 195, 203,
204, 207–220, 222–235,
237, 238, 243, 244,
247–252, 254, 255,
257–259, 270, 271, 298
Edward Tufte, 11
effect, 10, 98, 101, 208
effectiveness, 99, 111, 154, 172, 181,
182, 188, 190, 197, 204,
241, 249, 276
efficacy, 72, 285
efficiency, 51, 77, 89, 93, 99–101,
107, 118, 122, 123, 142,
146, 148, 152, 157, 158,
165, 166, 168, 172, 174,
176–178, 182, 185, 269,
270, 273
effort, 30, 46, 49, 71, 133, 244, 298
egalitarianism, 259
electricity, 156, 256
electronic, 92, 101
electronics, 127, 132, 137, 210
element, 220
Elon Musk, 8, 31, 36, 49
Elon Musk's, 36, 38, 39
Elon Musk, 30

embrace, 1, 24, 30, 48, 77, 124, 144, 145, 149, 162, 271, 290, 298
emergence, 2, 3, 5, 80, 116
emission, 138
emotion, 112
emphasis, 31, 78, 135, 194, 195, 210, 229–232, 234, 256, 260
empire, 289
employability, 209, 215, 216, 219, 224, 225, 235
employee, 35, 149
employment, 5, 6, 40, 77, 143, 167, 178, 181, 194, 208, 235, 243, 290
empowerment, 103, 250, 252, 256
encryption, 102
end, 48, 57, 82, 121, 226, 235
energy, 27, 35, 59, 73–77, 137, 138, 142, 143, 146–148, 156–159, 164, 167, 168, 264–266, 272, 273
enforcement, 134
engagement, 78, 115, 158, 213, 230, 249, 265
engine, 5, 59
engineering, 18, 30, 71, 72, 264, 282–286
enhancement, 51, 141
enrollment, 13, 249, 257
entertainment, 32, 77, 79
enthusiasm, 23
entrance, 210
entrepreneur, 8, 20, 23, 26, 31, 36, 40, 48, 49
entrepreneurship, 4, 8, 17, 20–23, 26, 31, 36, 42–48, 132, 146, 194, 244, 270

entry, 78, 102
environment, 4, 8, 22, 24, 27, 30, 43, 44, 46, 47, 64, 73, 76, 110–112, 117, 119, 130, 134–136, 141, 144–146, 149, 152, 157, 162, 167–169, 174, 181, 212, 230, 231, 233, 234, 252, 257, 268, 270–272, 275
environmentalist, 160
equality, 194, 195, 229, 231, 240, 257–261
equipment, 233
equity, 142, 145, 176–178, 185, 210, 225
era, 3, 83, 113
eradication, 147
error, 122
establishment, 88, 92, 130, 132, 133, 135, 136, 257
estimate, 9, 13
ethnicity, 237
ethos, 160
Europe, 3, 5, 91, 116, 117
evaluation, 111, 204, 205
event, 5, 98, 209
evidence, 7, 8, 12, 111, 181, 235, 267
evolution, 5, 35, 82, 88, 91, 93
examination, 7, 8
examining, 5–8, 12, 16, 17, 113, 289
example, 3, 6–8, 10, 13, 14, 30, 31, 42, 48, 49, 66, 82, 90, 91, 98, 100–103, 108, 109, 117, 122, 142, 143, 145, 146, 156, 166, 167, 184, 185, 204, 214, 217–219, 224, 232, 241, 244, 252, 269, 288–290, 298
excellence, 6, 7, 32, 33, 111, 112, 232

exchange, 44, 113, 114, 116, 118, 120, 124, 174, 191, 268, 295, 298
exclusion, 142, 146, 237
exercise, 14, 107
existence, 87
expansion, 3, 5, 82, 88, 92, 129, 137, 290
expenditure, 11, 13, 193
expense, 141, 144
experience, 6, 10, 23, 29, 31–33, 44, 48–50, 57, 78–80, 84, 133, 157, 208, 210, 212, 214, 217, 220, 234, 235, 279
experimentation, 24, 135
expertise, 4, 30, 111, 112, 128, 148, 214, 268, 295, 298
exploit, 129
exploitation, 5, 129, 131
exploration, 2, 5, 22, 30, 31, 36, 37, 39
explore, 2, 7, 9, 10, 13, 17–19, 23, 26, 29, 33, 36, 40, 43, 48, 51, 53, 55, 67, 69, 71, 73–76, 79, 83, 87, 90, 101, 104, 106, 110, 113, 115–118, 121, 123, 124, 136, 141, 144, 156, 158, 160, 165–167, 171, 178, 182, 183, 185, 190, 193, 196, 207, 209, 223–226, 232, 239, 242, 244, 247, 253, 255, 256, 259, 263, 265, 266, 272, 282, 287, 288, 291, 295
export, 14, 124–128, 130–132, 137, 138, 257
exporter, 127, 137
exposure, 97

extension, 256
extent, 237, 239, 241
extreme, 101, 265

face, 19, 21, 24, 26–31, 35, 44, 47, 49, 82, 96, 102, 161, 180, 188–190, 193, 195, 227, 230, 232, 236, 244, 247, 254, 265, 270, 284, 290
facilitation, 127, 130
fact, 108
factor, 34, 41, 88, 132, 133, 135, 214, 235
factory, 127, 137
failure, 13, 23, 24, 28, 30, 48, 50
fairness, 101, 182, 185, 281
fall, 289
family, 209, 220, 259, 260
farming, 3, 270, 273
fashion, 123
fear, 28
fee, 83
feedback, 24, 28, 30, 49, 108, 110, 111, 123, 230
fermentation, 72
fertility, 273
fertilizer, 273
field, 5, 23, 24, 38, 71, 73, 100, 107, 158, 208, 219, 224, 241, 279, 282, 283, 285
film, 51, 77–79
finance, 4, 17, 27, 28, 45, 90–93, 96, 110, 111, 135, 146, 172, 185, 190, 264, 269, 275, 287, 289
financing, 45, 91, 134, 191, 194, 204
finding, 177
Finland, 13, 173, 193, 209–211, 229–231

fintech, 92, 135
firm, 110, 111
flexibility, 173, 209, 220, 229
Florence, 91
flow, 27, 87, 93, 96, 113, 116, 118–120, 122, 129
flowing, 156
focus, 6, 29, 32, 33, 36, 104, 124, 125, 127, 130, 132, 133, 135, 138, 147, 152, 157, 210, 211, 213, 214, 219, 224, 230–234, 252, 254, 260, 273
food, 163, 240, 256, 264, 273, 284
footprint, 76, 79, 143, 167
foray, 32, 34
force, 23, 34, 51, 53, 77, 137, 212
forecasting, 122, 281
forefront, 74, 77, 132, 135, 163, 234
foresight, 6
forest, 167
forestry, 167
form, 97, 173, 191, 208, 209, 224, 234, 244, 251
format, 8
formation, 91, 212, 214
formulation, 146, 178, 196, 199
fossil, 38, 73, 143, 148, 156–158, 272, 273
foster, 1, 4, 22, 41, 44, 45, 47, 70, 77, 111, 129, 138, 149, 174, 189, 219, 232, 233, 249, 265, 267, 271, 291, 295, 296, 298
foundation, 3, 110, 133, 136, 137, 210, 229, 232, 258, 267, 279, 290
founder, 31, 33, 34, 48, 49, 110
founding, 30

fraction, 208
fragmentation, 100
frame, 91
framework, 9, 12, 18, 58, 109, 110, 134, 135, 148, 207, 219, 251
fraud, 103, 264
freedom, 3, 229
frenzy, 109
frequency, 17, 99–101
frustration, 80
fuel, 44, 132, 145, 148, 158
fulfillment, 34
function, 190
functionality, 57
functioning, 88, 93, 95, 185
fund, 34, 100, 194, 244
fundamental, 9, 68, 108, 109, 111, 152, 171, 207, 212, 214, 241, 247, 249
funding, 23, 26, 29, 43–48, 204, 229, 233, 245
future, 1, 2, 7, 8, 18, 23, 24, 27, 31, 33, 35–39, 54, 59, 70, 73, 77, 79, 91, 92, 99, 107, 109, 120, 121, 124, 134–136, 141, 144, 148, 152, 155, 159, 161, 166, 169, 198, 199, 207, 210, 211, 213, 229, 231, 236, 239, 243, 252, 260, 261, 263, 265, 267, 268, 271, 272, 274, 275, 277, 282, 286, 289, 291, 294, 298

gain, 1, 5–8, 10–12, 16, 27, 40, 90, 107, 109, 129, 137, 205, 234, 240–242, 289
gaming, 232

gap, 38, 49, 88, 102, 133, 195, 209, 223, 260
Gary Becker, 215
gas, 38, 73, 75, 148, 156, 157, 265, 272, 273
gear, 160
gender, 10, 11, 195, 213, 236, 237, 247, 257–261
Gene, 71
gene, 71–73, 284
generation, 17, 79, 133, 141, 142, 146, 152, 153, 155, 158, 162, 164, 182, 185, 193, 245, 250, 265
genetic, 18, 71, 72, 264, 282–286
genocide, 255
genome, 71
George Soros, 107
George Soros', 109
Germany, 13, 158, 210, 211, 225, 234–236
Germany, 158, 225
ggplot2, 12
giant, 34
gig, 269
Gini, 237, 240, 241
globalization, 2, 4, 5, 16–18, 92, 113–121, 237
globe, 113, 222
goal, 25, 36, 37, 77, 147, 223, 295
good, 247
governance, 4, 134, 174, 195, 254, 255, 258, 266, 267, 275, 277
government, 2–4, 8, 16–18, 43, 44, 47, 57, 95, 127, 131–133, 135, 137, 138, 144, 167, 168, 171–174, 177, 178, 182, 184, 185, 190–193, 195, 196, 198, 203, 204, 232–234, 236, 249, 254–257, 259, 260, 294
grant, 52
graph, 8, 11
Great Britain, 5
Greece, 90
green, 92, 156–159, 167, 265
greenhouse, 38, 73–75, 145, 148, 156, 157, 265, 272, 273
grid, 157, 158
ground, 85
groundbreaking, 3, 31, 32, 36, 43, 53, 57, 66, 71, 132
groundwork, 117, 261
group, 240, 241, 251, 252
growth, 1–6, 8, 13, 16–19, 22, 23, 28–30, 34, 35, 39, 40, 43–48, 51, 54, 59, 73, 76, 77, 79, 82, 85, 87, 89, 91, 93, 96, 109, 113–117, 119, 124–134, 136–139, 141, 142, 144, 146–148, 152, 155, 157, 166, 167, 169, 171–174, 178, 181, 185, 189, 191, 193, 195, 196, 198, 199, 203, 207, 208, 211–215, 218, 219, 224, 226, 228, 232, 234–239, 241, 243, 244, 246, 247, 249–251, 254–256, 258, 263, 265–271, 275, 289–291, 294, 295, 298
Guay C. Lim, 12
guidance, 8, 12, 28, 30, 48, 50, 133, 148, 224
guide, 1, 5, 11, 12, 18, 99, 147, 152, 178, 274, 284, 291

hand, 88, 89, 121, 124, 143, 172, 191, 237, 240, 250, 268–270, 279, 295, 296
happiness, 195, 230
hardware, 33
harmony, 275
harness, 67, 70, 74, 270, 271, 277
hazard, 98
health, 71, 73, 95, 145, 147, 148, 163, 174, 203, 204, 208, 230, 247, 259, 282, 285
healthcare, 18, 32, 73, 142, 145, 173, 177, 178, 190, 194, 204, 208, 224, 238, 240, 243, 244, 247–250, 252, 254, 257–259, 264, 269, 270, 283
heart, 255
heat, 11, 156
heating, 156
helm, 25
help, 1, 2, 8, 24, 28, 29, 45, 46, 83, 88, 95, 99, 112, 129, 148, 152, 157, 172, 178, 213, 225, 227, 236, 248, 251, 260, 261, 267, 273, 290, 294
heritage, 168
highlight, 67, 76, 117, 158, 178, 198, 209, 222, 225, 267, 275, 289
hiking, 167
history, 2–5, 32, 90, 92, 102, 103, 136, 160, 251, 267, 289, 290
holding, 98, 123
home, 42, 85, 194, 282
Hong Kong, 135
hope, 285

hospital, 194
hospitality, 84, 85
host, 128, 129, 131
hotel, 49, 84
housing, 84, 98, 109, 142
how, 1, 6, 9, 12, 17, 19, 23, 31, 51, 54, 59, 77, 78, 89, 101, 117, 118, 121, 131, 144, 148, 166, 231, 252, 263, 266, 269, 296
Huawei, 138
hub, 130, 133–135, 173, 199
human, 1, 2, 38, 40, 71, 89, 93, 122, 132, 133, 144, 163, 174, 195, 199, 203, 205, 207, 208, 211–215, 247, 249, 258, 268, 269, 273, 279, 282, 283, 285, 290
humanity, 39
hurdle, 29
hydropower, 156, 273
hypothesis, 9, 11, 13, 108

ice, 272
Iceland, 173, 193
idea, 23, 80, 83, 141, 160
identification, 29, 203
identity, 33
immigrant, 261
impact, 1, 2, 5–12, 14, 17, 23, 29, 32, 35, 36, 38, 39, 43, 53, 55, 56, 67, 68, 70, 71, 73, 80, 82–84, 87, 90, 95, 98, 112, 115, 117, 121, 124, 130, 138, 144–146, 148, 149, 160–162, 165, 168, 173, 174, 183, 189, 190, 204, 207, 209, 217, 219, 222, 231, 234, 242, 245,

Index 313

253, 259, 261, 263, 269–271, 273, 281
imperative, 211
implementation, 41, 92, 98, 124, 148, 149, 155, 157, 178, 195, 205, 245, 246, 264, 280
import, 14, 119
importance, 2, 4, 6, 9, 10, 17, 18, 22, 25, 33–35, 48, 49, 51, 54, 67, 73, 98, 110–112, 121, 123, 124, 137, 142, 147–149, 152, 156, 168, 171, 185, 190, 193, 194, 211, 223, 225, 226, 231, 235, 237, 241, 247, 266, 268, 271, 272, 275, 291, 295
imposition, 172
improvement, 30, 31, 52, 57, 59, 111, 112, 128, 148, 228, 298
in, 1–9, 11–14, 17–20, 22–49, 51, 52, 54, 57, 67, 69, 71–73, 76–80, 82–85, 87–104, 107–114, 116–125, 127–130, 132–138, 141–149, 152, 154, 156–161, 163, 164, 166–168, 171–174, 176–178, 182, 185, 186, 188–191, 193, 195, 196, 199, 200, 203–205, 207–215, 217–220, 222–242, 244–247, 249, 250, 252, 254–261, 263–272, 274–276, 279, 281–285, 287, 289–291, 294, 295, 298

incentive, 98
inclusion, 45, 89, 101–103, 145, 203, 204, 229, 244, 249–252, 257, 259, 261, 264, 287, 289
inclusivity, 84, 145, 258
income, 10, 11, 19, 84, 91, 102, 117, 120, 133, 136, 138, 146, 172–174, 184, 191, 194, 203, 205, 237, 240, 244, 247, 250, 251, 254, 255, 269, 270, 290
increase, 28, 50, 78, 108, 118, 146, 178, 184, 191, 207, 238, 244, 251, 256, 270–272, 287
independence, 103, 172, 196
India, 14, 249
individual, 1, 2, 5–8, 11, 13, 70, 78, 97, 144, 171, 208, 211, 212, 214, 220, 224, 230, 235, 244, 250, 267, 273, 275, 285
industrialization, 5, 130, 131, 133, 136, 138
industry, 6, 17, 24, 27, 28, 30–33, 35, 37, 38, 45, 46, 48, 49, 51, 53, 59, 71, 77–80, 82–85, 97, 98, 110–112, 123, 132–134, 138, 143, 145, 148, 168, 169, 177, 209, 211, 212, 223–225, 235, 236, 257, 269–271, 298
inequality, 4, 5, 116, 117, 120, 133, 138, 142, 145, 146, 172–174, 195, 203–205, 213, 237–247, 254, 266, 269, 270, 290, 291

inflation, 13, 172, 185
influence, 2, 14, 18, 25, 77, 82, 108, 109, 111, 138, 144, 172, 186, 188, 189, 241, 290
influx, 195
information, 8–11, 24, 52, 72, 100, 102, 108, 113, 114, 116, 118, 122, 124, 171, 177, 178, 204, 210, 232, 266, 285, 295, 298
infrastructure, 3, 8, 13, 34, 44, 45, 100, 102, 127, 128, 130, 133–135, 137, 138, 146, 148, 157, 158, 168, 171, 173, 190, 191, 199, 213, 232, 233, 247, 249, 251, 255–258, 265, 266, 272, 289
infringement, 67
ingenuity, 93
initiation, 136
initiative, 12, 225, 233, 249
innovation, 1, 3, 4, 6, 8, 17, 19, 22–24, 27, 30–36, 38, 40–46, 48–59, 63–65, 67, 69, 70, 72, 76, 77, 82, 83, 85, 89, 92, 101, 112, 116, 118, 127, 129–136, 138, 142, 146, 149, 152, 157, 159, 165, 173, 195, 196, 199, 207, 211, 212, 214, 224, 232–235, 244, 247, 254, 264, 265, 267–271, 290, 295, 296, 298
innovator, 36
input, 46
insecurity, 27
inspiration, 5–8, 31, 33, 82, 133, 254
instability, 29, 136, 191

installation, 157
instance, 8, 72, 91, 284, 285
instruction, 210, 223–225, 230
instrument, 99
insulin, 72
insurance, 88, 93, 97, 146, 250, 272
integration, 4, 33, 92, 113, 116, 121–124, 129, 137, 146, 149, 157, 159, 195, 213, 225, 264, 271, 279, 293
integrity, 92, 95, 100, 101, 124, 286
intelligence, 18, 28, 38, 40, 121, 135, 138, 198, 232, 233, 263, 279
interconnectedness, 4, 18, 98, 100, 113, 116, 118
interdependence, 113, 116–118
interest, 91, 97, 172, 173, 186, 189, 191, 220, 288, 289
interface, 32
intermediary, 97
intermittency, 157
internet, 4, 32, 45, 77–79, 101, 102, 109, 114, 116, 118, 121, 220, 232, 263, 269
interplay, 6, 7, 17, 42, 144, 263, 268
interpretation, 10, 14
intersectionality, 260
intervention, 89, 171, 172, 174, 176–178, 269
interview, 8
introduction, 3, 12, 32, 35, 78, 269
inundation, 272
invention, 5
inventory, 122, 123
invest, 3, 30, 49, 64, 79, 87, 91, 103, 104, 124, 142, 168, 208, 250, 271, 289, 290

investing, 27, 38, 77, 79, 97, 104–107, 110, 128, 129, 131, 133, 159, 174, 208, 211, 218, 219, 233, 234, 249, 261, 298
investment, 18, 42, 45, 52, 67, 88, 90, 92–94, 103, 105, 106, 108–113, 116, 117, 119, 121, 127, 129–134, 136, 138, 148, 172, 173, 193, 199, 208, 215, 219, 254, 256, 257, 271
investor, 45, 105, 107, 130, 290
Ireland, 130
irrigation, 256
isolation, 57
Israel, 8
issue, 47, 84, 89, 133, 204, 213, 242, 249, 260

Japan, 193
Jeff Bezos, 6, 35, 36, 48
Jeff Bezos, 33, 34
job, 17, 19, 39–43, 75, 77, 128, 130, 131, 137, 146, 148, 157, 194, 209, 210, 212, 214, 215, 219, 223–225, 234–237, 250, 257, 264, 266, 269–271, 290
Joe Gebbia, 83
journey, 6–8, 24, 26, 28–31, 33, 35, 48, 49, 82, 90, 93, 138, 166, 209, 228, 268
journeyman, 235
judgment, 109, 111
juggernaut, 36
justice, 145

Kenya, 103

Kieran Healy, 12
know, 34, 282, 296
knowledge, 1, 6, 7, 22, 24, 28, 43–45, 48, 59, 64, 103, 112, 129–132, 148, 207–215, 220, 223, 224, 226, 228, 229, 247, 255, 266, 268, 295–298

labor, 5, 35, 117, 119, 122, 127, 129, 130, 137, 142, 143, 145, 173, 193–195, 209, 212–215, 219, 223, 225, 234–236, 259, 271, 281
laboratory, 285
lack, 45, 46, 98, 237, 239, 240, 247, 250
land, 158, 167, 237, 273
landscape, 3, 6, 18, 24, 45, 49, 73, 82, 92, 101, 103, 118, 120, 135, 136, 152, 200, 208, 211, 245, 263, 285, 287, 290
language, 212, 232
launch, 32
laundering, 134
law, 195
layout, 67
lead, 10, 17, 23, 30, 54, 57, 59, 108–112, 122, 123, 142, 173, 177, 178, 184, 224, 228, 232, 237, 264, 268, 272
leader, 31, 35, 135, 143, 160, 163, 210, 233, 234, 260
leadership, 7, 25, 32, 34, 36, 166, 168, 255, 258, 260
leakage, 204, 205

learning, 24–26, 28, 30, 31, 48, 50,
111, 112, 166, 193,
209–214, 219–223,
225–231, 233–236, 254,
268, 270, 271, 279, 281,
290, 291, 295
leave, 33, 259–261
ledger, 264, 286
legacy, 33, 112
lending, 87–90, 96, 97, 109,
250–252, 288
lens, 17
lesson, 49
level, 11, 24, 34, 84, 100, 147, 158,
168, 177, 191, 195, 203,
216, 219, 240, 251, 252,
265
leverage, 6, 29, 30, 79, 85, 102, 124,
131, 198, 268, 271, 295
liberalization, 14, 113, 117–121,
136
library, 78, 79
licensing, 44, 67
life, 1, 7, 16, 23, 28, 72, 78, 123, 144,
145, 153, 194, 195, 209,
226, 230, 250, 260, 294
lifetime, 208
light, 6
lightning, 89
likelihood, 285
line, 8, 10, 11, 160–162, 203, 240,
241, 271
lining, 167
link, 143
liquidity, 88, 89, 93, 97, 99–101, 288
literacy, 13, 103, 204, 213, 250–252
livelihood, 252
living, 1, 19, 71, 83, 114, 163, 215,
237, 239, 241, 250, 282

loan, 26
location, 102, 130, 135, 247, 252
locomotive, 5
lodging, 83
logo, 67
look, 25, 124, 147, 211, 238, 298
loop, 152
Lorenz, 240
loss, 255, 272, 291
love, 230
loyalty, 142, 149
luck, 6

machine, 5, 38, 110
machinery, 3, 137, 269
magnitude, 216
mail, 77
mailbox, 77
mainstream, 32
maintenance, 157, 271
makeup, 282
making, 1, 2, 7, 9, 12, 14, 24, 32, 33,
36, 57, 82, 107, 110–112,
123, 146, 148, 163, 168,
181, 188, 208, 212, 220,
235, 240, 251, 257, 259,
260, 266, 285, 291, 298
management, 34, 95, 98, 99, 110,
119, 122, 127, 131, 134,
142, 145, 167, 171, 190,
193, 250, 251, 264, 266,
298
managing, 27, 31, 79, 93, 96, 100,
138, 173, 174, 185, 193
manipulation, 89, 100, 101
manner, 8, 13, 287
manufacturer, 123
manufacturing, 3, 5, 18, 107, 116,
121–124, 127, 129, 130,

Index

    137, 143, 157, 198, 210, 257, 269, 270
map, 71
mark, 6, 33
market, 2–4, 16–19, 23, 24, 27–35, 38, 40, 49, 54, 57, 66, 79, 82, 85, 87–90, 92, 95–101, 104, 107–110, 112, 117, 122–124, 129, 136–138, 142, 144, 171–174, 176–178, 181, 189, 193–196, 209, 212–215, 219, 223, 225, 234–236, 244, 246, 259, 270, 271, 281, 290
marketing, 7, 23, 26–28, 59, 84
marketplace, 35, 91, 118
Mars, 37, 39
mass, 5
master, 27
material, 71, 121, 145, 220, 282
mathematics, 212, 229, 232, 279
maturity, 91, 97, 191
mean, 13
means, 14, 91, 122, 147, 152, 177, 210, 212, 214
measure, 8, 109, 240, 241
measurement, 146, 239, 241
mechanism, 174
media, 49, 78, 84
medicine, 71, 73, 282, 283, 285
meeting, 49, 141
melting, 272
mentality, 8
mentoring, 44, 212
mentorship, 45, 48
mercantilism, 3
meritocracy, 110, 112
Mesopotamia, 90

method, 12
micro, 84
microfinance, 45, 146, 251, 252, 257
microstructure, 99
milestone, 88, 91
million, 78, 252, 255
mindset, 1, 7, 8, 17, 19, 23, 28, 30, 31, 33, 34, 36, 39, 45, 110, 112, 144, 209, 228
miracle, 131–133
mission, 49
mitigation, 143, 168
mix, 2, 75, 147, 157, 193
ML, 281
mobile, 32, 101–103, 118, 232, 251, 257, 269
mobility, 83, 119, 173, 211–214, 232, 238, 247
model, 9, 10, 32, 59, 78–80, 82–85, 127, 152, 161, 162, 169, 173, 193, 195, 225, 229, 231, 236, 251, 252, 261, 265
modification, 282, 284
moment, 14
money, 64, 91, 97, 102, 103, 134, 172, 186, 189, 191, 257
monitoring, 67, 181, 203–205
morbidity, 247
mortality, 247, 257
mortar, 35, 269
mortgage, 89, 96–99, 109
motivation, 6, 30
motive, 3
move, 12, 111
movement, 101, 121, 133, 256, 298
movie, 77, 78
Muhammad Yunus, 251
multifactor, 102

multimedia, 220
multitude, 28
music, 32, 33
Musk, 8, 30, 31, 36, 38, 39, 49
myriad, 2

name, 33
Nathan Blecharczyk, 83
nation, 2, 131, 199, 210
nature, 2, 14, 55, 93, 98, 109, 157, 158, 163, 167, 213, 220, 226, 237, 241, 289, 291, 298
need, 5, 6, 10, 14, 27, 28, 35, 70, 73, 78, 79, 83, 87, 92–94, 98, 100, 102, 117, 120, 122–124, 126, 128, 129, 135, 138, 139, 142, 144–146, 148, 156, 158, 164, 168, 174, 193, 195, 196, 204, 209, 213, 214, 224, 235, 236, 241, 244, 245, 251, 264, 269–271, 280, 289, 290
neighborhood, 84
net, 134, 194, 245, 250, 259
network, 25, 30, 44, 48, 50, 137, 252, 286, 289
networking, 25, 29, 44, 45, 220
neurotechnology, 38, 39
neutrality, 35
news, 100
niche, 57
noise, 158
North America, 5
Norway, 173, 193
note, 4, 129, 187, 241
notion, 6, 107, 141, 144
novelty, 56

novice, 105
number, 8, 84, 97, 167, 271
nursing, 194
nutrition, 204

objective, 108, 112, 178
obligation, 91
obsession, 33
obstacle, 26, 30
off, 163, 259
offer, 1, 2, 6, 7, 18, 23, 29, 34, 48, 73, 75, 78, 82, 85, 88, 94, 117, 123, 126, 148, 154–157, 167, 180, 194, 214, 220, 221, 224, 257
offering, 57, 73, 77, 79, 82, 84, 101, 102, 223, 225, 235, 283, 285
office, 44
Omaha, 103
one, 4, 33, 34, 36, 49, 82, 83, 89, 92, 103, 110, 131, 138, 144, 147, 171, 196, 203, 209, 226, 229, 232, 244, 255, 270
online, 18, 34, 78, 83, 85, 89, 101–103, 208, 209, 211, 213, 220–222, 232, 269
open, 24, 26, 110–112, 172, 189, 298
opening, 136, 193
openness, 13, 14, 298
operating, 33, 101, 124, 298
operation, 157
opinion, 245
opportunity, 24, 28, 48, 50, 220, 229
Oprah Winfrey, 49
optimization, 122, 193
option, 220, 225

order, 2, 4, 7, 12, 26, 27, 99, 138, 144, 237, 242, 289, 290
organ, 285
organism, 282
orientation, 107
other, 5, 9, 10, 12, 14, 33, 37, 44, 45, 57, 72, 82, 85, 88, 89, 91, 96, 101, 110, 117, 121, 124, 127, 129, 133–135, 138, 172, 190, 191, 200, 208, 209, 230, 231, 236, 237, 240, 241, 250–252, 257, 258, 261, 269, 270, 272, 279, 289, 295, 296
outcome, 171
output, 122, 207, 269, 271
outreach, 225
overextension, 289
oversight, 92, 98–100
overtourism, 168
overview, 2, 97
ownership, 3, 39, 83, 88

pace, 5, 73, 92, 113, 116, 135, 213, 220, 225, 230, 271, 290
package, 32
pain, 49
panel, 9, 13
paradigm, 32
parenting, 204
part, 28, 48, 78, 127, 196, 210, 232
participation, 194, 195, 259, 277, 298
partnership, 234, 235
passion, 1, 23, 24, 31, 33
past, 2, 4, 5, 8, 11, 78, 99, 117, 118, 127, 193, 203, 263, 267, 268, 270, 290
Patagonia, 143, 160–162

path, 1, 5, 26, 28, 127, 128, 133, 258
pathway, 144, 155, 205, 209, 214, 223, 224
patience, 107
patient, 71, 72, 177, 270, 283, 285
pattern, 237
Paul Kagame, 255, 258
Paul Newbold, 12
pay, 80, 83, 97, 177, 191, 195, 260, 288
payment, 88, 94
peak, 290
peer, 83, 251, 264, 286
penetration, 232
pension, 97
people, 32, 34, 49, 78, 82, 83, 116, 127, 133, 137, 147, 160, 162, 239, 247, 249, 255, 269
percentage, 240
perfectionism, 31
performance, 8, 12, 14, 57, 122, 144–147, 149, 172, 229, 230, 279
period, 3, 5, 52, 91, 99, 109, 258, 289
perseverance, 6, 24, 31, 33
persistence, 24, 26, 30, 31, 49, 50
personalization, 34
perspective, 6, 8, 12, 18, 84, 104, 107, 129, 212
pesticide, 273
pharmaceutical, 72, 73, 130, 163
phase, 290
phenomenon, 4, 17, 113, 116
philanthropic, 142, 145
philanthropist, 107
philanthropy, 149
philosophy, 3, 34, 103, 106, 110

phone, 32
pie, 11
pioneer, 2, 160
pipeline, 135
piracy, 67
pitch, 40, 45
place, 39, 52, 88, 101, 102, 194, 232, 260
plan, 23, 255, 260
planet, 145, 147, 160, 162, 163, 268
planning, 27, 134, 171, 173, 174, 178–181, 193, 196–200, 281
platform, 32, 49, 80, 83–85, 88, 277, 288, 289
play, 1, 7, 12, 17, 19, 40, 44, 46–48, 73, 87, 88, 93–96, 101, 103, 108, 121, 130, 145, 171, 172, 174, 176–178, 185, 189, 190, 223, 234, 239, 246, 251, 266, 270, 271, 275, 290, 291, 295
player, 32, 78, 79, 127, 137
playing, 91, 100, 118, 158
plot, 9, 11
point, 3, 11, 116, 136, 290
policy, 1, 12, 14, 43, 44, 47, 117, 130, 131, 136, 146, 147, 158, 171, 172, 181, 185–190, 193, 249, 267, 274, 290, 293
pollution, 82, 138, 142, 145, 157, 172, 291
pool, 88, 97, 288, 296
pooling, 88, 98
popularity, 10, 214, 220
population, 103, 146, 193–195, 237, 241, 244, 255, 256, 259, 264

portfolio, 67, 88, 165
portion, 103, 210, 241, 256
position, 34, 35, 78, 79, 108, 111, 116, 134, 135, 291
possibility, 285
potential, 1, 6, 8, 10–12, 14, 18, 29, 30, 34, 37–40, 43, 59, 67, 71, 73, 75, 77, 79, 83, 85, 89, 92, 95, 101, 103, 109, 111, 116, 121, 127, 129–131, 143, 145, 149, 156, 158, 166, 196, 204, 207, 208, 211, 213–215, 222, 224, 245, 249, 251, 252, 263–265, 268–271, 275, 279–285, 288, 289
poverty, 49, 102, 103, 127, 137, 142, 146, 147, 174, 178, 203–205, 210, 213, 237–242, 246, 247, 250, 252–259, 261, 291
power, 1–3, 5, 17, 31, 36, 46, 51, 54, 70, 73, 74, 78, 82, 83, 103, 107, 110, 112, 117, 124, 133, 148, 156, 158, 159, 163, 166, 178, 211, 258, 264, 265, 268, 269, 271, 289, 298
powerhouse, 6, 34, 133, 136, 138, 211
practice, 195
precipitation, 168
precision, 71, 121, 123, 269, 270
predictability, 157
premium, 67
preparation, 210
preschool, 259
presence, 14, 35, 43, 44, 72, 134, 135, 158

Index

present, 9, 11, 13, 18, 79, 120, 123, 141, 151, 267, 288, 291, 294
preservation, 134, 141, 144, 167
pressure, 28, 79, 195, 230, 233
prevention, 283
price, 78, 79, 89, 91, 99, 100, 107, 108, 157, 174, 185
pricing, 27, 79, 82
principal, 91, 97, 191
principle, 99, 104, 110–112, 145–147, 244
priority, 97, 246
privacy, 35, 39, 72, 267
probability, 9
problem, 30, 98, 208, 210, 212, 213, 230, 256, 269
process, 17, 20, 34, 51, 54, 59, 97, 98, 111, 118, 209, 210, 226, 282, 298
processing, 132
product, 7, 26, 27, 34, 35, 59, 67, 121, 123, 124, 153, 160, 165
production, 3, 5, 27, 72, 78, 79, 117–124, 130, 136, 137, 141, 143, 147, 152, 163, 164, 172, 269, 271, 272
productivity, 5, 19, 32, 45, 51, 121, 124, 128, 129, 136, 146, 148, 178, 207, 208, 211, 212, 214, 215, 219, 224, 235, 247, 256, 269, 271, 272, 298
professional, 23, 27, 28, 30, 32, 225, 226, 228
professionalism, 231
proficiency, 224
profile, 285

profiling, 72
profit, 3, 52, 79, 91, 99, 108, 109, 160
profitability, 27, 142, 143, 162
program, 84, 171, 173, 174, 203–205
programming, 78, 79, 214, 271
progress, 3, 5, 22, 37, 46, 48, 51, 141, 145, 147, 148, 157, 195, 210, 247, 252, 254, 255, 258, 260, 268
project, 71, 158
proliferation, 2, 92, 220
prominence, 36, 209
promise, 264, 284, 285, 289
promotion, 92, 130, 131, 133, 213, 219, 258, 260
property, 4, 17, 51, 52, 54, 63–67, 124, 130, 138
prophecy, 108
proportion, 244
proposition, 27
prosperity, 3–5, 7, 13, 18, 40, 116, 124, 128, 133, 139, 141, 146, 166, 173, 174, 185, 193–195, 200, 207, 211, 214, 249, 263, 266, 267, 277, 289, 291–294
protection, 4, 17, 51, 52, 54, 64–67, 88, 130, 134, 203–205, 250, 258, 267, 273, 291, 294
protectionism, 266
provision, 101, 172, 177, 233, 256
proximity, 43, 119
public, 1, 78, 88, 95, 158, 169, 171, 172, 177, 178, 182, 190, 191, 195, 244, 245, 259, 260, 264, 298

purchase, 96, 97, 191
purification, 273
purpose, 24, 95
pursuit, 2, 6, 7, 20, 24, 28, 33, 34, 112, 124, 244, 281

quality, 10, 14, 33, 38, 67, 77, 98, 104, 107, 111, 112, 121, 124, 144, 145, 147, 157, 160, 177, 194, 210, 213, 214, 219, 220, 229, 238, 247–249, 254, 259, 270, 271, 298
question, 11
quo, 20, 59

R. Carter Hill, 12
race, 237
rail, 137
randomness, 9
range, 2, 12, 27, 33, 51, 57, 71, 78, 79, 82, 88, 91, 93, 94, 98, 118, 134, 143, 147, 149, 163, 164, 166, 179, 181, 186, 189, 194, 220, 229, 259, 272, 273
rank, 111, 195
rate, 148, 172, 184, 189, 211, 225, 240, 241
ratio, 173
rationale, 111
Ray Dalio, 110, 112
Ray Dalio's, 110
reach, 35, 79, 117, 118, 203, 269
readiness, 224
reading, 43, 281
reality, 36, 79, 108, 109
realization, 39
realm, 31, 33

reasoning, 111
recession, 109, 267, 290
recognition, 67, 138, 143, 166, 229, 291
recommendation, 34, 78
record, 26, 112
recovery, 153, 189, 267
recruiting, 30
recycle, 152, 155
recycling, 142, 145, 265
redistribution, 172, 203, 244–246
reduce, 38, 44, 73, 75, 121–123, 142, 144–146, 148, 152, 155, 157, 172, 174, 178, 191, 213, 238, 244, 251, 254, 256, 259, 264, 265, 270, 273, 285
reduction, 145, 146, 152–155, 168, 203–205, 252–255, 258
reevaluation, 98
reference, 240, 241
reflection, 108
reflexivity, 107–110
reforestation, 167
reform, 136, 231
region, 42, 135
registry, 203
regression, 9, 10
regulation, 35, 82–84, 88, 92, 95, 98, 100, 172
rehabilitation, 194
reinforcement, 281
rejection, 285
relationship, 8–11, 13, 14, 32, 40, 108, 113, 131, 141, 185, 207, 215, 219
release, 78, 272
relevance, 213, 236
reliability, 10, 14

Index

reliance, 73, 127, 143, 157, 245, 250, 273
reminder, 33, 112
removal, 113
rent, 83
rental, 77
renting, 83
repayment, 91, 191, 251
reporting, 146, 148
representation, 257, 260
reputation, 66, 104, 142, 143, 145, 149, 152, 211
research, 2, 8–11, 13, 14, 16, 17, 20, 23, 27, 29, 37, 38, 43, 44, 49, 51, 52, 54, 64, 67, 71, 107, 130, 132, 135, 138, 148, 166, 188, 231–234, 264, 268, 270, 271, 285, 298
reserve, 172, 189
reshape, 36, 38, 39, 92, 216, 289
reshaping, 6, 17, 87, 271
resilience, 6, 17, 19, 24, 26, 30, 31, 48–50, 157, 230, 250, 265–268
reskilling, 220, 236, 271
resort, 173, 190
resource, 39, 83, 122, 138, 142, 145, 146, 152, 153, 155, 156, 199, 265, 270, 291
response, 84, 92, 117, 123, 203
responsibility, 35, 142–145, 147, 149, 160, 162, 230
result, 117, 128, 172, 190, 215, 218, 249, 271, 272, 289
retail, 6, 32, 34, 269
retailer, 123
return, 88, 97, 191, 215
reuse, 145, 152, 155

revenue, 35, 79, 143, 172, 182, 183, 185, 190, 191, 193, 245
review, 46, 148, 173
revolution, 6, 32, 33, 74, 77, 80, 82, 116, 163, 166, 269
ride, 80–83, 269
right, 1, 30, 77, 91, 172, 177, 247, 249, 258
rigor, 8, 111
rise, 3, 5, 6, 32, 34–36, 77, 79, 80, 83, 84, 88, 92, 98, 109, 118, 136–138, 168, 265, 269, 272, 289
risk, 6, 8, 19, 27, 43, 59, 72, 87–89, 92, 93, 95–101, 110, 124, 132, 251, 265, 266, 272, 285
road, 256
robotic, 270
rock, 160
role, 1–4, 6–9, 12, 16, 17, 19, 22, 31, 40, 43, 44, 46–49, 51, 54, 67, 72, 73, 78, 87–91, 93–96, 101–103, 118, 121, 124, 130, 132, 136, 137, 144, 145, 156, 166, 167, 171–174, 176–178, 182, 185, 189, 190, 196, 207, 210, 211, 213, 214, 218, 223, 229, 233–236, 239, 246, 250, 251, 256, 259, 261, 263, 266, 270, 271, 274, 275, 290, 291, 295
Rome, 90
room, 83
rule, 195
run, 10, 76, 149
Rwanda, 255–258

safeguard, 52, 95, 102, 144
safety, 72, 82, 85, 138, 177, 194, 244–246, 250, 254, 259, 270, 271
salary, 234
sample, 10, 11
sampling, 10
San Francisco, 83
sandbox, 135
satellite, 37
satisfaction, 34–36, 122, 195, 230
saving, 72, 167, 172
scalability, 220, 264
scale, 113, 116, 118, 120, 137, 158, 251
scarcity, 156
scatter, 9, 11
scenario, 107, 218
school, 45, 174, 203, 210, 235, 249, 257, 259
science, 3, 212, 229, 232, 279
scope, 55, 245
sea, 168, 265, 272
second, 14, 225
section, 2, 7, 9, 17, 23, 26, 29, 34, 36, 40, 43, 48, 53, 67, 71, 73, 80, 83, 101, 104, 110, 116, 118, 121, 124, 131, 134, 136, 144, 152, 156, 160, 166, 174, 178, 182, 185, 190, 193, 196, 200, 215, 223, 226, 229, 232, 234, 239, 241, 242, 244, 247, 253, 255, 259, 263, 265–267, 272, 275, 282, 291, 295
sector, 5, 19, 32, 38, 130, 135, 136, 147, 157, 171, 177, 256
securitization, 17, 96–99, 119
security, 39, 75, 77, 89, 102, 103, 138, 148, 157, 194, 256, 264, 267, 273, 284, 289
segment, 244
self, 11, 28, 108, 111, 220, 250, 251
sell, 88, 89, 91, 99, 101, 117
selling, 91, 99
seniority, 111
sense, 24, 67, 195, 220, 230
separation, 98
sequencing, 285
sequestration, 273
series, 9, 10, 78, 196
server, 298
service, 27, 77–80, 82, 103
set, 20, 23, 31–34, 38, 68, 70, 95, 110, 134, 137, 145, 147, 148, 160, 194, 218, 229, 258
setback, 23, 26
setting, 138, 150, 178, 181
Shanghai, 135
shape, 1, 12, 18, 33, 39, 46, 54, 121, 263, 268, 286, 291
share, 64, 125, 129, 142, 147, 247, 296, 298
sharing, 43, 44, 59, 64, 80–83, 85, 110, 129, 131, 148, 220, 236, 266–269, 295–298
shelter, 240
shift, 32, 38, 73, 78, 138, 144, 148, 209, 265, 269
shipbuilding, 132
shipping, 114, 117, 118
shop, 34, 269
shortage, 224, 285
side, 285
significance, 2, 10, 19, 33, 47, 110, 268, 275

Index

Silicon Valley, 8, 42, 43
Silicon Valley's, 43
simplicity, 33
simplify, 44
Singapore, 134–136, 171, 173, 174, 196–200, 225
Singapore, 225
situation, 4
size, 4, 173
skill, 129, 224, 225, 254
smartphone, 33, 80, 117
snapshot, 14
society, 19, 36, 39, 40, 51, 59, 67, 70, 76, 133, 138, 141, 142, 144, 145, 147–149, 152, 162, 172, 175, 185, 195, 207, 211, 223, 226, 237, 239, 240, 244, 247, 249, 255, 256, 261, 272, 284
socio, 142, 173, 210, 225, 229
software, 33, 214, 271, 298
soil, 273
solidarity, 195, 259
solution, 101, 103
Soros, 107–109
source, 6, 7, 156, 298
sourcing, 117, 124, 149
South Korea, 13, 132, 133, 210, 211, 232–234
South Korea's, 131–133, 210, 232, 234
space, 30, 31, 36, 37, 39
spacecraft, 31
SpaceX, 36
specialist, 194
specificity, 72
spectrum, 56, 57
speed, 45, 100, 137, 163, 232, 269

spending, 172, 173, 182, 190, 191, 193, 208, 290
spillover, 157
spin, 163
spirit, 6
spread, 4, 5, 88, 91, 99
stability, 3, 19, 27, 28, 88, 92, 93, 95, 98, 99, 101, 135, 146, 157, 185, 189, 190, 250, 266, 267, 275, 290
staff, 167, 252
stage, 32, 43
stagnation, 136, 237
stakeholder, 124, 148
standard, 13, 162, 237, 239
standout, 167
start, 8, 57, 229, 250, 270, 290
startup, 40, 43
state, 90, 137, 173, 193–195, 259, 261
statistic, 240
status, 20, 59, 194, 229
steam, 3, 5, 156
stem, 285
step, 172
Steve Jobs, 6, 7, 31, 33, 48
Steve Jobs', 31
Steve Jobs, 31
stewardship, 142, 160
stock, 88, 91, 100, 107, 108, 207, 214, 215
stone, 2, 48
stop, 34
storage, 77, 91, 122, 156, 157
store, 34, 103
story, 6, 11, 30, 33, 49, 80, 82, 83, 131, 135, 200
strategy, 33, 48, 79, 104, 109, 127, 137, 141, 149, 218, 255,

257, 258
stream, 78
streaming, 32, 77–79
strength, 10
stress, 28, 95, 100, 233, 250
structure, 27, 132
student, 210, 230, 231
study, 2, 4, 5, 7, 8, 26, 160, 200, 219, 230, 241, 254, 270, 291
subfield, 279
subject, 95, 229
subscription, 79
subset, 250
subsistence, 3
success, 1–14, 16–36, 38, 40–43, 46, 48–51, 54, 57, 59, 65, 67, 70, 73, 75–78, 82, 83, 85, 87, 89–91, 99, 105, 107, 110, 112, 113, 115–118, 120, 121, 123–125, 127, 128, 131–138, 141, 143–147, 152, 154–156, 158–162, 164, 166, 171, 173, 174, 181–185, 193, 195, 196, 198–200, 205, 207, 209–211, 213, 214, 216, 219, 222, 223, 229–236, 238, 239, 249, 252–255, 258, 259, 261, 263–268, 270–272, 275, 279, 281, 288–292, 295, 296, 298
suit, 38, 101
summary, 8, 13, 240
sunlight, 157
superpower, 136–138
supervision, 92, 95
supply, 27, 34, 72, 116, 121–124, 127, 137, 143, 157, 172, 174, 186, 189, 264, 289
support, 8, 10, 11, 23, 25, 28–30, 43, 44, 47, 48, 91, 132, 133, 138, 142, 145, 148, 173, 194, 198, 205, 224, 226, 230, 233, 245, 246, 249, 251, 252, 260, 261, 270
surface, 156
surplus, 193
surrounding, 39, 48, 117
survey, 11
sustainability, 17, 35, 92, 124, 142, 143, 145–147, 149, 156, 159, 163, 165, 166, 168, 172, 173, 178, 185, 195, 196, 204, 205, 245, 246, 251, 254, 265, 267, 268, 272–275, 291
Sweden, 173, 193, 259–261
Switzerland, 225
system, 4, 33, 34, 78, 83, 88, 92–95, 98, 102, 134, 136, 148, 152, 157, 158, 174, 193, 203, 204, 210, 211, 225, 229–236, 244, 250, 252, 259, 261, 265, 286, 298

tablet, 32
tackle, 18, 205
taking, 6, 8, 19, 24, 43, 59, 88, 92, 132, 148, 149
tale, 6
talent, 4, 27, 29, 42, 44–46
tap, 4, 79, 129, 132
target, 27, 49, 147, 148, 193
targeting, 82, 203, 205, 246, 258
tariff, 14
task, 27, 109

tax, 45, 127, 132, 168, 172, 173, 184, 185, 193, 194, 244
taxation, 171–173, 182, 184, 185, 191, 194, 244, 245
taxi, 80, 82, 269
taxis, 82
teacher, 213, 231
teaching, 213, 229–231
team, 6, 23, 26, 29, 110
tech, 35, 42, 82
technique, 9, 11
technology, 3, 4, 6, 18, 30, 32, 36, 38, 44, 59, 66, 67, 72, 77, 80, 83, 85, 95, 100, 103, 113, 116, 118, 119, 128–131, 135, 138, 158, 208, 210, 213, 214, 220, 224, 232, 234, 251, 252, 263, 264, 268–271, 275, 282–284, 286, 288–290, 296, 298
telecommunications, 32, 118, 138
telegraph, 5
temperature, 272
tenacity, 49
tenure, 111
term, 18, 27, 30, 34, 35, 37, 49, 54, 73, 75, 77, 84, 85, 96, 98, 99, 104, 107, 116, 124, 127, 128, 139, 141, 142, 145, 147, 152, 157, 168, 173, 181, 185, 193–196, 198, 199, 204, 205, 208, 214, 216, 218, 219, 249, 250, 255, 267, 273, 288, 291–294, 298
test, 11, 13, 46, 109
testament, 82, 83, 93, 107, 133, 134
testing, 9, 72, 230, 231, 251
textile, 5

the Dutch Republic, 289
the Osa Peninsula, 167
The Roman Empire, 289
the United States, 3, 88, 91, 109, 117, 217, 219
theater, 78
Theil, 240, 241
theme, 17
theory, 9, 107–109, 207, 211, 215, 219, 290
therapy, 71, 73
think, 18, 24, 34, 82, 121
thinking, 6, 23, 33, 39, 40, 107, 110, 208, 210, 212, 213, 230
thirst, 28
threat, 135, 168
threshold, 240, 241
time, 2, 8–10, 14, 27, 30, 49, 64, 87, 90, 91, 95, 100, 102, 107, 114, 118, 119, 122, 123, 145, 156, 189, 191, 209, 210, 245, 259, 271, 279, 289
today, 1, 24, 30, 34, 49, 90, 121, 124, 152, 226, 228, 275, 295
Tokyo, 135
tolerance, 24
toll, 28
tool, 9, 71, 191, 213, 284
tooling, 122
topic, 166, 185, 190
tourism, 37, 85, 143, 144, 166–169, 257
track, 26, 112
tracking, 148, 269
trade, 3–5, 13, 14, 18, 52, 87, 91, 92, 113, 114, 116–121, 124–129, 132, 133,

136–138, 177, 193, 223, 224, 266, 275, 289
trading, 18, 88, 90–92, 99–101, 173, 289
traffic, 82
trailblazer, 158
training, 1, 44, 45, 124, 194, 207, 209–214, 219, 223–225, 229, 234–236, 249, 251, 252, 281
trajectory, 290
transaction, 93, 96, 99–101, 251
transfer, 44, 89, 128, 203, 204, 244, 296
transformation, 3, 17, 54, 57, 73, 77, 130, 133–136, 138, 210, 258, 271
transition, 5, 73, 75, 127, 136, 138, 148, 152, 157–159, 210, 216, 235, 264, 265, 274
transparency, 95, 98–100, 110–112, 134, 147, 258, 287, 298
transplantation, 285
transportation, 4, 5, 32, 37–40, 51, 80, 82, 83, 113, 114, 116–119, 122, 137, 148, 244, 269
travel, 4, 31, 49, 83–85, 114
Travis Kalanick, 80
treatment, 72, 194, 247, 270, 283, 285
trend, 11
trough, 290
trust, 67, 95, 103, 124, 134, 195, 264, 267
tuition, 208
tumor, 285
turn, 3, 136, 215
turning, 3, 116, 136

type, 156

U.S., 100
uncertainty, 9, 24, 29
underestimation, 98
underinvestment, 172
understanding, 1, 2, 5–9, 11–14, 16–18, 22, 27–29, 34, 40, 49, 71, 96, 99, 107, 109, 110, 117, 185, 200, 207, 219, 230, 239–242, 251, 263, 271, 275, 283, 288, 291
unemployment, 11, 194, 196, 208, 211, 215, 217–219, 225, 235, 236, 244, 259, 270, 290
unionization, 35
United States, 42
universality, 147
unrest, 195, 272
up, 4, 8, 18, 24, 71, 96–98, 108, 109, 134, 136, 137, 163, 193, 203, 225, 235, 245, 282, 290
updating, 235
upgrade, 130, 224
upheaval, 136
upskilling, 214, 220, 225, 236, 271
urbanization, 136, 138
usage, 249
use, 2, 9–11, 27, 29, 32, 66, 71, 72, 78, 98, 103, 121, 135, 142, 145, 146, 148, 152, 158, 163, 167, 172, 185–187, 189, 220, 267, 269, 273, 281, 284, 285, 287
user, 31–33, 49, 50, 57, 67, 78, 103
utilization, 39, 83, 265

vacation, 85
vaccination, 203
value, 6, 20, 27, 33, 48, 57, 91, 96,
    104–108, 124, 129, 130,
    144, 152, 225, 265
variety, 1, 163
vehicle, 38, 123
Venice, 91
venture, 23, 26, 27, 29, 40, 43–45
viability, 273
video, 77
Vietnam, 117
view, 10, 24, 28, 30, 48, 108
viewer, 78
viewing, 78, 79
village, 251
virus, 72
visa, 45
visibility, 84, 122
vision, 20, 24, 30, 34, 36–39, 78,
    148, 255, 258
visitor, 168
visualization, 2, 7–13
voice, 35
volatility, 100, 157
volume, 99–101, 118
vulnerability, 250

wage, 224, 237
wallet, 103
war, 131, 133
warning, 267
Warren Buffett, 48, 103, 104
Warren Buffett's, 105–107
waste, 122, 124, 141–143, 145, 146,
    152–156, 164, 168, 265,
    270
water, 138, 142, 143, 156, 167, 168,
    273

wave, 109
way, 3, 8, 9, 23, 24, 31, 32, 34, 38,
    49, 71, 73, 77–80, 82, 83,
    87, 88, 96, 101, 110, 118,
    141, 145, 146, 163, 166,
    191, 193, 208, 211, 232,
    252, 268, 269, 283, 285,
    286, 289, 294
wealth, 1, 3, 17, 107, 133, 134, 145,
    178, 237, 240, 244
weather, 157, 265, 272
web, 298
weight, 31
weighting, 10
welfare, 145, 171, 173, 174, 191,
    193–196, 230, 252, 254,
    259, 261
well, 1, 7, 28, 30, 35, 40, 59, 80, 83,
    87, 107, 109, 111, 112,
    138, 141, 144–147, 149,
    162, 171, 172, 178, 181,
    185, 194, 195, 199, 200,
    204, 211, 213, 214, 224,
    229–231, 233, 234, 239,
    241, 247, 249, 250, 252,
    259, 272, 282, 291, 292,
    294
Western Europe, 3
whole, 36, 80, 145, 172, 175, 223,
    239, 261, 268, 284
wildlife, 167
William E. Griffiths, 12
William L. Carlson, 12
willingness, 144
wind, 73, 148, 156–158, 265, 273
wisdom, 24
wood, 156
work, 10, 23, 28, 30–32, 45, 172,
    194, 209, 210, 213, 220,

224, 234, 235, 244, 245, 259, 260, 277, 290, 298
worker, 82
workforce, 35, 43, 124, 130, 173, 195, 207, 209–212, 219, 223–226, 234–236, 247, 270, 271, 281
working, 5, 28, 35, 107, 142, 145, 148, 260, 295, 298
workplace, 209, 223, 260, 261
world, 1–4, 6, 7, 11, 12, 18, 31, 33, 36, 42, 43, 59, 70, 77, 82, 90–93, 96, 98, 102, 103, 110, 113, 116–118, 120, 127, 131, 133, 135, 137, 148, 154, 156, 160, 167, 169, 177, 178, 190, 196, 203, 209, 211, 213, 217, 219, 226, 228, 230, 232, 238, 244, 247, 265–268, 270, 272, 275, 281, 286, 288, 290, 295, 296, 298
worth, 2, 35, 134, 188

x, 11

y, 11
year, 191, 193
youth, 211, 225, 235, 236
Yvon Chouinard, 160

Zara, 123
zip, 167

Milton Keynes UK
Ingram Content Group UK Ltd.
UKHW020102181024
449757UK00011B/695